Crime Writers

Recent Titles in the
Author Research Series
Jen Stevens, Series Editor

Fantasy Authors: A Research Guide
Jen Stevens and Dorothea Salo

Science Fiction Authors: A Research Guide
Maura Heaphy

Women's Fiction Writers: A Research Guide
Rebecca Vnuk

Romance Authors: A Research Guide
Sarah E. Sheehan

Crime Writers:
A Research Guide

Elizabeth Haynes

Author Research Series
Jen Stevens, Series Editor

LIBRARIES UNLIMITED

AN IMPRINT OF ABC-CLIO, LLC
Santa Barbara, California • Denver, Colorado • Oxford, England

Library of Congress Cataloging-in-Publication Data

Haynes, Elizabeth (Dorothy Elizabeth)
    Crime Writers : A Research Guide / Elizabeth Haynes.
        p. cm. — (Author Research Series)
    Includes bibliographical references and index.
    ISBN 978-1-59158-914-3 (pbk. : acid-free paper)   1. Detective and mystery stories, American—Bio-bibliography—Dictionaries.   2. Detective and mystery stories, English—Bio-bibliography—Dictionaries.   3. Crime—Fiction—Bibliography.   4. Crime in literature—Bibliography.   I. Title.
    PS374.D4H39   2011
    813'.087209003—dc22
    [B]   2010047200

ISBN: 978-1-59158-914-3
EISBN: 978-1-59158-919-8

15   14   13   12   11   1   2   3   4   5

This book is also available on the World Wide Web as an eBook.
Visit www.abc-clio.com for details.

Libraries Unlimited
An Imprint of ABC-CLIO, LLC

ABC-CLIO, LLC
130 Cremona Drive, P.O. Box 1911
Santa Barbara, California 93116-1911

This book is printed on acid-free paper ∞

Manufactured in the United States of America

Dedicated to Lucinda and Skip Nelson for their constant
friendship and support over the years.

Contents

Acknowledgments

I want to thank the following persons for their assistance:

- Edmand Pace for copying, finding sources, and checking URLs
- Cathy J. Pruitt for making some gentle suggestions to improve my prose
- James Latta for assistance at the beginning of the project
- Jen Stevens and Barbara Ittner for their encouragement and help

Introduction: Crime Fiction Writers: A Research Guide

Crime Fiction as a Genre

One of the most popular genres, crime fiction, with its many permutations and subgenres, encompasses many of the authors who are perennial bestsellers. Mike Ashley, in *The Mammoth Encyclopedia of Modern Crime Fiction,* defines crime fiction as that about "the breaking and enforcement of the law" (xi), and that is as good a definition as any. Crime fiction is frequently synonymous with mystery fiction but is more encompassing than just the traditional mystery format. It deals not only with stories of crime and law enforcement but also with the deeper motivations of the human mind and heart.

In some respects, the crime narrative reaches back as far as the biblical story of Cain and Abel. Humans have always been fascinated with crime and transgression. The eighteenth century was marked by cynicism on the part of the populace about law and justice being only for the rich—an attitude that later found some expression in the hard-boiled crime works of the twentieth century. But the first modern crime author is thought to be Edgar Allan Poe who used many of the characteristics of the crime novel. His amateur detective C. Auguste Dupin had a profound effect on later authors although he appeared in only three stories, the best known of which is "The Murders in the Rue Morgue."

Besides Poe, other nineteenth-century authors who contributed to the development of the crime novel include Dickens (*Bleak House, The Mystery of Edwin Drood*) and Wilkie Collins (*The Woman in White, The Moonstone*). Female authors were also making their mark, with authors Katherine Green and Seeley Register (a pseudonym for Metta Victoria Fuller Victor) establishing conventions such as the private detective.

Short stories became popular during the late nineteenth and early twentieth centuries, with Conan Doyle's stories about Sherlock Holmes being the best known. The popularity of the short-story form declined after the First World War, and the 1920s are considered the beginning of the "golden age" of crime novels. Crime novelists now considered to be classic began publishing during this period, including Agatha Christie, Dorothy L. Sayers, John Dickson Carr, Ngaio Marsh, and Margery Allingham. These well-known English writers established the format and conventions for what is today considered the cozy format of the traditional puzzle mystery, with its circumscribed group of characters, mannered society, and emphasis on clues and brain power.

The Depression era saw the rise of a contrasting type of novel in the United States that reflected the realities of life during that time: hard-boiled stories began in the pulp magazines and depicted cynical detectives, gangsters, and brutal life on the streets. Preeminent authors in this category were Dashiell Hammett, Raymond Chandler, and Mickey Spillane. The modern crime novel, as opposed to detective puzzle novels, began with this group.

Police procedural novels became popular in the mid-twentieth century. These novels focused on the methods used by law enforcement to solve crimes, with an emphasis on one or more individual officers. Ed McBain was one of the best-known practitioners of this form of fiction.

Private investigators took center stage again in the late twentieth century, but these novels tended not to be as gritty as the hard-boiled fiction of the 1930s and 1940s. This period also saw the rise in popularity of female private eyes, with series characters introduced by Marcia Muller, Sara Paretsky, and Sue Grafton becoming immensely popular. Diversity of characters was also on the increase as well. Gay and lesbian protagonists were featured by authors such as Laurie R. King. Main characters from different races and ethnic groups became common, including the African American protagonists of Walter Mosley's works and the Native Americans of Tony Hillerman's novels.

Another popular category that continues today is the legal novel. Works by John Grisham and David Baldacci regularly top bestseller lists and focus on legal and political maneuvering, both in the courtroom and behind the scenes. Historical crime fiction is also currently popular, with a thriving subgenre that turns historical characters into detectives. Eras depicted range from the time of ancient Egypt, Greece, and Rome up through World War II.

Crime fiction, probably more than any other fictional genre, is largely identified with the concept of series. Stand-alone novels are certainly not uncommon, but series of novels built around one or more main characters are the standard for the genre. Series may run to many volumes or may be relatively short-lived, but almost every successful crime novelist faces the pressure to continue the adventures of popular characters through multiple outings.

Crime fiction has fascinated readers since its beginnings. Fans may be attracted by the intellectual challenge of solving a crime from the clues furnished by the author. They may be fanatically loyal to particular categories or individual series. They may seek out fiction with a resolution that (usually) restores order and peace to the community. They may admire the writing of certain authors. These and other reasons continue to draw readers into this multifaceted category of reading.

Crime Fiction Timeline

Early Forays

Literary Events

1841—Edgar Allan Poe: "The Murders in the Rue Morgue"
1868—Wilkie Collins: *The Moonstone*
1870—Charles Dickens: *The Mystery of Edwin Drood*
1887—Sir Arthur Conan Doyle: "A Study in Scarlet"

World Events

1846–1848—Mexican War
1853–1856—Crimean War
1861–1865—U.S. Civil War
1876—Custer's defeat at Little Big Horn
1894—Dreyfus case, France

The Golden Age (1920–1949)

The traditional mystery, emphasizing clues and detection, came to fruition during this period, when authors published works that are considered classic and that had a profound impact on subsequent authors and the field as a whole.

Literary Events

1920—Agatha Christie: *The Mysterious Affair at Styles*
1923—Dorothy L. Sayers: *Whose Body?*
1934—Ngaio Marsh: *A Man Lay Dead*
1934—Rex Stout: *Fer-de-Lance*
1939—Raymond Chandler: *The Big Sleep*

World Events

1920—Nineteenth Amendment gives women the vote
1927—Lindbergh crosses the Atlantic nonstop
1929—U.S. stock market collapse

1934—Hitler becomes leader of Germany
1939–1945—World War II
1945—Franklin D. Roosevelt dies
1946—Winston Churchill gives "iron curtain" speech

1950–1969

A relatively quiet period in crime fiction history, this era saw the rise of police procedurals, but traditional mysteries by golden-age authors were still being published.

Literary Events

1956—Ed McBain: *Cop Hater*
1962—P. D. James: *Cover Her Face*
1962—Dick Francis: *Dead Cert*
1964—Ruth Rendell: *From Doon with Death*

World Events

1952—Elizabeth II becomes Queen of Great Britain
1957—Sputnik launched
1961—Berlin Wall built
1963—President Kennedy assassinated
1964—Civil Rights Act passed
1968—Martin Luther King assassinated

1970–1989

These two decades have been considered a second golden age. Female crime novelists came back into their own with the formation of Sisters in Crime and the popularity of several series devoted to female private detectives. Reflecting events in society, crime novels began to feature increasing diversity in characters and settings. Besides those listed here, authors who started publishing during this period include James Lee Burke, Mary Higgins Clark, Robert Crais, Aaron Elkins, Elizabeth George, Carolyn Hart, Carl Hiaasen, J. A. Jance, Elmore Leonard, Peter Lovesey, Margaret Maron, James Patterson, Anne Perry, Elizabeth Peters, Nancy Pickard, and Scott Turow.

Literary Events

1970—Tony Hillerman: *The Blessing Way*
1974—Robert B. Parker: *The Godwulf Manuscript*
1977—Marcia Muller: *Edwin of the Iron Shoes*
1982—Sara Paretsky: *Indemnity Only*
1986—Sue Grafton: *A Is for Alibi*

1987—Sisters in Crime formed
1989—John Grisham: *A Time to Kill*
1990—Patricia Cornwell: *Postmortem*

World Events

1974—Watergate scandal; President Nixon resigns
1975—South Vietnam surrenders to North Vietnam
1978—First personal computers
1981—President Reagan becomes President
1986—*Challenger* explodes after launch
1989—End of Cold War

1990–2010

This period saw the increase in popularity in forensics novels, historical mysteries, and the continued ascendancy of female crime fiction authors. Authors who started to publish during this period include Donna Andrews, David Baldacci, Nevada Barr, Lee Child, Michael Connelly, Deborah Crombie, Diane Mott Davidson, Tess Gerritsen, Charlaine Harris, Laurie R. King, Laura Lippman, and Kathy Reichs.

Literary Events

1990—Walter Mosley: *Devil in a Blue Dress*
1993—Minette Walters: *The Sculptress*
1994—Janet Evanovich: *One for the Money*
1994—Dennis Lehane: *A Drink Before the War*
1998—Alexander McCall Smith: *The No. 1 Ladies Detective Agency*
2003—Jacqueline Winspear: *Maisie Dobbs*

World Events

1991—Gulf War
1993—World Wide Web
1997—NASA lands spacecraft on Mars
2001—Terrorist attack on 9/11
2003—Iraq War begins
2009—Barack Obama becomes first black U.S. president

About the Writers

It's difficult to narrow a list of writers of crime fiction down to fifty names. Many readers may quarrel with the final choices, and it's true that a volume such as this could include two or even three times as many writers who are worthy of consideration. The final choices were based on a mix of authors: some who are considered classic; some who have been writing for a number of years but are still publishing; newer authors who are popular with readers; representative authors from various categories of the genre; and award winners. I hope that the author you are looking for is included in this book. If not, it's only because I couldn't include all who perhaps deserved to be here.

Organization of Entries

Authors are listed alphabetically under the name that appears on their works. In cases in which a writer has published in the crime fiction genre under more than one pen name, cross-references point to the main entry under the best-known name. Pen names may be used to allow an author to try out a new series without having to face the expectations attached to the better-known name. Or they may be used regularly for different categories within the overall genre. An example of this is Barbara Mertz, who writes as both "Elizabeth Peters" and "Barbara Michaels." In this book, she will be found under the entry for "Elizabeth Peters."

Quotation and Biography

Each entry begins with a quotation characteristic of the writer's style. This is followed by a short biography and a brief description of the type of work for which the writer is known.

Category Tags

Category tags are found after the biographical sketch for each author. These tags signify categories into which the author's works fall. The tags were developed according to categories given in Diana Tixier Herald's *Genreflecting* (6th ed.) There is a complete "List of Authors by Category" presented at the end of the book.

Awards

Major awards won by the writer are listed. Information about award winners was taken from award listings on the Web sites of the various organizations that administer the awards. Unless otherwise indicated, awards for crime authors are given in multiple categories. Additional information about the awards can be found in the "Major Awards" section. The awards listed include the following (in alphabetical order):

- Agatha: Given by attendees of the annual Malice Domestic convention, emphasizing cozy mystery fiction
- Anthony: Given by attendees of Bouchercon, the world mystery convention

- Barry: Given by the editors of Deadly Pleasures magazine and presented at Bouchercon
- Dagger: Given by the Crime Writers association in the United Kingdom
- Edgar: Given by the Mystery Writers of America (MWA)
- Grand Master: Given for lifetime achievement by the MWA
- Macavity: Given by members of Mystery Readers International
- Shamus: Given by the Private Eye Writers of America
- Nero: Given by members of the Wolfe Pack to a work that represents the spirit of the Nero Wolfe novels
- Lefty: Given by attendees of the Left Coast Crime convention for the best humorous mystery

Major Works

Next comes a listing of the author's series (with titles), titles of major stand-alone works, short-story collections, and any nonfiction works by the author that it is important to understand in relation to the crime fiction field. Short-story anthologies edited by the author and omnibus collections of novels are not listed.

Research Sources

Research sources fall into two categories: primary and secondary. Primary sources are those sources that are in the author's own words, including non-fiction works, essays, and interviews. Secondary sources provide information and interpretation by persons other than the author. Sources given in the listings include both primary and secondary sources if available. Research sources are listed under the following headings for each author.

Encyclopedias and Handbooks

Abbreviations are given for common sources in this category, but other sources may also be listed. A list of abbreviations for common sources follows this section. Works included here may include basic biographical information, summary information about works, and so on. Some works that include critical analyses are also found in this section. Entries in some sources may be brief.

Bibliographies

Again, abbreviations are given for common sources in this category. These sources provide lists of works by or about an author and may include

Web sites. Sources such as the author's official Web site that may have biblio-graphical information are not included in this section.

Biographies and Interviews

This section includes print and online interviews (including audio and video interviews) and works with a significant biographical component. Interviews may focus on a particular work or period in the author's life or may be more comprehensive.

Criticism and Readers' Guides

These works range from entire books devoted to a single author and his or her works to scholarly articles and essays that have appeared in journals and books. Bio-critical works, such as volumes of the Dictionary of Literary Biography, are included in this section. There is not much critical material available yet on a few of the newer authors, whereas there is an abundance of critical material available on authors such as Christie or Chandler. Sources are selected for this section on the basis of scholarly worth and likelihood of availability in U.S. libraries.

Web Sites

Web sites included here are the author's official Web site, fan-run Web sites if they include useful information, and other Web sites that may be of interest to those wishing to learn about a particular author. Even classic authors who are no longer living may have one or more Web sites devoted to their lives and works. As noted earlier, some types of Web sites appear in many entries. General features of such Web sites are given here to avoid repetitive annotations within entries.

- Official Web site: Common elements of these Web sites include bio-graphical information, comprehensive lists of works, links to interviews and articles, book excerpts, appearance schedule, and press informa-tion. Some sites may also include blogs, personal photos, essays, and similar material.
- Fan sites: These vary in content but may include bibliographies, links to interviews, critical essays, book reviews, and discussion forums.
- Blogs: Author blogs may appear on the official Web site or be separate. They may or may not be frequently updated.
- Facebook: Authors seem to be just beginning to take advantage of this social networking site. Only a few writers have well-developed Face-book entries at the time of this writing. but those are listed.

All URLs were checked during November 2010.

Read-Alike Lists

Entitled "If You Like…Then You Might Like…," lists of read-alike authors have been created for selected authors throughout the book. Authors listed in the read-alikes have written works that are similar in category, feel, milieu, or theme to those of another author and may be of interest to those who are researching the original author.

What's Not Included

Materials not included are individual book reviews and short interviews (unless there is little else available).

Abbreviations

Following is a list of abbreviations used for works frequently referred to in the entries for the writers. Full citations for these and other works are given in the General Bibliography found near the end of the book.

- 100: Drew's *100 Most Popular Genre Fiction Authors*
- BEA: *Beacham's Analyses Series*
- BEB: *Beacham's Biography Series*
- BYA: Swanson and James's *By a Woman's Hand,* 2nd ed.
- CA: *Contemporary Authors*
- CANR: *Contemporary Authors, New Revision*
- CLC: *Contemporary Literary Criticism*
- EMM: Murphy's *Encyclopedia of Murder and Mystery*
- GWM: Lindsay's *Great Women Mystery Writers,* 2nd ed.
- MCF: Ashley's *The Mammoth Encyclopedia of Modern Crime Fiction*
- OCC: Herbert's *Oxford Companion to Crime and Mystery Writing*
- STJ: Pederson's *St. James Guide to Crime and Mystery Writers*
- TCLC: *Twentieth-Century Literary Criticism*
- WWW: Herbert's *Whodunit? A Who's Who in Crime & Mystery Writing*

Bibliographies

- FF: *FantasticFiction.co.uk* (http://FantasticFiction.co.uk accessed April 27, 2010)
- OM: *Omnimystery* (http://authors.omnimystery.com/ accessed April 27, 2010)

How to Use This Book

This book is intended for a variety of audiences and needs:

Students

You can browse through the book to get ideas for authors to use for your projects and papers. The "Major Works" section of each entry will give you a quick idea of what each author has published and when.

To find out more about an author's life, check the biographical resources listed for the entry. These might include interviews with the author, books and articles about the author's life, and collected letters to or by the author. Some authors have even written autobiographies. We've listed a number of author Web sites and blogs under "Web Sites"; these can give you even more information about an author (and his or her opinions!).

To get information about the books that the authors wrote, consult the "Criticism and Readers' Guides" section. There, you'll find literary criticism (discussions and interpretations of the novels and stories). Some of these articles are formal academic essays, while others may be more informal articles and "reader's guides." Incidentally, literary criticism is often referred to as "secondary" sources (as opposed to "primary" sources—novels, short stories, letters, and other things that were actually written by the authors themselves).

Teachers

You can browse through the book to find potential authors to use in your curriculum and syllabi planning. More specifically, the "Major Works" section of each entry will help you select specific novels and short stories to teach or to recommend to students for free reading. The "Biographical Sketch" and the "Criticism and Reader's Guides" sections suggest essays and books that you can use in planning lectures and lessons or for directing student research. Although many of the Web sites listed under "Web Sites" may be less academic, they can provide an additional angle. Students may especially enjoy the immediacy of reading authors' blogs.

A "General Bibliography" that you can consult for broader sources for the fantasy genre as a whole is also included.

Librarians

The "Major Works" provide quick lists to consult in Reader's Advisory questions. Some entries even include a "If You Like … Then You Might Like …" section that you can consult to find books for the patron who has read all of his or her favorite author's books and needs more. These lists may also be helpful for collection development.

In turn, the "Biographical Sketch" and the "Criticism and Readers' Guides" sections will prove useful for reference questions concerning writers and their works. You can also use them, as well as the "General Bibliography," for collection development.

Book Club Leaders

You can browse through the book to find authors and books that your book club might be interested in. The "Biographical Sketch" sections may be especially helpful to you for background information as you prepare for book club discussions. We've listed a number of author Web sites that you can use to see what your authors are working on now (they can also be a lot of fun to read!).

Going Beyond This Book

Authors keep writing books, and researchers keep writing books and articles about them. Although the listed sources will remain useful, you may want to look for more current ones. Here are some tips:

- Check the bibliography: A number of reference books, indexes, and Web portals that you can use to find additional sources are listed within the entries and in the "General Bibliography."
- One good source deserves another: If you find a book or Web site that you like (or even halfway like), look in the index, foot notes, bibliography, or "Web Sites" for more sources.
- Talk to your local reference librarian: Librarians may have ideas for further searching or know about new sources and updates.

Of course, you can also search the Web, which leads to …

Getting Beyond Google or Wikipedia

One of the reasons for this book is that doing author research online can be really hard. The first few (or several) pages of Google results are often full of hits from online book vendors, genealogy charts, or, sad to say, Web sites that tend to all say the same thing. You can use a variety of techniques to search for more in-depth articles:

- Think about your search terms: Try combining various terms such as "interview" or "article" along with the author name (e.g., "Agatha Christie" AND "interview"). Putting the author's name in quotation marks will also tell the search engine to keep the names together (so you don't end up with hits for every "Sharon" when all you wanted was "Sharon McCone").
- Look for links on Web sites: Even so-so Web sites can provide links to really great ones. Crime writer association and journal Web sites are often especially helpful for this (e.g., the "International Thriller Writers"). Author web sites can also be a great source.
- Check reference books: Many include recommended links (this also works for finding books and articles!)
- Check an index: Many indexes, such as the *Modern Language Bibliography* (MLA) and *Annual Biography of English Language and Literature* (ABELL) are starting to include Web sites.

EVALUATING WHAT YOU FIND

Anyone can post a Web site, and (almost) anyone can edit a Wikipedia entry. Even books aren't always trustworthy. As you do research, consider these factors:

- *Currency*

How old is the information? Does it matter? Currency tends to be more important for authors who are still alive (and publishing).

- *Authority*

Who wrote the book or created the Web site? What makes them qualified to do so? Do they list credentials? When in doubt, check to see if you can find the same information in at least two other sources (this is also known as "triangulation").

- *Point of view*

A publisher's Web site and a *Publishers Weekly* article may have very different points of view. Publisher sites are generally focused on selling books, while Web sites, books, and articles produced by third parties are more likely to be neutral or even critical. Look for sources from a variety of viewpoints.

- *Audience*

Who is the article written for? Who is the Web site produced for? Web sites and articles directed at fans often differ from those directed at scholars and critics. In general, *scholarly* Web sites and publications tend to be more focused and specialized. They may also assume prior knowledge of the author and their books.

What to Do If the Web Site Links Don't Work

Every effort has been made to ensure that the Web site links included in this book are current, but Web site URLs do often change over time. If you should come across an URL that doesn't work, try the following:

- First, try a different Web browser. Some pages won't work in particular browsers.
- Next, try looking up the title of the page on an Internet search engine such as www.google.com. Google also caches sites, so try the cache link if the current link doesn't work.
- If it's a page from a publisher Web site, try doing an internal search in the Web site (publishers have a habit of rearranging their sites and URLs every so often).
- Finally, try looking up the nonworking URL in the Internet Archive (www.archive.org), an online archive for both active and obsolete Web sites. The Archive doesn't have every page that's ever been online, but it has a large number of them.

Alphabetical List of Authors

Andrews, Donna
Baldacci, David
Barr, Nevada
Burke, James Lee
Chandler, Raymond
Child, Lee
Christie, Agatha
Clark, Mary Higgins
Connelly, Michael
Cornwell, Patricia
Crais, Robert
Crombie, Deborah
Davidson, Diane Mott
Elkins, Aaron
Evanovich, Janet
Francis, Dick
George, Elizabeth
Gerritsen, Tess
Grafton, Sue
Grisham, John
Harris, Charlaine
Hart, Carolyn
Hiaasen, Carl
Hillerman, Tony
James, P. D.
Jance, J. A.

King, Laurie R.
Lehane, Dennis
Leonard, Elmore
Lippman, Laura
Lovesey, Peter
Maron, Margaret
Marsh, Ngaio
McBain, Ed (aka Evan Hunter)
Mosley, Walter
Mullar, Marcia
Paretsky, Sara
Parker, Robert B.
Patterson, James
Perry, Anne
Peters, Elizabeth (aka Barbara
    Mertz, Barbara Michaels)
Picard, Nancy
Reichs, Kathy
Rendell, Ruth (aka Barbara Vine)
Sayers, Dorothy L.
Smith, Alexander McCall
Stout, Rex
Turow, Scott
Walters, Minette
Winspear, Jacqueline

Crime Writers

Andrews, Donna

If Michael still believed we'd reach dry land soon, I wasn't going to discourage him. Even though deep down, I knew that we really had boarded the Flying Dutchman, and were doomed to sail up and down the coast for all eternity, or at least until we ran out of fuel and had to be rescued by the Coast Guard.

—*Murder with Puffins*, 2000

Biographical Sketch

Donna Andrews was born in Yorktown, Virginia, and attended the University of Virginia, where she majored in English and drama with a concentration in writing and developed an interest in mysteries. After graduating, she joined the communications staff of a large financial organization in the Washington, D.C., area, where she worked for two decades and "developed a profound understanding of the criminal mind through her observation of interdepartmental politics" (official Web site). Her communications background was useful when she decided to try her hand at writing crime fiction and submitted a manuscript for the Malice Domestic/St. Martin's Press contest for best first traditional mystery. She won that contest, and that manuscript went on to win three major awards (Agatha, Anthony, and Barry) for best first novel. Several subsequent books have been award nominees.

Andrews writes in two series thus far. The books in the Meg Langslow series are noted for their humor, family involvement, and interesting characters, as well as for the creative titles involving birds. *Publisher's Weekly* described one book as having "a smile on nearly every page and at least one chuckle per chapter." Her other series has a unique twist with the introduction of an artificial intelligence, Turing Hopper, as the primary character. Turing believes she may be developing sentience, and her thoughts on this as well as her plans make her appealing for tech-conscious readers.

Categories: Amateur Detective, Cozy

Awards

Agatha Award, Best First Novel (*Murder with Peacocks,* 1999)
Agatha Award, Best Novel (*You've Got Murder,* 2002)
Agatha Award, Best Short Story ("A Rat's Tale," *Ellery Queen Mystery Magazine,* September–October 2007)
Anthony Award, Best First Novel (*Murder with Peacocks,* 2000)
Barry Award (*Murder with Peacocks,* 2000)
Lefty Award, Funniest Mystery (*Murder with Peacocks,* 2000; *We'll Always Have Parrots,* 2005)

Major Works

Meg Langslow series: *Murder with Peacocks* (1999), *Murder with Puffins* (2000), *Revenge of the Wrought-Iron Flamingos* (2001), *Crouching Buzzard, Leaping Loon* (2003), *We'll Always Have Parrots* (2004), *Owls Well That Ends Well* (2005), *No Nest for the Wicket* (2006), *The Penguin Who Knew Too Much* (2007), *Cockatiels at Seven* (2008), *Six Geese a-Slaying* (2008), *Swan for the Money* (2009), *Stork Raving Mad* (2010)
Turing Hopper series: *You've Got Murder* (2002), *Click Here for Murder* (2003), *Access Denied* (2004), *Delete All Suspects* (2005)

Research Sources

Encyclopedias and Handbooks: CA (254), CANR (174), GWM

Bibliographies: FF, OM

Biographies and Interviews

Bloom, Tayler. "Interview: Donna Andrews." Personal blog. December 30, 2007. http://blogs.myspace.com/index.cfm?fuseaction=blog.view&friend ID=167182571&blogID=342446542 (accessed November 1, 2010).
"Donna Andrews." *Booksnbytes.com.* May 2006. http://www.booksnbytes. com/authors/andrews_donna.html (accessed November 1, 2010).
"Donna Andrews." *Cozy Library.* 2006. http://www.cozylibrary.com/default. aspx?id=123 (accessed November 1, 2010).
"Donna Andrews." *FreshFiction.com.* 2010. http://freshfiction.com/author. php?%20id=185 (accessed November 1, 2010).
Webb, Betty. "Interview with Donna Andrews." *WebbsBlog.* January 3, 2008. http://bloggingwebb.blogspot.com/2008/01/interview-with-donna-andrews.html (accessed November 1, 2010).

Criticism and Reader's Guides

Cogdill, Oline. "Funny Bones: Donna Andrews Tickles Readers with Her Witty and Wacky Novels." *Mystery Scene* 107 (2008): 32–34.

"Donna Andrews." *Romantic Times Book Reviews.* n.d. http://www.rtbook reviews.com/author/donna-andrews (accessed November 1, 2010).
"Donna Andrews: The Meg Lanslow Mysteries." *A Woman of Mystery.* March 7, 2007. http://awomanofmystery.wordpress.com/2007/03/07/ donna-andrews-the-meg-lanslow-books/ (accessed November 1, 2010).

Web Site

Official Web site: http://www.donnaandrews.com/ (accessed November 1, 2010).

Baldacci, David, 1960–

There are four acknowledged ways of meeting your maker: . . . . However, if you live in Washington, D.C., there is a fifth way of kicking the bucket: the political death. It can spring from many sources: frolicking in a public fountain with an exotic dancer who is not your wife; stuffing bags of money in your pants when the payer unfortunately happens to be the FBI; or covering up a bungled burglary when you call 1600 Pennsylvania Avenue home.

—*Simple Genius*, 2007

Biographical Sketch

David Baldacci was born in Richmond, Virginia. He attended Virginia Commonwealth University, where he received a bachelor's degree in political science, and law school at the University of Virginia. He was a trial and corporate lawyer for nine years in Washington, D.C. During this time, he was also writing stories and screenplays during his spare time. His first published novel, *Absolute Power*, was a best seller, won the Gold Medal Award from the Southern Writers' Guild, and was adapted into a movie starring Clint Eastwood.

Baldacci's fast-paced novels fall into the category of political and legal thrillers, and he has been compared to John Grisham. Baldacci's books consistently appear on best-seller lists and have been translated into thirty languages. This immensely popular author has also been named in *People Magazine*'s 50 Most Beautiful People list. A strong supporter of literacy, Baldacci and his wife, Michelle, have started a foundation to fund family literacy efforts.

Categories: Legal, Thriller

Major Works

The King and Maxwell Mystery series: *Split Second* (2003), *Hour Game* (2004), *Simple Genius* (2007), *First Family* (2009)

The Camel Club Mystery series: *The Camel Club* (2005), *The Collectors* (2006), *Stone Cold* (2007), *Divine Justice* (2008), *Hell's Corner* (2010)
Shaw and James series: *The Whole Truth* (2008), *Deliver Us from Evil* (2010)
Nonseries novels: *Absolute Power* (1996), *Total Control* (1997), *The Winner* (1997), *The Simple Truth* (1998), *Saving Faith* (1999), *Last Man Standing* (2001), *The Collectors* (2006), *Wish You Well* (2007), *True Blue* (2009)

Research Sources

Encyclopedias and Handbooks: CA (187), CANR (179)

O'Brien, Carolyn. "David Baldacci." *Encyclopedia Virginia*. Virginia Foundation for the Humanities. June 15, 2009. http://www.encyclopediavirginia. org/Baldacci_David_1960-. (accessed November 1, 2010).

Bibliographies: FF, OM

Biographies and Interviews

Beck, Glenn. "Glenn Talks with Author David Baldacci." *The Glenn Beck Program*. April 20, 2009. http://www.glennbeck.com/content/articles/ article/196/24271/ (accessed November 1, 2010).
"David Baldacci." *Bookreporter.com*. November 2002. http://www.book reporter.com/authors/au-baldacci-david.asp#talk0211 (accessed November 1, 2010).
"David Baldacci: 2009 National Book Festival." (videocast) *Library of Congress*. September 26, 2009. http://www.loc.gov/today/cyberlc/feature_ wdesc.php?rec=4688 (accessed November 1, 2010).
"David Baldacci: Absolute Thriller." *Bitter Lawyer*. September 10, 2009. http://www.bitterlawyer.com/index.php/interviews/david_baldacci_ absolute_thriller_author_lawyer?entry_id=1301 (accessed November 1, 2010).
"David Baldacci: Book Fest 2007." (videocast) *Library of Congress*. September 29, 2007. http://www.loc.gov/today/cyberlc/feature_wdesc.php? rec=4136 (accessed November 1, 2010).
Kitto, Kris. "20 Questions with Author David Baldacci." *The Hill*. November 9, 2009. http://thehill.com/capital-living/67055-20-questions-david-baldacci (accessed November 1, 2010).
Milk, Leslie. "Mystery Man: David Baldacci." *Washingtonian.com*. August 1, 2007. http://www.washingtonian.com/articles/people/5044.html (accessed November 1, 2010).
Patrick, Bethanne. "A Conversation with David Baldacci." (videocast—3 parts) *WETA Book Studio*. January 25, 2010. http://www.thebookstudio. com/blog/bethanne/conversation-david-baldacci-0 (accessed November 1, 2010).

Shapiro, Ari. "A Conspiracy Around Every Corner in Baldacci's D.C." (audiocast) *Morning Edition, NPR.* July 17, 2009. http://www.npr.org/templates/story/story.php?storyId=106921382 (accessed November 1, 2010).

Thomas, Louisa. "Thriller Instinct," *Newsweek.* March 30, 2009. http://www.newsweek.com/id/190339/page/1 (accessed November 1, 2010).

Zibert, Eve. "The Secrets of His Success." *Book Page.* 2007. http://www.bookpage.com/0705bp/david_baldacci.html (accessed November 1, 2010).

Criticism and Reader's Guides

Murphy, Stephen M. *Their Word Is Law: Bestselling Lawyer-Novelists.* New York: Berkley Books, 2002. 14–27.

"Wish You Well." (reading guide) *ReadingGroupGuides.* 2010. http://www.readinggroupguides.com/guides_W/wish_you_well1.asp (accessed November 1, 2010).

Web Site

Official Web site: http://www.davidbaldacci.com (accessed November 1, 2010).

Barr, Nevada, 1952–

A tarantula the size of a woman's hand, the most horrifying of gentle creatures, wandered slowly across Anna's path. "As a Park Ranger I will protect and serve you." She talked to the creature from a safe three yards away. "But we'll never be friends. Is that going to be a problem?"

—*Track of the Cat,* 1993

Biographical Sketch

Although Barr was born in Nevada, there is some dispute as to whether she was named for the state or for one of her father's favorite book characters. Both of her parents were pilots, and she was raised near a small airport in California. She attended California Polytechnic State University at San Luis Obispo and received a master's degree in theater at the University of California at Irvine. Barr pursued a number of occupations, including stage and film acting in New York and Minneapolis, and worked in advertising before becoming first a part-time and then a full-time park ranger with the National Park Service. She attributes her becoming a ranger to her first husband, who was also a ranger and who aroused in her an interest in nature and conservation. She began writing her second published book and first mystery while working at Guadalupe Mountains National Park, and she eventually left the Park Service to write full time. Barr now lives in New Orleans and has remarried yet another former park ranger.

Barr's fame as a crime writer rests on her Anna Pigeon series, set in various national parks. Anna is middle aged and a loner for the most part, moving from park to park in her career. Although she falls in love twice and eventually marries, romantic relationships do not change her independent nature. Because of her position as a ranger, Anna is a law enforcement person, but she also can be characterized as an amateur detective. The Pigeon books defy being characterized as falling into one particular subgenre of crime fiction. Certainly, part of the attraction of this series is the variety of park settings, with Anna's adventures being characteristic of the different places where she works. Barr's latest work, *13 ½*, is a stand-alone psychological thriller.

Categories: Amateur Detective, Police Procedural

Awards

Anthony Award for Best First Novel (*Track of the Cat,* 1994)
Agatha Award for Best First Novel (*Track of the Cat,* 1994)
Barry Award for Best Novel (*Deep South,* 2001)

Major Works

Anna Pigeon series: *Track of the Cat* (1993), *A Superior Death* (1994), *Ill Wind* (1995), *Firestorm* (1996), *Endangered Species* (1997), *Blind Descent* (1998), *Liberty Falling* (1999), *Deep South* (2000), *Blood Lure* (2001), *Hunting Season* (2002), *Flashback* (2003), *High Country* (2004), *Hard Truth* (2005), *Winter Study* (2008), *Borderline* (2009), *Burn* (2010)
Nonseries novels: *13½* (2009)
Nonfiction: *Seeking Enlightenment... Hat by Hat: A Skeptic's Path to Religion* (2003)

Research Sources

Encyclopedias and Handbooks: 100, BYA, CA (161), CANR (95, 160), GWM, MCF, WWW

Bibliographies: FF, OM

Biographies and Interviews

Brunsdale, M. "'PW' Talks with Nevada Barr: Suffer the Little Children." *Publishers Weekly* 256.38 (2009): 31. http://www.publishersweekly.com/pw/by-topic/1-legacy/16-all-book-reviews/article/10547-pw-talks-with-nevada-barr-.html (accessed November 1, 2010).

"Nevada Barr." *The Mississippi Writers' Page*. July 30, 2007. http://www.ole miss.edu/mwp/dir/barr_nevada/index.html (accessed November 1, 2010).

Rowen, John. "The Booklist Interview: Nevada Barr." *Booklist* 95.16 (1999): 1462.

Shindler, Dorman T. "The Law of Nature: An Interview with Nevada Barr." *Armchair Detective: A Quarterly Journal Devoted to the Appreciation of Mystery, Detective, and Suspense Fiction* 28.3 (1995): 308–11.

Shindler, Dorman T. "Nevada Barr: Taking On History's Mysteries." *Publishers Weekly* 250.4 (2003): 230.

Silet, Charles L. P. "Nevada Barr." *Speaking of Murder, vol. 2: Interviews with the Masters of Mystery and Suspense*. Ed. Ed Gorman and Martin H. Greenberg. New York: Berkley Prime Crime, 1999. 78–88.

Criticism and Reader's Guides

Barr, Nevada. "How I Write." *The Writer* 117.6 (2004): 66.

Barr, Nevada. "Wolves, Moose, Researchers, and Me." *National Parks* 83.1 (2009): 24-5. http://books.google.com/books?id=o1wEAAAAMBAJ& pg=PA1&source=gbs_toc&cad=2#v=onepage&q&f=false (accessed November 1, 2010).

"Nevada Barr." (audiocasts) *Bill Thompson's Eye on Books*. n.d. http://eyeon books.com/iap.php?authID=334 (accessed November 1, 2010).

Pinckley, Diana "Nevada Barr: Not Just Another Day in the Park." *Mystery Scene* 104 (2008): 18–20.

Rancourt, Linda M. "Murder, She Writes." *National Parks* 69.9/10 (1995): 30.

Reynolds, Moira Davison. "Nevada Barr." *Women Authors of Detective Series: Twenty-One American and British Writers, 1900–2000*. Jefferson, NC: McFarland, 2001. 145–48.

Web Sites

Official Web site: http://www.nevadabarr.net/ (accessed November 1, 2010).

Facebook page: http://www.facebook.com/pages/Nevada-Barr/50882766478 (accessed November 1, 2010).

"Nevada Barr Resource Page" 14 June 2006. http://mindharp.tripod.com/ nbarr.html—Fan site that includes biography, lists of books, related links to national parks featured in books. Not updated since 2006 but still has some useful information (accessed November 1, 2010).

If You Like Nevada Barr

Barr depicts a number of very different natural settings through the eyes of her park ranger protagonist, Anna Pigeon. She portrays a somewhat lonely, independent woman who is nevertheless open to new experiences and relationships. The crimes that Anna investigates grow out of the natural settings in which the novels take place.

Then You Might Like

C. J. Box

Box has garnered critical acclaim for his series about Joe Pickett, a Wyoming game warden. The Pickett books involve social issues such as environmentalism, survivalists, and poaching and have vivid descriptions of the natural landscape in which they take place. *Blue Heaven* is the winner of the 2009 Edgar Award for Best Novel.

Sue Henry

Alex Jensen, an Alaska state trooper, and Jessie Arnold, a top woman musher in Alaskan dog sledding, are the protagonists in Henry's main series of novels, with later entries mainly revolving around Jessie. Her books are praised for their suspenseful plots and vivid descriptions of the Alaskan wilderness. The series begins with *Murder on the Iditarod Trail.*

Karen Kijewski

Kijewski writes a series about a woman private investigator, Kat Colorado. Kat is a strong protagonist, reminiscent of Anna Pigeon in her determination to solve the mystery at hand. Kat is involved romatically with a cop but has an off-again, on-again relationship and doesn't marry. Like Anna, Kat is independent and strong-willed. Titles include *Katwalk* and *Katapult,* the first two entries in the series.

Skye Kathleen Moody

Moody's protagonist, Venus Diamond, is an agent of the U.S. Fish and Wildlife Service. The series has a strong environmental message and takes place in various locales, as does Barr's series. Titles include *Rain Dance* and *Blue Poppy,* among others.

Dana Stabenow

Alaska is also the setting for Stabenow's books about Kate Shugak, an Aleutian Indian. Kate was formerly with the district attorney's office in Anchorage but now lives in a bus after receiving a serious injury. The books take place primarily in a fictional national park, and their vivid descriptions of the natural setting, along with strong characterizations and interesting plots, make them appealing to readers. Try *A Cold Day for Murder* and *Dead in the Water.*

Burke, James Lee, 1936–

My grandfather and his father were both violent men. Their eyes were possessed of a peculiar unfocused light that soldiers call the thousand-yard stare, and the ghosts of the men they had killed visited them in their sleep and stood in attendance by their deathbeds. When I was a young police officer in Houston, I swore their legacy would never be mine.

—Cimarron Rose, 1997

Biographical Sketch

James Lee Burke was born in Houston, Texas, and grew up on the coasts of Texas and Louisiana. He attended the University of Southwest Louisiana and later received his B.A. and M.A. degrees from the University of Missouri. Although he held various jobs such as surveyor, social worker, and newspaper reporter, Burke also was a college instructor at several institutions. After winning an award for a story written while he was a student at Southwest Louisiana, he began writing seriously. His first novel was published in 1965 and was soon followed by two more. After that, he wouldn't be published again for thirteen years.

Burke collected ninety-three rejection slips for his noncrime novel, *The Lost Get-Back Boogie,* which was eventually published by the Louisiana State University Press and garnered a Pulitzer Prize nomination. But before that book was published, Burke started writing a crime novel, which became *The Neon Rain,* the first Dave Robicheaux novel. Two of his subsequent novels have received Edgar awards for best novel, another a Gold Dagger Award, and Burke has been named a Grand Master by the Mystery Writers of America. Burke's books feature gritty plots, flawed protagonists, and a strong sense of the southern locales.

Burke and his wife, Pearl, have four children, and their daughter Alafair is also a published crime novelist.

Categories: Hard-Boiled, Police Procedural

Awards

Edgar Award for Best Novel (*Black Cherry Blues,* 1990; *Cimarron Rose,* 1998)
Gold Dagger Award (*Sunset Limited,* 1998)
Grand Master Award (Mystery Writers of America) (2009)

Major Works

Dave Robicheaux series: *The Neon Rain* (1987), *Heaven's Prisoners* (1988), *Black Cherry Blues* (1989), *A Morning for Flamingos* (1990), *A Stained White Radiance* (1992), *In the Electric Mist with Confederate Dead* (1993), *Dixie City Jam* (1994), *Burning Angel* (1995), *Cadillac Jukebox* (1996), *Sunset Limited* (1998), *Purple Cane Road* (2000), *Jolie Blon's Bounce* (2002), *Last Car to Elysian Fields* (2003), *Crusader's Cross* (2005), *Pegasus Descending* (2006), *The Tin Roof Blowdown* (2007), *Swan Peak* (2008)

Billy Bob Holland series: *Cimarron Rose* (1997), *Heartwood* (1999), *Bitterroot* (2001), *In the Moon of Red Ponies* (2004)
Hackberry Holland series: *Lay Down My Sword and Shield* (1995), *Rain Gods* (2009)

Research Sources

Encyclopedias and Handbooks: 100, CA (13–16R), CANR (7, 22, 41, 64, 106, 176), EMM, MCF, STJ, WWW

Bibliographies: FF, OM

Biographies and Interviews

"James Lee Burke." *Bookreporter.com*. July 23, 1997. http://www.bookreporter. com/authors/au-burke-james-lee.asp (accessed November 1, 2010).

"James Lee Burke: 'Last Car to Elysian Fields.'" (audiocast) *Day to Day, NPR*. October 22, 2003. http://www.npr.org/templates/story/story.php? storyId=1474880 (accessed November 1, 2010).

"James Lee Burke's Fictional Take on Katrina." (audiocast) *Day to Day, NPR*. July 30, 2007. http://www.npr.org/templates/story/story.php?storyId= 12303974 (accessed November 1, 2010).

Jackson, Martin. "James Lee Burke's New Orleans." *Telegraph.co.uk*. August 22, 2008. http://www.telegraph.co.uk/travel/destinations/north america/usa/2591004/James-Lee-Burkes-New-Orleans-Three-years-after-Hurricane-Katrina.html (accessed November 1, 2010).

Kaminsky, Stuart, and Laurie Roberts. "James Lee Burke." *Behind the Mystery: Top Mystery Writers Interviewed*. Cohasset, MA: Hot House, 2005. 104–19.

Kogan, Deen. "James Lee Burke: An Interview and Appreciation." *Irish Edition*. September 25, 2008. http://irishedition.com/2008/09/25/james-lee-burke-an-interview-and-appreciation/ (accessed November 1, 2010).

McCone, Arthur. "Meet the Writers: James Lee Burke." *Barnes and Noble*. 2002. http://www.barnesandnoble.com/writers/writerdetails.asp?cid= 968834#bio (accessed November 1, 2010).

Peters, Barbara. "James Lee Burke." (videocast—6 parts) *The Poisoned Pen*. n.d. http://www.poisonedpen.com/interviews/james-lee-burke; also available at http://www.youtube.com/watch?v=QL9vnrLk1ZE (accessed November 1, 2010).

Rainone, Anthony. "James Lee Burke." *January Magazine*. October 2004. http://januarymagazine.com/profiles/jlburke.html (accessed November 1, 2010).

Welch, David. "Author Interviews: James Lee Burke." *Powells Books*. August 4, 2000. http://www.powells.com/authors/burke.html (accessed November 1, 2010).

Wertheimer, Linda. "The Burke Family Business Is a Mystery." (audio-cast) *All Things Considered, NPR.* June 13, 2004. http://www.npr.org/templates/story/story.php?storyId=1952890 (accessed November 1, 2010).

Womack, Steven "A Talk with James Lee Burke." *Armchair Detective: A Quarterly Journal Devoted to the Appreciation of Mystery, Detective, and Suspense Fiction* 29.2 (1996): 138–43.

Criticism and Reader's Guides

Bogue, Barbara. *James Lee Burke and the Soul of Dave Robicheaux: A Critical Study of the Crime Fiction. Series.* Jefferson, NC: McFarland, 2006.

Carney, Rob "Clete Purcel to the Rampaging Rescue: Looking for the Hard-Boiled Tradition in James Lee Burke's Dixie City Jam." *Southern Quarterly: A Journal of the Arts in the South* 34.4 (1996): 121–30.

Easterling, Thomas "'All Our Stories Begin Here': Heroism and Sense of Place in James Lee Burke's Dave Robicheaux Mystery Series." *Songs of the New South: Writing Contemporary Louisiana.* Ed. Suzanne Disheroon Green and Lisa Abney. Westport, CT: Greenwood, 2001. 57–65.

Engel, Leonard, ed. *A Violent Conscience: Essays on the Fiction of James Lee Burke.* Jefferson, NC: McFarland, 2009.

Geherin, David. "James Lee Burke: Southern Louisiana." *Scene of the Crime: Importance of Place in Crime and Mystery Fiction.* Jefferson, NC: McFarland, 2008. 93–108.

Hall, Dean G. "James Lee Burke." *American Hard-Boiled Crime Writers* (*Dictionary of Literary Biography* 226). Ed. George Parker Anderson and Julie B. Anderson. Detroit, MI: Gale, 2000. 19–30.

Pridgen, Allen "James Lee Burke's Dave Robicheaux: A Search for Home." *Southern Quarterly: A Journal of the Arts in the South* 41.1 (2002): 67–79.

Shelton, Frank W. "James Lee Burke's Dave Robicheaux Novels." *The World Is Our Home: Society and Culture in Contemporary Southern Writing.* Ed. Jeffrey J. Folks and Nancy Summers Folks. Lexington: University Press of Kentucky, 2000. 232–43.

Wilson, Anthony. "James Lee Burke." *Twenty-First-Century American Novelists: Second Series* (*Dictionary of Literary Biography* 350). Ed. Wanda H. Giles and James R. Giles. Detroit, MI: Gale, 2009. 39–45.

Web Sites

Official Web site: http://www.jamesleeburke.com/ (accessed November 1, 2010).

Facebook page: http://www.facebook.com/pages/James-Lee-and-Alafair-Burke/64090488440 (accessed November 1, 2010).

Chandler, Raymond, 1888–1959

But down these mean streets a man must go who is not himself mean, who is neither tarnished nor afraid. The detective in this kind of story must be such a man. He is the hero, he is everything. He must be a complete man and a common man and yet an unusual man. He must be, to use a rather weathered phrase, a man of honor. . . .

—"The Simple Art of Murder," 1944

Biographical Sketch

Raymond Chandler was born in Chicago but moved to England at the age of seven with his mother after his parents divorced. He attended school there and, in 1905, spent a year on the continent studying French and German. He became a naturalized British citizen but returned to the United States in 1912, settling in Los Angeles. He worked at a number of different jobs and served briefly in World War I. In 1919, he became involved with a married woman, Cissy Pascal, who was 18 years his senior. He married her in 1924, after her divorce and his mother's death. Chandler's depression and alcoholism contributed to his checkered work history, and, after being fired from a highly paid managerial position at the Dabney Oil Syndicate, he began writing short stories for the pulp magazines. He later reworked some of these stories into his Philip Marlowe crime novels. Chandler also wrote several screenplays for Hollywood movies and received two Academy Award nominations (for *Double Indemnity* in 1944 and *The Blue Dahlia* in 1946). In 1954, Cissy Chandler died, causing Chandler's alcoholism and depression to worsen and leading to at least one attempt at suicide. He later became romantically involved with Helga Greene, his literary agent, and was engaged to her at the time of his death, in 1959.

Chandler was one of the early practitioners of the hard-boiled school of detective fiction. His essay "The Simple Art of Murder" is considered a classic in the literature on private-eye fiction. Although the critical reception of his work was mixed during his lifetime, Chandler is considered today to be a major American author.

Categories: Hard-Boiled, Private Detective

Awards

Edgar Award for Best Novel (*The Long Goodbye,* 1954)

Major Works

Philip Marlowe series: *The Big Sleep* (1939), *Farewell, My Lovely* (1940), *The High Window* (1942), *The Lady in the Lake* (1943), *The Little Sister*

(1949), *The Long Goodbye* (1953), *Playback* (1958), *Poodle Springs* (1989, completed by Robert B. Parker)

Screenplays: *Double Indemnity* (1944, with Billy Wilder), *And Now Tomorrow* (1944, with Frank Partos), *The Unseen* (1945, with Hagar Wilde), *The Blue Dahlia* (1946; published as a book in 1976, edited by Matthew Bruccoli)

Short-story collections: *Five Murders* (1944), *Five Sinister Characters* (1945), *Red Wind: A Collection of Short Stories* (1946), *Spanish Blood* (1946), "Finger Man" *and Other Stories* (1947), *The Simple Art of Murder* (1950), *Trouble Is My Business: Four Stories from* "The Simple Art of Murder" (1951), *Pick-up on Noon Street* (1952), *Pearls Are a Nuisance* (1953), *Killer in the Rain* (1964), *The Smell of Fear* (1965), *Raymond Chandler: Collected Stories* (2002—includes all short stories)

Short stories: "Blackmailers Don't Shoot" (1933), "Smart-Aleck Kill" (1934), "Finger Man" (1934), "Killer in the Rain" (1935), "Nevada Gas" (1935), "Spanish Blood" (1935), "Guns at Cyrano's" (1936), "The Man Who Liked Dogs" (1936), "Noon Street Nemesis" (1936, also known as "Pick-up on Noon Street"), "Goldfish" (1936), "The Curtain" (1936), "Try the Girl" (1937), "Mandarin's Jade" (1937), "Red Wind" (1938), "The King in Yellow" (1938), "Bay City Blues" (1938), "The Lady in the Lake" (1939), "Pearls Are a Nuisance" (1939), "Trouble Is My Business" (1939), "I'll Be Waiting" (1939), "The Bronze Door" (1939), "No Crime in the Mountains" (1941), "Professor Bing's Snuff" (1951), "English Summer" (1957; first printed in 1976), "Marlowe Takes on the Syndicate" (1959; also known as "Philip Marlowe's Last Case," "The Pencil," and "Wrong Pidgeon")

Essays (selected): "The Simple Art of Murder (December 1944, *The Atlantic Monthly*), "Writers in Hollywood" (November 1945, *The Atlantic Monthly*), "The Simple Art of Murder" (April 15, 1950, *Saturday Review of Literature;* revised version of the *Atlantic Monthly* article), "A Couple of Writers" (1951; first published in *Raymond Chandler Speaking,* 1984), "Ten Per Cent of Your Life" (February 1952, *The Atlantic Monthly*)

Other: *Raymond Chandler: Stories and Early Novels* (Frank MacShane, ed., Library of America, 1995); *Later Novels and Other Writings: The Lady in the Lake; The Little Sister; The Long Goodbye; Playback; Double Indemnity; Selected Essays and Letters* (Frank MacShane, ed., Library of America, 1995)

Nonfiction: *Raymond Chandler Speaking* (Dorothy Gardiner and Kathrine Sorley Walker, eds., 1962; letters, criticism, and fiction), *The Raymond Chandler Papers: Selected Letters and Non-fiction, 1909–1959* (Frank MacShane and Tom Hiney, eds. 2001)

Research Sources

Encyclopedias and Handbooks: BEA, BEB, CA (129), CANR (60, 107), EMM, OCC, STJ, TCLC (1, 7 179), WWW

Bibliographies: FF

Biographies and Interviews

"Authors and Creators: Raymond Chandler." *Thrilling Detective.* n.d. http://www.thrillingdetective.com/trivia/chandler.html (accessed November 1, 2010).

Fleming, Ian. "Interview with Raymond Chandler." (audiocast of an interview with Chandler in 1958 for the BBC—4 parts) *BBC.* 1958. http://www.youtube.com/watch?v=Zj6cc0T1z7I (accessed November 1, 2010).

Freeman, Judith. "The Big Sleep: Raymond Chandler, 50 Years Dead." *LA Weekly.* March 25, 2009. http://www.laweekly.com/2009-03-26/art-books/thebig-sleep/ (accessed November 1, 2010).

Freeman, Judith. *The Long Embrace: Raymond Chandler and the Woman He Loved.* New York: Pantheon, 2007.

Hartlaub, Joe. "Raymond Chandler." *BookReporter.com.* n.d. http://www.bookreporter.com/authors/au-chandler-raymond.asp (accessed November 1, 2010).

Hiney, Tom. *Raymond Chandler: A Biography.* New York: Atlantic Monthly Press, 1997.

"Judith Freeman Uncovers the Mystery of Chandler's Life." (videocast) *USC College.* March 11, 2008. http://www.youtube.com/watch?v=usLo5LyjLNU (accessed November 1, 2010).

MacShane, Frank. *The Life of Raymond Chandler.* New York: Dutton, 1976.

Routledge, Chris. "Raymond Chandler's Early Life." *ChrisRoutledge.co.uk.* March 26, 2009. http://chrisroutledge.co.uk/2009/03/raymond-chandlers-early-life/ (accessed November 1, 2010).

Silet, Charles P. "Raymond Chandler Profile Bio and Essay." *MysteryNet.com.* n.d. http://www.mysterynet.com/books/testimony/chandler/ (accessed November 1, 2010).

Walton, James. "Raymond Chandler's Los Angeles." *Telegraph.co.uk.* January 9, 2009. http://www.telegraph.co.uk/travel/destinations/northamerica/usa/4206216/Raymond-Chandlers-Los-Angeles.html (accessed November 1, 2010).

Criticism and Reader's Guides

Arden, Leon. "A Knock at the Backdoor of Art: The Entrance of Raymond Chandler." *Art in Crime Writing: Essays on Detective Fiction.* Ed. Bernard Benstock. New York: St. Martin's, 1983. 73–96.

Babener, Liahna K. "Raymond Chandler's City of Lies." *Los Angeles in Fiction: A Collection of Original Essays*. Ed. David Fine. Albuquerque: University of New Mexico Press, 1984. 109–31.

Barra, Allen. "The Case for Raymond Chandler." *Salon.com*. July 31, 2002. http://www.salon.com/books/feature/2002/07/31/chandler/index.html (accessed November 1, 2010).

Durham, Philip. *Down These Mean Streets a Man Must Go: Raymond Chandler's Knight*. Chapel Hill: University of North Carolina Press, 1963.

Hadley, Mary. "Raymond Chandler's 'The Big Sleep.'" *American Writers: Classics, vol. 2*. Ed. Jay Parini. New York: Scribner's, 2004. 55–68.

Hickman, Miranda B., and Michael D. Sharp, eds. "The Legacy of Raymond Chandler: Neither Tarnished nor Afraid." *Studies in the Novel* 35.3 (2003): 285–426.

Hume, Mick. "Why Marlowe Is Still the Chief of Detectives." *Spiked Review of Books*. December 2009. http://www.spiked-online.com/index.php/site/reviewofbooks_article/7851/ (accessed November 1, 2010).

Irwin, John T. "Being Boss: Raymond Chandler's 'The Big Sleep.'" *Southern Review* 37.2 (2001): 211–48.

Kerridge, Jake. "Raymond Chandler's Novels under the Magnifying Glass." *Telegraph.co.uk*. March 19, 2009. http://www.telegraph.co.uk/culture/books/bookreviews/5017441/Raymond-Chandlers-novels-under-the-magnifying-glass.html (accessed November 1, 2010).

Knight, Stephen. "'A Hard Cheerfulness': An Introduction to Raymond Chandler." *American Crime Fiction: Studies in the Genre*. Ed. Brian Docherty. New York: St. Martin's, 1988. 71–87.

"Los Angeles History: 1930s Crime; Raymond Chandler." (videocast—3 parts) No producer. July 27, 2009. http://www.youtube.com/watch?v=LIbFzcdOKUo (accessed November 1, 2010).

MacDonald, Susan Peck. "Chandler's American Style." *Style* 39.4 (2005): 448–68.

Madden, David W. "Anne Riordan: Raymond Chandler's Forgotten Heroine." *The Detective in American Fiction, Film, and Television*. Ed. Jerome H. Delamater and Ruth Prigozy. Westport, CT: Greenwood, 1998. 3–11.

Madden, David W. "Raymond Chandler." *100 Masters of Mystery and Detection, vol. 1*. Ed. Fiona Kelleghan. Pasadena, CA: Salem Press, 2001. 117–26.

Marling, William. *Raymond Chandler*. Boston: Twayne, 1986.

Moss, Robert F. "Raymond Chandler." *American Hard-Boiled Crime Writers* (*Dictionary of Literary Biography* 226). Ed. George Parker Anderson and Julie B. Anderson. Detroit, MI: Gale, 2000. 70–91.

Moss, Robert F., ed. *Raymond Chandler: A Documentary Volume*. Detroit, MI: Gale, 2002.

Rzepka, Charles J. *Detective Fiction*. Cambridge, U.K: Polity Press, 2005. 201–19.

Skinner, Robert E. *The Hard-Boiled Explicator: A Guide to the Study of Dashiell Hammett, Raymond Chandler, and Ross Macdonald.* Metuchen, NJ: Scarecrow Press, 1985.

Speir, Jerry. *Raymond Chandler.* New York: Ungar, 1981.

Tate, James O. "Raymond Chandler's Pencil." *The Detective in American Fiction, Film, and Television.* Ed. Jerome H. Delamater and Ruth Prigozy. Westport, CT: Greenwood, 1998. 27–34.

Van Dover, J. K., ed. *The Critical Response to Raymond Chandler.* Westport, CT: Greenwood, 1995.

Weisenburger, Steven. "Order, Error, and the Novels of Raymond Chandler." *The Detective in American Fiction, Film, and Television.* Ed. Jerome H. Delamater and Ruth Prigozy. Westport, CT: Greenwood, 1998. 13–26.

Widdicombe, Toby. *A Reader's Guide to Raymond Chandler.* Westport, CT: Greenwood, 2001.

Wolfe, Peter. *Something More Than Night: The Case of Raymond Chandler.* Bowling Green, OH: Popular Press, 1985.

Zseleczky, Joan. "Raymond Chandler." *Mystery and Suspense Writers: The Literature of Crime, Detection, and Espionage, I.* Ed. Robin W. Winks and Maureen Corrigan. New York: Scribner's, 1998. 143–68.

Web Site

Moss, Robert F. *The Raymond Chandler Website.* http://home.comcast.net/~ mossrobert/—Site maintained by a Raymond Chandler scholar. Includes links to critical essays and other resources (accessed November 1, 2010).

If You Like Raymond Chandler

Raymond Chandler was one of the foremost authors of the hard-boiled private-eye story. His protagonists deal with the seamy underside of everyday life but have a distinct moral code and a certain gallantry of manner. His writing combined street idiom with a more literary style.

Then You Might Like

Lawrence Block

Block's Matthew Scudder series portrays an ex-police officer who quit after accidentally shooting an innocent person. Although he is not a licensed private eye, he sometimes investigates as a favor for someone. The series is regarded as offering excellent hard-boiled depictions of the seamier side of New York as seen through the eyes of a morally devastated man. The first title in the series, *A Death at the Slaughterhouse,* won an Edgar Award for Best First Novel.

James Cain

Writing about the same time as Chandler, Cain also depicted tough protagonists, but they are not detectives and seem like antiheroes. Cain is regarded as an early noir writer, and he had a profound influence on authors such as Camus. Two of his best-known novels are *The Postman Always Rings Twice* and *Double Indemnity* (adapted by Chandler for the screen).

James Ellroy

Ellroy's works, especially the earlier ones, are reminiscent of Chandler in their southern California settings, dense plotting, and hard-boiled characters. Start with *Brown's Requiem.*

Dashiell Hammett

Hammett is regarded as the founder of the hard-boiled private-eye school: Chandler himself regarded Hammett as his predecessor. His best-known work is *The Maltese Falcon,* with its anti-hero, Sam Spade, who is surrounded by a fascinating, although morally deficient, group of characters. This book, along with Hammett's other work, had a profound impact on how the private detective would be depicted henceforward in American fiction. Other titles include *Red Harvest, The Dain Curse,* and *The Thin Man.*

Ross Macdonald

Macdonald, whose real name was Kenneth Millar, is frequently mentioned as the third in the triumvirate of authors who inaugurated the hard-boiled private-eye genre. His series about Lew Archer features strong characterizations that drive the plot and provide psychological and moral emphasis. He won Edgar awards for *The Wycherly Woman* and *The Zebra-Striped Hearse.*

Child, Lee, 1954–

> *She was white and probably in her forties. She was plain. She had black hair, neatly but unstylishly cut and too uniformly dark to be natural. She was dressed all in black. I could see her fairly well....*
>
> *Not a perfect view, but good enough to ring every bell on the eleven-point list. The bullet headings lit up like cherries on a Vegas machine.*
>
> *According to Israeli counterintelligence I was looking at a suicide bomber.*

—*Gone Tomorrow,* 2009

Biographical Sketch

Lee Child was born in 1954 in Coventry, England. He attended law school in Sheffield, England, and worked as a television director for Granada Television for a number of years. After being fired in 1995, he started writing *Killing Floor.* In 1998, he moved to the United States with his wife, Jane. They have one daughter, Ruth.

Child's novels feature a tough-guy, ex-military policeman protagonist, as well as nonstop action. Critical reception has been mixed, but the books have become increasingly popular with the public. In addition to receiving two Barry awards, Child's books have also been nominated for best novel for the Anthony Award (*Bad Luck and Trouble*) and the Macavity Award (*One Shot*).

Categories: Hard-Boiled, Thriller

Awards

Barry Award, Best First Novel (*Killing Floor,* 1998)
Barry Award, Best Novel (*The Enemy,* 2005)

Major Works

Jack Reacher series: *Killing Floor* (1997), *Die Trying* (1998), *Tripwire* (1999), *Running Blind* (2000), *Echo Burning* (2001), *Without Fail* (2002), *Persuader* (2003), *The Enemy* (2004), *One Shot* (2005), *The Hard Way* (2006), *Bad Luck and Trouble* (2007), *Nothing to Lose* (2008), *Gone Tomorrow* (2009), *61 Hours* (2010)

Research Sources

Encyclopedias and Handbooks: CA (194), CANR (160, 194), MCF

"Child, Lee—Author, Career, Sidelights, Selected writings." *Online Encyclopedia.* n.d. http://encyclopedia.jrank.org/articles/pages/3931/Child-Lee.html. (accessed November 1, 2010).

Bibliographies: FF, OM

Biographies and Interviews

Child, Lee. "The Origin of the Thriller." *Powells Books.* n.d. http://www.powells.com/essays/child.html (accessed November 1, 2010).
Cochran, Stacey. "Lee Child Interview." (videocast) *The Artist's Craft: Raleigh Television Network.* May 26, 2009. http://www.youtube.com/watch?v=6aeUckSeZLg (accessed November 1, 2010).
Donahue, Dick "Late to the Crime Scene." *Publishers Weekly* 251.22 (May 31, 2004): 44–45. http://www.publishersweekly.com/pw/print/20040531/37605-late-to-the-crime-scene-.html (accessed November 1, 2010).
Donahue, Dick, and Jeff Zaleski "PW Talks with Lee Child." *Publishers Weekly* 249.16 (April 22, 2002): 48.
Jordan, Jon. "Interviews with Lee Child." *BooksnBytes.com.* April 21, 2002. http://www.booksnbytes.com/auth_interviews/lee_child.html; http://www.booksnbytes.com/auth_interviews/lee_child_2.html (accessed November 1, 2010).

Karim, Ali. "Child of His Times." *Rapsheet*. May 13, 2009. http://therap sheet.blogspot.com/2009/05/child-of-his-times.html (accessed November 1, 2010).

Karim, Ali. "The Persuasive Lee Child." *January Magazine*. May 2003. http://januarymagazine.com/profiles/leechild.html (accessed November 1, 2010).

"Lee Child." *Bookeporter.com*. 19 May 2006. http://www.bookreporter.com/authors/au-child-lee.asp (accessed November 1, 2010).

"Lee Child: 2009 National Book Festival." (videocast) *Library of Congress*. September 26, 2009. http://www.loc.gov/today/cyberlc/feature_wdesc.php?rec=4653 (accessed November 1, 2010).

McGrath, Charles "Creating a Don Quixote of the Cheap Motel Circuit." *New York Times*. June 3, 2008. http://www.nytimes.com/2008/06/03/books/03child.html?_r=1 (accessed November 1, 2010).

Neary, Lynn. "Mysteries' Colorful Characters Reel in Readers." (audiocast) *All Things Considered, NPR*. July 20, 2007. http://www.npr.org/templates/story/story.php?storyId=12131219 (accessed November 1, 2010).

Peters, Barbara. "Lee Child Interview." (videocast—6 parts) *Poisoned Pen*. n.d. http://www.poisonedpen.com/interviews/lee-child. Also available at http://www.youtube.com/watch?v=KgJIVudKe6M (accessed November 1, 2010).

Sachs, Andrea. "Q&A: Author Lee Child." *Time*. June 11, 2007. http://www.time.com/time/arts/article/0,8599,1631477,00.html (accessed November 1, 2010).

Wertheimer, Linda. "'Reaching' Back to a Murky Past." (audiocast) *Weekend All Things Considered, NPR*. June 6, 2004. http://www.npr.org/templates/story/story.php?storyId=1919715 (accessed November 1, 2010).

Criticism and Reader's Guides

Child, Lee. "Jack Reacher." *The Lineup: The World's Greatest Crime Writers Tell the Inside Story of Their Greatest Detectives*. Ed. Otto Penzler. New York: Little, Brown, 2009. 29–43.

Maslin, Janet. "Tough Guy at the Border Of Hope and Despair." *New York Times*. June 2, 2008. http://www.nytimes.com/2008/06/02/books/02masl.html (accessed November 1, 2010).

Web Site

Official Web site: http://www.leechild.com/ (accessed November 1, 2010).

Christie, Agatha, 1890–1976

In her sleep Mrs. Bantry frowned. Something disturbing was penetrating through the dream state, something out of its time. Footsteps along the

*passage, footsteps that were too hurried and too soon. Her ears listened
unconsciously for the chink of china, but there was no chink of china.*

   *The knock came at the door.... Out of the dim green light Mary's voice
came, breathless, hysterical. "Ooh, ma'am, oh, ma'am, there's a body in
the library!"*

—The Body in the Library, 1942

Biographical Sketch

Agatha Miller, the daughter of Frederick Alvah and Clarissa Miller, was born
in Torquay, Devon. She did not attend school but was taught at home by her
mother; she later studied music in Paris. She served as a V.A.D.(Voluntary
Aide Detachment) nurse during World War I. In 1914, she married Archi-
bald Christie, a colonel in the Royal Air Force. It was not a happy marriage,
and the couple divorced in 1928 after having one daughter, Rosalind. After
the death of her mother and when it became apparent that the marriage was
on the rocks, Agatha Christie, in a mystery as puzzling as any of her books,
disappeared for eleven days. Many theories have been put forth as to the
cause of this, but no definitive answer has ever been established. After her
divorce, she traveled, and, while in the Middle East, she met Max Mallowan,
a young archaeologist. Although he was fourteen years younger than Agatha,
they found each other congenial company and were married in 1930. It was
a happy marriage, and she traveled with him annually to his excavation projects. Both served during World War II, he in the Royal Air Force in North
Africa and she in a London hospital. All the while, she continued her prolific
output of mysteries, plays, and juvenile stories. She was named a Commander
of the British Empire in 1956 and a Dame Commander, Order of the British
Empire, in 1971.

   Agatha Christie was rightly considered the queen of the crime novel during the first half of the twentieth century, and her books continue to sell
today in more than one hundred languages. It is said that only the Bible and
Shakespeare have sold more copies (*Contemporary Authors Online*). Although
her writing was often rated as pedestrian, her tightly woven puzzle plots and
sharp characterizations enchanted her reading public. Her two great character creations, the Belgian detective Hercule Poirot and the village spinster
Miss Marple, star not only in the books but also in numerous movies and
television adaptations. In addition to her crime novels, Christie also wrote
a number of plays that were very popular as well; *The Mousetrap* holds the
distinction of being the longest-running play in history—it is still being per-
formed. Although many of the mystery conventions introduced by Christie
seem like clichés today, it must be remembered that she had an enormous
influence on the crime novel. The Agatha awards presented by the Malice
Domestic annual convention are named in her honor.

Categories: Amateur Detective, Cozy, Private Detective

Awards

Edgar Grand Master Award for Lifetime Achievement (1955)

Major Works

Hercule Poirot series: *The Mysterious Affair at Styles* (1920), *The Murder on the Links* (1923), *Poirot Investigates* (short stories, 1934), *The Murder of Roger Ackroyd* (1926), *The Big Four* (1927), *The Mystery of the Blue Train* (1928), *The Under Dog, and Other Stories* (1929), *Peril at End House* (1932), *Thirteen at Dinner* (U.K. title *Lord Edgware Dies*, 1933), *Murder in Three Acts* (1934), *Murder on the Calais Coach* (aka *Murder on the Orient Express*, 1934), *Death in the Air* (1935), *The A.B.C. Murders* (1936), *Cards on the Table* (1936), *Murder in Mesopotamia* (1936), *Poirot Loses a Client* (1937), *Death on the Nile* (1937), *Dead Man's Mirror and Other Stories* (1937), *Appointment with Death* (1938), *Peril at End House* (1938), *Murder for Christmas* (1938), *The Patriotic Murders* (1940), *Sad Cypress* (1940), *Evil under the Sun* (1941), *Murder in Retrospect* (1942), *The Hollow* (1946), *The Labours of Hercules* (short stories, 1947), *There Is a Tide...* (1948), *The Mousetrap and Other Stories* (1949), *Mrs. McGinty's Dead* (1952), *Funerals Are Fatal* (1953), *Hickory, Dickory, Death* (1955), *Dead Man's Folly* (1956), *Cat among the Pigeons* (1960), *The Clocks* (1963), *Third Girl* (1966), *Hallowe'en Party* (1969), *Elephants Can Remember* (1972), *Hercule Poirot's Early Cases* (short stories, 1974), *Curtain: Hercule Poirot's Last Case* (1975), *Hercule Poirot's Casebook: 50 Stories* (1984)

Miss Marple series: *The Murder at the Vicarage* (1930), *The Body in the Library* (1942), *The Moving Finger* (1942), *A Murder Is Announced* (1950), *Murder with Mirrors* (1952), *A Pocket Full of Rye* (1953), *What Mrs. McGillicudy Saw!* (1957), *The Mirror Crack'd* (1962), *A Caribbean Mystery* (1964), *At Bertram's Hotel* (1965), *13 Clues for Miss Marple* (short stories, 1966), *Nemesis* (1971), *Sleeping Murder* (1976), *Miss Marple's Final Cases and Two Other Stories* (short stories, 1979), *Miss Marple: The Complete Short Stories* (1985)

Tommy and Tuppence Beresford series: *The Secret Adversary* (1922), *Partners in Crime* (short stories, 1929), *N or M?* (1941), *By the Pricking of My Thumbs* (1968), *Postern of Fate* (1973)

Nonseries novels: *The Man in the Brown Suit* (1924), *The Secret of Chimneys* (1925), *The Seven Dials Mystery* (1929), *The Murder at Hazelmoor* (1931), *The Boomerang Clue* (1935), *Easy to Kill* (1939), *And Then There Were None* (1939), *Death Comes As the End* (1944), *Towards Zero* (1944), *Remembered Death* (1945), *The Crooked House* (1949), *They Came to Baghdad* (1951), *So Many Steps to Death* (1954), *Ordeal by Innocence* (1959), *The Pale Horse* (1962), *Endless Night* (1968), *Passenger to Frankfurt* (1970), *Murder on Board* (1974)

Short-story collections: *The Mysterious Mr. Quin* (1930), *The Tuesday Club Murders* (1932), *The Hound of Death and Other Stories* (1933), *Mr. Parker Pyne, Detective* (1934), *The Listerdale Mystery and Other Stories* (1934), *Witness for the Prosecution and other Stories* (1948), *Double Sin, and Other Stories* (1961), *Surprise! Surprise!: A Collection of Mystery Stories with Unexpected Endings* (1965), *The Golden Ball and Other Stories* (1971)

Plays (selected): *Black Coffee* (1930), *Ten Little Indians* (1944), *Appointment with Death* (1945), *Little Horizon* (1945), *The Hollow* (1951), *The Mousetrap* (1952), *Witness for the Prosecution* (1953), *Spider's Web* (1954), *Towards Zero* (with Gerald Verner, 1956), *The Unexpected Guest* (1958), *Verdict* (1958), *Go Back for Murder* (1960)

Nonfiction: *Come, Tell Me How You Live* (1946), *Agatha Christie: An Autobiography* (1977)

Research Sources

Encyclopedias and Handbooks: BEA, BEB, CA (17–20R, 61–64), CANR (10,37,108), CLC (1, 6, 8, 12, 39, 48, 110), EMM, OCC, STJ, WWW

Bunson, Matthew. *The Complete Christie: An Agatha Christie Encyclopedia.* New York: Pocket Books, 2000.

Riley, Dick, and Pam McAllister, eds. *The Bedside, Bathtub & Armchair Companion to Agatha Christie.* New York: Ungar, 1979.

Sanders, Dennis, and Len Lovallo. *The Agatha Christie Companion: The Complete Guide to Agatha Christie's Life and Work.* New York: Delacorte, 1984.

Sova, Dawn B. *Agatha Christie A to Z: The Essential Reference to Her Life and Writings.* New York: Facts on File, 1996.

Bibliographies: FF

Delicious Death bibliography site (http://www.deliciousdeath.com/)— Bibliography of all works, with additional lists by detective series and cover images (accessed November 1, 2010).

Biographies and Interviews

Blackler, Keith. "Crime Does Pay." (documentary videocast—3 parts) 1990. http://www.youtube.com/watch?v=qlewYB0rGpA (accessed November 1, 2010).

Cade, Jared. *Agatha Christie and the Eleven Missing Days.* London: Peter Owen, 1998.

Christie, Agatha. *Agatha Christie: An Autobiography.* New York: Dodd, 1977.

Christie, Agatha. *Come, Tell Me How You Live.* Pleasantville, NY: Akadine Press, 2001.

Edwards, Austin. "Agatha Christie: Biography of an Author." *Essortment. com.* 2009. http://www.essortment.com/all/agathachristie_rlxk.htm (accessed November 1, 2010).

Gill, Gillian. *Agatha Christie: The Woman and Her Mysteries.* New York: Free Press, 1990.

Huntley, Dana. "Greenway House: At Home with Agatha Christie." *History-Net.* n.d. http://www.historynet.com/greenway-house-at-home-with-agatha-christie.htm (accessed November 1, 2010).

Keating, H. R. F. "Agatha Christie." *Concise Dictionary of British Literary Biography, vol. 6: Modern Writers 1914–1945.* Ed. Matthew J. Bruccoli. Detroit, MI: Gale, 1991. 69–83.

Morgan, Janet. *Agatha Christie: A Biography.* New York: Knopf, 1985.

Riviere, Francois, and Jean-Bernard Naudin, ill. *In the Footsteps of Agatha Christie.* North Pomfret, VT: Trafalgar Square, 1997.

Robyns, Gwen. *The Mystery of Agatha Christie.* New York: Doubleday, 1978.

Thompson, Laura. *Agatha Christie: An English Mystery.* London: Headline Review, 2007.

Thompson, Laura. "Agatha Christie's Private Life Would Have Stumped Even Poirot." *Telegraph.co.uk.* August 22, 2009. http://www.telegraph. co.uk/culture/books/6073273/Agatha-Christies-private-life-would-have-stumped-even-Poirot.html (accessed November 1, 2010).

Criticism and Reader's Guides

"The Agatha Christie Reading Group Guide." (pdf). n.d. http://www.waidev8. com/php/PDFS/STUDIO_v2_Asset_Library/974---PDF.pdf (accessed November 1, 2010).

"And Then There Were None." (teacher's guide—pdf). n.d. http://www. agathachristie.com/site-media/downloads/Holtzbrink%20ATTWN%20 teachers%20guide.pdf (accessed November 1, 2010).

Bargainnier, Earl F. *The Gentle Art of Murder: The Detective Fiction of Agatha Christie.* Bowling Green, OH: Popular Press, 1980.

Bayard, Pierre, and Carol Cosman. *Who Killed Roger Ackroyd? The Mystery behind the Agatha Christie Mystery.* New York: New Press, 2000.

Birns, Nicholas, and Margaret Boe Birns. "Agatha Christie: Modern and Modernist." *The Cunning Craft: Original Essays on Detective Fiction and Contemporary Literary Theory.* Ed. Ronald G. Walker and June M, Frazer. Macomb: Western Illinois University Press, 1990. 120–34.

Curran, John. "Ordeal by Analysis: Agatha Christie's The Thirteen Problems." *Twentieth-Century Suspense: The Thriller Comes of Age.* Ed. Clive Bloom. New York: St. Martin's, 1990. 80–96.

Curran, John. "The Top 10 Agatha Christie Mysteries." *Guardian.co.uk.* September 18, 2009. http://www.guardian.co.uk/books/2009/sep/15/top-10-agatha-christie-novels (accessed November 1, 2010).

Devas, Angela. "Murder, Mass Culture, and the Feminine: A View from the 4.50 from Paddington." *Feminist Media Studies* 2.2 (2002): 251–65.

DuBose, Martha Hailey. "Agatha Christie: The Queen of Crime." *Women of Mystery: The Lives and Works of Notable Women Crime Novelists.* New York: St. Martin's Minotaur, 2000. 86–160.

Fitzgibbon, Russell H. *The Agatha Christie Companion.* Bowling Green, OH: Popular Press, 1980.

Grossvogel, David I. "Death Deferred: The Long Life, Splendid Afterlife and Mysterious Workings of Agatha Christie." *Art in Crime Writing: Essays on Detective Fiction.* Ed. Bernard Benstock. New York: St. Martin's, 1983. 1–17.

Hari, Johann. "Agatha Christie: Radical, Conservative Thinker." Personal Web site. October 3, 2003. http://www.johannhari.com/2003/10/04/agatha-christie-radical-conservative-thinker (accessed November 1, 2010).

Hart, Anne. *The Life and Times of Hercule Poirot.* New York: Putnam, 1990.

Hawkes, David. "Agatha Christie." *Mystery and Suspense Writers: The Literature of Crime, Detection, and Espionage, I.* Ed. Robin W. Winks and Maureen Corrigan. New York: Scribner's, 1998. 195–216.

Irons, Glenwood, and Joan Warthling Roberts. "From Spinster to Hipster: The 'Suitability' of Miss Marple and Anna Lee." *Feminism in Women's Detective Fiction.* Ed. Glenwood H. Irons. Toronto: University of Toronto Press, 1995. 64–73.

Keating, H.R.F. "Agatha Christie." *British Mystery Writers, 1920–1939 (Dictionary of Literary Biography* 77). Ed. Bernard Benstock and Thomas F. Staley. Detroit, MI: Gale, 1989. 68–82.

Keating, H.R.F., ed. *Agatha Christie: First Lady of Crime.* New York: Holt, 1977.

Knepper, Marty S. "Agatha Christie/Mary Westmacott." *Great Women Mystery Writers: Classic to Contemporary.* Ed. Kathleen Gregory Klein. Westport, CT.: Greenwood, 1994. 58–66.

Knepper, Marty S. "The Curtain Falls: Agatha Christie's Last Novels." *Clues: A Journal of Detection* 23.4 (2005): 69–84.

Knepper, Marty S. "Miss Marple's St. Mary Mead: A Geographical Mystery Solved?" *Clues: A Journal of Detection* 25.4 (2007): 37–51.

Knepper, Marty S. "Reading Agatha Christie's Miss Marple Series: The Thirteen Problems." *In the Beginning: First Novels in Mystery Series.* Ed. Mary Jean DeMarr. Bowling Green, OH: Popular Press, 1995. 33–57.

Lovitt, Carl R. "Controlling Discourse in Detective Fiction: Or, Caring Very Much Who Killed Roger Ackroyd." *The Cunning Craft: Original Essays on Detective Fiction and Contemporary Literary Theory.* Ed. Ronald G.

Walker and June M, Frazer. Macomb: Western Illinois University Press, 1990. 68–85.

Maida, Patricia D., and Nicholas B. Spornick. *Murder She Wrote: A Study of Agatha Christie's Detective Fiction.* Bowling Green, OH: Popular Press, 1982.

Makinen, Merja. *Agatha Christie: Investigating Femininity.* New York: Palgrave Macmillan, 2006.

Mann, Jessica. "Agatha Christie." *Deadlier Than the Male: Why Are Respectable English Women So Good at Murder?* New York: Macmillan, 1981. 121–53.

Miller, Kristine A. "Case Closed: Scapegoating in British Women's Wartime Detective Fiction." *The Devil Himself: Villainy in Detective Fiction and Film.* Ed. Stacy Gillis and Philippa Gates. Westport, CT.: Greenwood, 2002. 91–106.

Osborne, Charles. *The Life and Crimes of Agatha Christie: A Biographical Companion to the Works of Agatha Christie.* New York: St. Martin's, 2001.

Rosenblum, Joseph. "Agatha Christie." *100 Masters of Mystery and Detection, vol. 1.* Ed. Fiona Kelleghan. Pasadena, CA: Salem Press, 2001. 154–63.

Reynolds, Moira Davison. "Agatha Christie." *Women Authors of Detective Series: Twenty-One American and British Authors 1900–2000.* Jefferson, NC: McFarland, 2001. 16–32.

Rowland, Susan. *From Agatha Christie to Ruth Rendell: British Women Writers in Detective and Crime Fiction.* New York: Palgrave, 2001.

Rushing, Robert. "Traveling Detectives: The 'Logic of Arrest' and the Pleasures of (Avoiding) the Real." *Yale French Studies* 108 (2005): 89–101.

Shaw, Marion, and Sabine Vanacker. *Reflecting on Miss Marple.* New York: Routledge, 1991.

Wagoner, Mary S. *Agatha Christie.* Boston: Twayne, 1986.

Zemboy, James. *The Detective Novels of Agatha Christie: A Reader's Guide.* Jefferson, NC: McFarland, 2008.

Web Sites

Official Web site: http://www.agathachristie.com/ (accessed November 1, 2010).

"Agatha Christie": http://www.youtube.com/watch?v=dTX9Wurap34 —Videocast composed of montage of many different pictures of Christie at various stages of her life (accessed November 1, 2010).

"Agatha Christie." *Literature Collection.* http://www.literaturecollection. com/a/agatha-christie/ —Biography and links to full text of two of Christie's mysteries (accessed November 1, 2010).

All about Agatha Christie fansite: http://www.all-about-agatha-christie.com/ —Includes biographical information, information about books, and links to two audio interviews with Christie (accessed November 1, 2010).

Hercule Poirot Central and Other Agatha Christie Info fansite: http://www. poirot.us/index.php —Includes information about Poirot and other Christie detectives. Nicely arranged and attractive site (accessed November 1, 2010).

World of Agatha Christie fansite: http://www.angelfire.com/fl/christianx/ page14.html (accessed November 1, 2010).

Clark, Mary Higgins, 1929–

The crack of her head on the hardwood floor sent waves of pain radiating through her skull, but she could still see that he was wearing a plastic raincoat and plastic over his shoes. "Please," she said, "please." She held up her hands to protect herself from the pistol he was pointing at her chest. The click as he pushed down the safety catch was his answer to her plea.

—*Just Take My Heart,* 2009

Biographical Sketch

Mary Higgins was born in New York (some sources say that her birth date was in 1931). Her father died when she was eleven, and her mother struggled financially in raising Mary and her brothers. She attended secretarial school so that she could work and help the family finances. After working for three years in an advertising agency, she became an flight attendant. A year later, she married Warren Clark, a neighbor whom she had known since she was sixteen, but was left a widow with five children when Warren died of a heart attack, in 1964. She decided to try writing; her first novel was about George Washington. In 1975, her first crime thriller was published and was immediately successful. With the resulting financial security, she was able to finally attend college and graduated from Fordham University at Lincoln Center summa cum laude. In 1996, she married John Conheeny. Her daughter Carol is a best-selling crime novelist in her own right.

Clark's best-selling novels depict everyday life situations but with suspense and terror lurking around the corner. She has been well received by critics and is the recipient of many awards and honors, including thirteen honorary doctorates. Her books continue to appear on best-seller lists in many countries as soon as they are published.

Categories: Romantic Suspense, Thrillers

Awards

Agatha Malice Domestic Lifetime Achievement Award (2010)
Grandmaster Lifetime Achievement Award (2000)

Major Works

Nonseries novels: *Where Are the Children?* (1975), *A Stranger Is Watch-ing* (1978), *The Cradle Will Fall* (1980), *A Cry in the Night* (1982), *Stillwatch* (1984), *Weep No More, My Lady* (1987), *While My Pretty One Sleeps* (1989), *Loves Music, Loves to Dance* (1991), *All Around the Town* (1992), *I'll Be Seeing You* (1993), *Remember Me* (1994), *Silent Night* (1995), *Let Me Call You Sweetheart* (1995), *Moonlight Becomes You* (1996), *Pretend You Don't See Her* (1997), *All Through the Night* (1998), *You Belong to Me* (1998), *We'll Meet Again* (1999), *Before I Say Goodbye* (2000), *On the Street Where You Live* (2001), *Daddy's Little Girl* (2002), *The Second Time Around* (2003), *Nighttime Is My Time* (2004), *No Place Like Home* (2005), *Two Little Girls in Blue* (2006), *I Heard That Song Before* (2007), *Where Are You Now?* (2008), *Dashing through the Snow* (2008), *Just Take My Heart* (2009), *The Shadow of Your Smile* (2010)

Novels with Carol Higgins Clark: *Deck the Halls* (2000), *He Sees You When You're Sleeping* (2001), *The Christmas Thief* (2004), *Santa Cruise: A Hol-iday Mystery at Sea* (2006)

Short-story collections: *The Anastasia Syndrome and Other Stories* (1989), *The Lottery Winner: The Alvirah and Willie Stories* (1994), *My Gal Sun-day* (1996)

Nonfiction: *Kitchen Privileges: A Memoir* (2002)

Research Sources

Encyclopedias and Handbooks: 100, BEA, BEB, BYA, CA (81–84), CANR (16, 36, 51, 76, 102, 133, 174), EMM, GWM, MCF, OCC, STJ, WWW

Bibliographies: FF

Biographies and Interviews

Abbe, Elfrieda. "Mary Higgins Clark: a Diabolical Mind at Work…" *The Writer* 117.12 (December 2004): 20–23.

Clark, Mary Higgins. "Touched by an Angel." *The Writing Life: Writers on How They Think and Work*. Ed. Marie Arana. New York: PublicAffairs, 2003. 35–38.

Dixit, Jay. "Mary Higgins Clark on Failure." (online blog) *Psychology Today*. May 20, 2009. http://www.psychologytoday.com/blog/brainstorm/200905/mary-higgins-clark-failure (accessed November 1, 2010).

Fakih, Kimberly Olson. "The Reassuring Triumph of the Good." *Library Journal* 115.5 (March 15, 1990): 34–37.

"Final Analysis: Mary Higgins Clark." *Psychology Today* 37.2 (April 2004): 96.

Freeman, Lucy. "Mary Higgins Clark." *Armchair Detective: A Quarterly Journal Devoted to the Appreciation of Mystery, Detective, and Suspense Fiction* 18.3 (1985): 228–37.

Grape, Jan. "A Conversation with Mary Higgins Clark." *Deadly Women: The Woman Mystery Reader's Indispensable Companion.* Ed. Jan Grape et al. New York: Carroll & Graf, 1998. 46–53.

Grape, Jan. "Mary Higgins Clark." *Speaking of Murder: Interviews with the Masters of Mystery and Suspense.* Ed. Ed Gorman and Martin H. Greenberg. New York: Berkley Prime Crime, 1998. 15–28.

Gray, Barbara. "Mary Higgins Clark." (videocast—2 parts) Around Cincinnati. May 12, 2009. http://www.youtube.com/watch?v=Q6W4pR6b4p0 (accessed November 1, 2010).

"Mary Higgins Clark." *Bookreporter.com.* May 5, 2000. http://www.bookreporter.com/authors/au-clark-mary-higgins.asp (accessed November 1, 2010).

"Mary Higgins Clark: National Book Festival." (videocast – 3 parts) *Library of Congress.* October 12, 2002. http://www.loc.gov/today/cyberlc/feature_wdesc.php?rec=3468 (part 1); http://www.loc.gov/today/cyberlc/feature_wdesc.php?rec=3469 (part 2); http://www.loc.gov/today/cyberlc/feature_wdesc.php?rec=3467 (part 3) (accessed November 1, 2010).

Smiley, Tavis. "Mary Higgins Clark." (videocast) *PBS.* May 1, 2009. http://www.pbs.org/kcet/tavissmiley/archive/200905/20090501.html (accessed November 1, 2010).

Swaim, Don. "Mary Higgins Clark." (audiocasts) *Wired for Books.* http://wiredforbooks.org/maryhigginsclark/ (accessed November 1, 2010).

Welch, Dave. "Author Interviews: Mary Higgins Clark." *Powells Books.* May 1999. http://www.powells.com/authors/higginsclark.html (accessed November 1, 2010).

White, Claire E. " A Conversation with Mary Higgins Clark." *Writers Write: The Internet Writing Journal.* May 2000. http://www.writerswrite.com/journal/may00/clark.htm (accessed November 1, 2010).

Criticism and Reader's Guides

Arant, Wendi. "Mary Higgins Clark." *American Mystery and Detective Writers* (*Dictionary of Literary Biography* 306). Ed. George Parker Anderson. Detroit, MI: Thomson Gale, 2005. 66–75.

De Roche, Linda. *Revisiting Mary Higgins Clark: A Critical Companion.* Westport, CT: Greenwood, 2003.

DuBose, Martha Hailey. "Mary Higgins Clark: Damsels in Distress." *Women of Mystery: The Lives and Works of Notable Women Crime Novelists.* New York: St. Martin's Minotaur, 2000. 374–85.

"*I Heard That Song Before*: Reading Group Guide." *Simon and Schuster.* n.d. http://books.simonandschuster.com/I-Heard-That-Song-Before/Mary-

Higgins-Clark/9780743497305/reading_group_guide (accessed November 1, 2010).

"*Just Take My Heart*: Reading Group Guide." *Simon and Schuster*. n.d. http://books.simonandschuster.com/Just-Take-My-Heart/Mary-Higgins-Clark/9781416570875/reading_group_guide (accessed November 1, 2010).

Pelzer, Linda Claycomb. *Mary Higgins Clark*. Westport, CT.: Greenwood, 1995.

"The Shadow of Your Smile: Reading Group Guide." *Simon and Schuster*. n.d. http://books.simonandschuster.com/Shadow-of-Your-Smile/Mary-Higgins-Clark/9781439172261/reading_group_guide (accessed November 1, 2010).

"Two Little Girls in Blue: Reading Group Guide." *Simon and Schuster*. n.d. http://books.simonandschuster.com/Two-Little-Girls-in-Blue/Mary-Higgins-Clark/9780743264907/reading_group_guide (accessed November 1, 2010).

"We'll Meet Again: Reading Group Guide." *Simon and Schuster*. n.d. http://books.simonandschuster.com/WE%27LL-MEET-AGAIN/Mary-Higgins-Clark/9780671004569/reading_group_guide (accessed November 1, 2010).

"Where Are You Now?: Reading Group Guide." *Simon and Schuster*. n.d. http://books.simonandschuster.com/Where-Are-You-Now/Mary-Higgins-Clark/9781416570882/reading_group_guide (accessed November 1, 2010).

Web Site

Official Web site: http://www.maryhigginsclark.com/ (accessed November 1, 2010).

Connelly, Michael, 1956–

A trial is a contest of lies.... The trick if you are sitting at the defense table is to be patient. To wait. Not for any lie. But for the one you can grab onto and forge like hot iron into a sharpened blade. You then use that blade to rip the case open and spill its guts out on the floor.

—*The Brass Verdict,* 2008

Biographical Sketch

Michael Connelly was born in Philadelphia. He graduated from the University of Florida with a major in journalism and started working for newspapers in Florida, primarily on the crime beat. After a magazine article he cowrote with two other reporters was a finalist for the Pulitzer Prize for feature writing, he moved to Los Angeles to work for the *Los Angeles Times* as a crime reporter. While in college, he had read and admired the work of Raymond Chandler, and the move to L.A. heightened his interest. Three years later, he published his first novel, based in part on an actual crime that had occurred in L.A. Connelly currently lives with his family in Florida.

Connelly's work has been well received by critics, and he has won a number of awards, both in the United States and internationally. His longest-running series is that featuring detective Harry Bosch, but he has also created several characters who cross over into various books among his multiple series.

Categories: Legal, Private Detective

Awards

Anthony Award for Best Novel (*The Poet*, 1997; *Blood Work*, 1999; *City of Bones*, 2003; *The Brass Verdict*, 2009)
Barry Award for Best Novel (*Trunk Music*, 1998; *City of Bones*, 2003)
Edgar Award for Best First Novel (*The Black Echo*, 1993)
Macavity Award for Best Novel (*Blood Work*, 1999; *The Lincoln Lawyer*, 2006)
Nero Award (*The Poet*, 1997)
Shamus Award for Best Novel (*The Lincoln Lawyer*, 2006)

Major Works

Harry Bosch series: *The Black Echo* (1992), *The Black Ice* (1993), *The Concrete Blonde* (1994), *The Last Coyote* (1995), *Trunk Music* (1997), *Angels Flight* (1999), *A Darkness More Than Night* (2001), *City of Bones* (2002), *Lost Light* (2003), *The Narrows* (2004), *The Closers* (2005), *Echo Park* (2006), *The Overlook* (2007), *Nine Dragons* (2009)
Mickey Haller series: *The Lincoln Lawyer* (2005), *The Brass Verdict* (2008), *The Reversal* (2010)—the last two titles also feature Harry Bosch
Nonseries novels: *The Poet* (1996), *Blood Work* (1998), *Void Moon* (2000), *Chasing the Dime* (2002), *The Scarecrow* (2009)
Nonfiction: *Crime Beat: A Decade of Covering Cops and Killers* (2006)

Research Sources

Encyclopedias and Handbooks: CA (158), CANR (91, 180), EMM, MCF, STJ, WWW

Bibliographies: FF, OM

Biographies and Interviews

Anderson, Karen G. "Michael Connelly Interview." *January Magazine.* February 1999. http://januarymagazine.com/profiles/connelly.html (accessed November 1, 2010).

Ayers, Jeff. "In the 'Lab' with Michael Connelly." *The Writer* 122.10 (October 2009): 20–23.

Cochran, Stacey. "Michael Connelly: The Artist's Craft." Raleigh Television network, October 24, 2008. (videocast) http://www.youtube.com/watch?v=1NECw_d0Tpc (accessed November 1, 2010).

"Novelist Connelly Revisits His 'Crime Beat' Days." (audiocast) *NPR Weekend Edition Saturday*. April 29, 2006. http://www.npr.org/templates/story/story.php?storyId=5368001 (accessed November 1, 2010).

Kaminsky, Stuart, and Laurie Roberts. "Michael Connelly." *Behind the Mystery: Top Mystery Writers Interviewed*. Cohasset, MA: Hot House, 2005. 164–75.

Lewis, Georgie. "Author Interviews: Michael Connelly's Shades of Black." *Powells Books*. April 2002. http://www.powells.com/authors/connelly.html (accessed November 1, 2010).

Lugar, Austin. "Michael Connelly Reel Deal Interview." (videocast—2 parts) November 18, 2009. http://www.youtube.com/watch?v=LaZ5-X3SkGc (accessed November 1, 2010).

"Michael Connelly." *Bookreporter.com*. October 2009. http://www.bookreporter.com/authors/au-connelly-michael.asp (accessed November 1, 2010).

"Michael Connelly: National Book Festival 2009." *Library of Congress*. September 26, 2009. podcast: http://www.loc.gov/podcasts/bookfest09/podcast_connelly.html. videocast: http://www.loc.gov/today/cyberlc/feature_wdesc.php?rec=4700. Also available at http://www.youtube.com/watch?v=—WfetBu_-Q (accessed November 1, 2010).

Ott, Bill. "Michael Connolly's Los Angeles." *Booklist* 100.17 (May1, 2004): 1576.

Minar, Jennifer. "An Interview with Bestselling Novelist Michael Connelly." *WritersBreak.com*. n.d. http://www.writersbreak.com/Interviews/articles/fiction/interviews_fiction_connelly_1.htm (accessed November 1, 2010).

Page, Benedicte. "Witnessing Hell: Michael Connelly, Creator of Detective Harry Bosch, Tells about His First Encounter with Murder—at the Age of 16." *The Bookseller* 5216 (February 10, 2006): 21.

Roth, Evan. "L.A. Avenger: A Interview with Michael Connelly." *Armchair Detective: A Quarterly Journal Devoted to the Appreciation of Mystery, Detective, and Suspense Fiction* 28.4 (1995): 398–402.

Shay, Christopher. "U.S. Writer Tackles a Real Hong Kong Cold Case." *Time.com*. November 10, 2009. http://www.time.com/time/world/article/0,8599,1937140,00.html (accessed November 1, 2010).

Swartley, Ariel. "Michael Connelly Doesn't Live Here Anymore...." *Book* (November-December 2002): 48–51.

Sykes, Jerry. "An Interview with Michael Connelly." *Speaking of Murder, vol. 2: Interviews with the Masters of Mystery and Suspense*. Ed. Ed Gorman and Martin H. Greenberg. New York: Berkley Prime Crime, 1999. 196–201.

Usery, Stephen. "WYPL Book Talk: Michael Connelly." (videocast—4 parts) *WYPL Book Talk*. December 7, 2008. http://www.youtube.com/watch?v=DPY5PNuEl5A (accessed November 1, 2010).

See also official Web site for additional links to interviews: http://www.michaelconnelly.com/Biography/Interviews/interviews.html (accessed November 1, 2010).

Criticism and Reader's Guides

Connelly, Michael. " Hieronymus Bosch." *The Lineup: The World's Greatest Crime Writers Tell the Inside Story of Their Greatest Detectives*. Ed. Otto Penzler. New York: Little, Brown, 2009. 45–59.

Gregoriou, Christiana. "Criminally Minded: The Stylistics of Justification in Contemporary American Crime Fiction." *Style* 37.2 (2003): 144–59.

Gregoriou, Christiana. "Demystifying the Criminal Mind: Linguistic, Social and Generic Deviance in Contemporary American Crime Fiction." *Working with English: Medieval and Modern Language, Literature and Drama* 1 (2003): 1–15.

Oates, J. C. "L.A. Noir: Michael Connelly." *Uncensored*. New York: Ecco, 2005. 101–5.

Solimini, Cheryl. "The Trouble with Harry." *Mystery Scene* 90 (2005): 18–22.

Web Site

Official Web site:—http://www.michaelconnelly.com/ (accessed November 1, 2010).

Cornwell, Patricia, 1956–

> *Brain tissue clung like wet, gray lint to the sleeves of Dr. Kay Scarpetta's surgical gown, and the front of it was splashed with blood. Stryker saws whined, running water drummed, and bone dust sifted through the air like flour. Three tables were full. More bodies were on the way. It was Tuesday, January 1, New Year's Day.*

—*Scarpetta*, 2008

Biographical Sketch

Born in Miami, Florida, Patricia Cornwell grew up in Montreat, North Carolina. She graduated from Davidson College and started working for the Charlotte *Observer*, winning an award for investigative reporting for a series on prostitution and crime. She married Charles Cornwell in 1980 and was later divorced. In 1984, she began working as a technical writer and computer analyst for the Office of the Chief Medical Examiner in Richmond, Virginia, and remained in that position until 1990. Her first crime novel was published in 1991 after being rejected by seven publishers. *Postmortem* went on to win four major crime fiction awards and was the start of the highly successful Kay Scarpetta series. In 2005, Cornwell married her female partner, Staci Gruber. She has several active philanthropic interests, including animal rescue, criminal justice, and literacy.

Cornwell is best known for her Kay Scarpetta series, about a medical examiner who solves crimes with forensic sleuthing. Her books were among the forerunners of the current popularity of forensic analysis and scene-of-the-crime detection in fiction and on television. She has two other series and has also authored a compelling but controversial nonfiction book about Jack the Ripper, in which she concluded that artist Walter Sickert committed the crimes.

Categories: Forensic, Police Procedural

Awards

Anthony Award for Best First Novel (*Postmortem*, 1991)
Gold Dagger Award (*Cruel and Unusual*, 1993)
John Creasey Dagger Award (*Postmortem*, 1990)
Edgar Award for Best First Novel (*Postmortem*, 1991)
Macavity Award for Best First Novel (*Postmortem*, 1991)

Major Works

Kay Scarpetta series: *Postmortem* (1990), *Body of Evidence* (1991), *All That Remains* (1992), *Cruel and Unusual* (1993), *The Body Farm* (1994), *From Potter's Field* (1995), *Cause of Death* (1996), *Unnatural Exposure* (1997), *Point of Origin* (1998), *Black Notice* (1999), *The Last Precinct* (2000), *Blow Fly* (2003), *Trace* (2004), *Predator* (2005), *Book of the Dead* (2007), *Scarpetta* (2008), *The Scarpetta Factor* (2009)
Andy Brazil series: *Hornet's Nest* (1997), *Southern Cross* (1998), *Isle of Dogs* (2001)
Win Garano series: *At Risk* (2006), *The Front* (2008)
Nonfiction: *Scarpetta's Winter Table* (1998), *Portrait of a Killer: Jack the Ripper–Case Closed* (2002)

Research Sources

Encyclopedias and Handbooks: 100, BEA, BEB, BYA, CA (134), CANR (53, 131, 195), CLC (155), EMM, GWM, MCF, STJ, WWW

Bibliographies: FF, OM

Biographies and Interviews

Duncan, Paul. "Interview with Patricia Cornwell." *Deadly Women: The Woman Mystery Reader's Indispensable Companion.* Ed. Jan Grape et al. New York: Carroll & Graf, 1998. 119–23.

Duncan, Paul. "Patricia Cornwell." *Speaking of Murder: Interviews with the Masters of Mystery and Suspense*. Ed. Ed Gorman and Martin H. Greenberg. New York: Berkley Prime Crime, 1998. 235–42.

Herbert, Rosemary. "Patricia D. Cornwell." *The Fatal Art of Entertainment: Interviews with Mystery Writers*. New York: G. K. Hall, 1994. 136–61.

Jardine, Cassandra. "Patricia Cornwell: 'Finally I Feel Rooted Somewhere.'" *Telegraph.co.uk.* November 26, 2007. http://www.telegraph.co.uk/culture/books/3669542/Patricia-Cornwell-Finally-I-feel-rooted-somewhere.html (accessed November 1, 2010).

O…, Heather Aimee. "Interview with Patricia Cornwell." *AfterEllen*. November 2, 2009. http://www.afterellen.com/people/2009/11/patricia-cornwell (accessed November 1, 2010).

"Patricia Cornwell." *Bookreporter.com*. n.d. http://www.bookreporter.com/authors/au-cornwell-patricia.asp (accessed November 1, 2010).

"Patricia Cornwell: Inside the Mind of a Crime Writer." (videocast) *TimesOnline*. April 22, 2008. http://www.youtube.com/watch?v=exgk7FlEKMA (accessed November 1, 2010).

"Patricia Cornwell on the Future of Crime Fiction." (videocast) *Galleycat.org*. December 3, 2008. http://www.mediabistro.com/galleycat/authors/exclusive_video_patricia_cornwell_on_the_future_of_crime_fiction_102274.asp (accessed November 1, 2010).

"Patricia Cornwell: Stalking the Ripper." (videocast—6 parts) *BBC*. 2002. http://www.youtube.com/watch?v=CXSheBgPO4w (accessed November 1, 2010).

Shindler, Dorman T. "Reticent Writer." *The Writer* 114.3 (March 2001): 30–33.

Turner, Janice. "Patricia Cornwell's Extraordinary Life." *TimesOnline.co.uk*. April 19, 2008. http://entertainment.timesonline.co.uk/tol/arts_and_entertainment/books/article3743717.ece (accessed November 1, 2010).

Wilson, Jacque. "The Monster That Patricia Cornwell Created." (videocast) *CNN*. December 15, 2008. http://edition.cnn.com/2008/SHOWBIZ/books/12/15/patricia.cornwell.scarpetta/index.html (accessed November 1, 2010).

Criticism and Reader's Guides

Bleiler, Ellen. "Patricia Cornwell." *Mystery and Suspense Writers: The Literature of Crime, Detection and Espionage, I*. Ed. Robin W. Winks and Maureen Corrigan. New York: Scribner's Sons, 1998. 243–50.

Cargill, Ann Sanders. "Chief Medical Examiner Kay Scarpetta." *Clues: A Journal of Detection* 22.2 (2001): 35–48.

Collins, Gerard. "Contagion and Technology in Patricia Cornwell's Scarpetta Novels." *The Devil Himself: Villainy in Detective Fiction and Film*. Ed. Stacy Gillis and Philippa Gates. Westport, CT.: Greenwood, 2002. 159–69.

Cornwell, Patricia. "The Passionate Researcher." *The Writing Life: Writers on How They Think and Work*. Ed. Marie Arana. New York: PublicAffairs, 2003. 152–55.

DuBose, Martha Hailey. "Patricia Cornwell: Dangerous Dissection." *Women of Mystery: The Lives and Works of Notable Women Crime Novelists.* New York: St. Martin's Minotaur, 2000. 393–99.

Etheridge, Charles L., Jr. "Patricia (Daniels) Cornwell." *American Mystery and Detective Writers* (*Dictionary of Literary Biography* 306). Ed. George Parker Anderson. Detroit, MI: Thomson Gale, 2005. 76–86.

Ford, Susan Allen. "Tracing the Other in Patricia D. Cornwell: Costs and Other Accommodations." *Clues: A Journal of Detection* 20.2 (1999): 27–34.

Lucas, Rose. "Anxiety and Its Antidotes: Patricia Cornwell and the Forensic Body." *Lit: Literature Interpretation Theory* 15.2 (2004): 207–22.

Messent, Peter. "Authority, Social Anxiety and the Body in Crime Fiction: Patricia Cornwell's Unnatural Exposure." *The Art of Detective Fiction.* Ed. Warren L. Chernaik et al. Basingstoke, England; New York: Macmillan; St. Martin's, with Institute of English Studies, School of Advanced Study, University of London, 2000. 124–37.

Messent, Peter. "Patricia Cornwell's 'Unnatural Exposure' and the Representation of Space: Changing Patterns in Crime Fiction." *Clues: A Journal of Detection* 21.2 (2000): 37–45.

Reynolds, Moira Davison. "Patricia Cornwell." *Women Authors of Detective Series: Twenty-One American and British Writers, 1900–2000.* Jefferson, NC: McFarland, 2001. 149–54.

Robinson, Bobbie. "Playing Like the Boys: Patricia Cornwell Writes Men." *Journal of Popular Culture* 39.1 (2006): 95–108.

Ryder, Stephen P. "Patricia Cornwell and Walter Sickert: A Primer." *Casebook.org.* n.d. http://www.casebook.org/dissertations/dst-pamandsickert.html (accessed November 1, 2010).

Strengell, Heidi. "'My Knife Is So Nice and Sharp I Want to Get to Work Right Away if I Get a Chance': Identification between Author and Serial Killer in Patricia Cornwell's Kay Scarpetta Series." *Studies in Popular Culture* 27.1 (2004): 73–90.

Summers-Bremner, Eluned. "Post-Traumatic Woundings: Sexual Anxiety in Patricia Cornwell's Fiction." *New Formations: A Journal of Culture/Theory/Politics* 43 (2001): 131–47.

Web Site

Official Web site: http://www.patriciacornwell.com/ (accessed November 1, 2010).

If You Like Patricia Cornwell

Cornwell's crime novels revolve around the forensic investigations of a pathologist. A hallmark of a Cornwell novel is a suspenseful plot with plenty of detailed explanations of investigative procedures.

Then You Might Like

Sarah Andrews

The Em Hanson series has a female forensic geologist as the primary protagonist. The series features strong female friendships as well as romantic relationships with various males. Titles include *Tensleep, A Fall in Denver,* and *Bone Hunter*.

Beverly Connor

Connor's Lindsay Chamberlain series has as its protagonist an archaeologist and forensic anthropologist. Chamberlain is an expert on Native American remains but proves to be adept at interpreting modern remains as well, leading her to become involved in various criminal investigations. Titles include *A Rumor of Bones* and *One Grave Too Many*.

Jeffrey Deaver

Deaver's Lincoln Rhyme novels feature a NYPD forensic specialist who is also a quadriplegic. Rhyme does his work with the help of special tools and his assistant Amelia Sachs, who is also his lover. The novels feature twisty plots and much forensic detail. Two titles are *The Bone Collector* and *The Broken Window*.

Linda Fairstein

Alexandra Cooper is a sex-crimes prosecutor in Manhattan. The crime cases recounted in the novels feature strong descriptions of investigative procedures and tense plots. Detailed forensic description adds to the veracity of the novels.

Robert W. Walker

Dr. Jessica Coran is a forensic pathologist working for the FBI. Her cases involve brutal and bloody murders and, like Scarpetta's, are not for the fainthearted. The series begins with *Killer Instinct,* followed by *Fatal Instinct* and other titles.

Crais, Robert, 1953–

> *Pike is wearing a gray sweatshirt with the sleeves cut off, faded Levi's and flat black pilot's glasses, which is the way he dresses every day of his life. His dark brown hair is cut short, and bright red arrows were tattooed on the outside of his deltoids long before tattoos were* au courant. *Watching Joe stand there, he reminds me of the world's largest two-legged pit bull.*

—*L.A. Requiem,* 1999

Biographical Sketch

A native of Louisiana, Robert Crais grew up living on the banks of the Mississippi in a family of oil refinery workers and policemen. Reading Raymond Chandler's novel *The Little Sister* as a teen had a profound influence on him and started his interest in crime fiction and Los Angeles. As an adult, he made amateur films and wrote short fiction before moving to Los Angeles, where he quickly was hired on as a television writer, working on such series as *Hill Street Blues, Cagney and Lacey,* and *Miami Vice.* In the mid-1980s, he quit television to try his hand at writing novels but was unsuccessful until the death of his father in 1985 inspired him to create the character of Elvis Cole. Crais lives near Los Angeles with his wife.

The Elvis Cole novels have been greeted with critical acclaim and, in addition to the awards listed here, have received numerous award nominations as well as making several "best of " lists. He received the Ross Macdonald Literary Award from the Santa Barbara Book Council in 2006. Crais attempts to combine good crime fiction with solid literary writing and continues to stretch himself as a writer.

Categories: Hard-Boiled, Private Detective

Awards

Anthony Award, Best Paperback Original (*The Monkey's Raincoat,* 1988)
Barry Award, Best Thriller (*The Watchman,* 2008)
Macavity Award, Best First Novel (*The Monkey's Raincoat,* 1988)
Shamus Award, Best Novel (*Sunset Express,* 1997)

Major Works

Elvis Cole/Joe Pike series: *The Monkey's Raincoat* (1987), *Stalking the Angel* (1989), *Lullaby Town* (1992), *Free Fall* (1993), *Voodoo River* (1995), *Sunset Express* (1996), *Indigo Slam* (1997), *L.A. Requiem* (1999), *The Last Detective* (2003), *The Forgotten Man* (2005), *The Watchman* (2007), *Chasing Darkness* (2008), *The First Rule* (2010)
Nonseries novels: *Demolition Angel* (2000), *Hostage* (2001), *The Two-Minute Rule* (2006)

Research Sources

Encyclopedias and Handbooks: 100, CA (187), CANR(163,194), MCF

Bibliographies: FF, OM

Biographies and Interviews

Ayers, Jeff. "Doing What He Loves: Top Crime Writer Robert Crais Left TV Scripts Behind to Make Good on His Lifelong Dream of Novel Writing." *The Writer* 122.5 (2009): 18–21.

Buckley, James, Jr. "Elvis Has Left the City." *BookPage.com*. 1999. http://www.bookpage.com/9906bp/robert_crais.html (accessed November 1, 2010).

Crais, Robert. "L.A. and Chasing Darkness." (videocast) July 10, 2008. http://www.youtube.com/watch?v=FD9O8Qd_3as (accessed November 1, 2010).

Foster, Jordan. "Slaying Dragons." *Publishers Weekly* 256.48 (2009): 27. http://www.publishersweekly.com/pw/by-topic/1-legacy/16-all-book-reviews/article/26044-pw-talks-with-robert-crais-.html (accessed November 1, 2010).

Grape, Jan. "Robert Crais." *Speaking of Murder, vol. 2: Interviews with the Masters of Mystery and Suspense*. Ed. Ed Gorman and Martin H. Greenberg. New York: Berkley Prime Crime, 1999. 140–52.

"Interview with Suspense Writer Robert Crais." (videocast) *Author Magazine*. March 6, 2009. http://www.youtube.com/watch?v=Epf1DIqIPpg (accessed November 1, 2010).

Signor, Randy Michael. "Robert Crais: Poster Boy." *Book* (September 2000): 18.

Smith, Kevin Burton. "The Explosive Talents of Robert Crais." *January Magazine*. May 2000. http://januarymagazine.com/profiles/rcrais.html (accessed November 1, 2010).

Thompson, Bill. "Listen to Robert Crais." (audiocasts) *Bill Thompson's Eye on Books*. n.d. http://www.eyeonbooks.com/iap.php?authID=275 (accessed November 1, 2010).

"Trust No One: Gregg Hurwitz and Robert Crais Interview for Borders." (videocast) August 21, 2009. http://www.youtube.com/watch?v=KLG3k4bTBFE (accessed November 1, 2010).

Criticism and Reader's Guides

Baye, Hagen. "Robert Crais: Chasing Darkness." *Mostly Fiction Book Reviews* (October 11, 2008). http://www.mostlyfiction.com/sleuths/crais.htm (accessed November 1, 2010).

Baye, Hagen. "Robert Crais: The Watchman." *Mostly Fiction Book Reviews* (July 15, 2005). http://www.mostlyfiction.com/spy-thriller/crais-pike.htm (accessed November 1, 2010).

Crais, Robert. "Elvis Cole and Joe Pike." *The Lineup: The World's Greatest Crime Writers Tell the Inside Story of Their Greatest Detectives*. Ed. Otto Penzler. New York: Little, Brown, 2009. 81–96.

Jenkins, Tom. "'… If the Day Got Any Better, My Cat Would Die.'" *Mystery Scene* 68 (2000): 38–41.

Mack, Deborah. "Review: L.A. Requiem." *Suite101.com* (September 30 2009). http://mysterycrimefiction.suite101.com/article.cfm?review_la_requiem (accessed November 1, 2010).

"Reading Group Guide for The Two Minute Rule." n.d. http://books.simo nandschuster.com/Two-Minute-Rule/Robert-Crais/9781416514961/ reading_group_guide (accessed November 1, 2010).

Web Site

Official Web site: http://www.robertcrais.com/ (accessed November 1, 2010).

Crombie, Deborah, 1952–

> *Then, on an impulse, she reached for the bold yellow-and-red teapot that sat in the place of honor above the Aga. It was daft to actually use such an expensive object, but it seemed to her that in a way it was sacrilege not to use it, and that Alex had understood. This pot had been lovingly designed and crafted for hands to grasp, for ordinary teas, for everyday lives—and those moments were all one had.*

—*And Justice There Is None,* 2002

Biographical Sketch

Deborah Crombie was born in Dallas, Texas, and grew up in the suburb of Richardson. Her only brother was ten years older than she, and her rather lonely childhood was alleviated by being taught to read by her grandmother. She graduated from Austin College in Sherman, Texas, with a degree in biology. She worked in newspapers and advertising, but a trip to England cemented her lifelong fascination with that country. She lived in Scotland and then England with her first husband, Peter Crombie. She returned to the United States to raise her daughter and started writing after working for several years. Crombie now lives in McKinney, Texas, with her husband, Rick Wilson, and travels to England and Scotland several times a year.

Crombie's works thus far are in a single series about Scotland Yard detectives Duncan Kincaid and Gemma James. As well as recounting various cases, the novels chart the developing romantic relationship between the two and the obstacles presented by their past lives. Her first novel, *A Share in Death,* received Agatha and Macavity nominations for best first novel. *Dreaming of the Bones* is her most acclaimed novel to date. It was nominated for an Edgar Award for best novel, won a Macavity Award for best novel, was named a *New York Times* notable book for 1997, and was included in the Independent Booksellers of America's "Top 100 Crime Novels of the Century."

Categories: Police Procedural

Awards

Macavity Award, Best Novel (*Dreaming of the Bones,* 1998)
Macavity Award, Best Novel (*Where Memories Lie,* 2009)

Major Works

Duncan Kincaid/Gemma James series: *A Share in Death* (1993), *All Shall Be Well* (1994), *Leave the Grave Green* (1995), *Mourn Not Your Dead* (1996), *Dreaming of the Bones* (1997), *Kissed a Sad Goodbye* (1999), *A Finer End* (2001), *And Justice There Is None* (2002), *Now May You Weep* (2003), *In a Dark House* (2004), *Water Like a Stone* (2006), *Where Memories Lie* (2008), *Necessary as Blood* (2009)

Research Sources

Encyclopedias and Handbooks: BYA, CA (187), CANR (179), GWM, MCF

Bibliographies: FF, OM

Biographies and Interviews

"Deborah Crombie." *Cozy Library.* 2009. http://www.cozylibrary.com/default.aspx?id=442 (accessed November 1, 2010).
"Deborah Crombie: Book Fest 07." (webcast.) *Library of Congress.* September 29, 2007. http://www.loc.gov/today/cyberlc/feature_wdesc.php?rec=4138 (accessed November 1, 2010).
Dingus, Anne. "Briterature." *Texas Monthly* 25.11 (1997): 26.
Ogle, Connie. "Writer Deborah Crombie Is Obsessed with Her Characters." *Miami Herald.* March 14, 2010. http://www.miamiherald.com/2010/03/14/1526346/writer-is-obsessed-with-her-characters.html (accessed November 1, 2010). A somewhat different version is available at http://www.popmatters.com/pm/article/122504-writer-deborah-crombie-is-obsessed-with-her-characters/ (accessed November 1, 2010).
Peters, Barbara.(webcast—6 parts) "Interview at Poisoned Pen." n.d. http://www.poisonedpen.com/interviews/deborah-crombie (accessed November 1, 2010).
"Talking with Deborah Crombie." *Audiofile.com.* June/July 2006. http://www.audiofilemagazine.com/features/A1650.html (accessed November 1, 2010).

Criticism and Reader's Guides

Graff, M. K. "Deborah Crombie: The Yellow Rose of Mystery." *Mystery Scene* 87 (2004): 18–19.

Hansson, Heidi. "Biography Matters: Carol Shields, Mary Swann, A. S. Byatt, Possession, Deborah Crombie, Dreaming of the Bones." *Orbis Litterarum: International Review of Literary Studies* 58.5 (2003): 353–70.

"Mystery Series 101: Fact Sheet on Deborah Crombie's Duncan Kincaid/Gemma James Mystery Series." November 10, 2009. http://www.examiner.com/x-27605-Mystery-Series-Examiner~y2009m11d10-crombie-slideshow-script (accessed November 1, 2010).

Web Sites

Official Web site: http://www.deborahcrombie.com/ (accessed November 1, 2010).

Facebook site: http://www.facebook.com/deborah.crombie (accessed November 1, 2010).

Davidson, Diane Mott, 1949–

A month before Christmas, I saw a ghost. This was not the ghost of Christmas past, present, or future. I didn't need to be reminded of bad things I'd done, nor, as far as I knew, of good things I ought to be doing. This wasn't, as my fifteen-year-old son, Arch, would say, any high woo-woo stuff either. I liked the past to stay in the past, thank you very much.

—*Sweet Revenge*, 2007

Biographical Sketch

Diane Mott Davidson was born in Hawaii and attended Wellesley College, then earned a B.A. at Stanford University and an M.A. from Johns Hopkins University. She also attended the Bishop's School of Theology and Ilif School of Theology. Davidson is a lay Episcopal preacher and has worked as a teacher, volunteer rape counselor, and volunteer tutor at a juvenile correctional facility. She is married to Jim Davidson, an electrical engineer, and has three sons.

Davidson had written for years but began focusing on mysteries only after her youngest son was in preschool. She spent time writing in a café that also had a catering service, which gave her the idea for her series of novels centered on a caterer. Davidson was one of the early writers in the genre focusing on food and cooking in her novels—a theme that has become increasingly popular. The Rocky Mountain Fiction Writers named her Writer of the Year in 1990.

Categories: Amateur Detective, Cozy

Awards

Anthony Award, Best Short Story ("Cold Turkey," *Sisters in Crime 5*, 1992)

Major Works

Goldy Schulz series: *Catering to Nobody* (1990), *Dying for Chocolate* (1992), *The Cereal Murders* (1993), *The Last Suppers* (1994), *Killer Pancake* (1995), *The Main Corpse* (1996), *The Grilling Season* (1997), *Prime Cut* (1998), *Tough Cookie* (2000), *Sticks and Scones* (2001), *Chopping Spree* (2002), *Double Shot* (2004), *Dark Tort* (2006), *Sweet Revenge* (2007), *Fatally Flaky* (2009), *Crunch Time* (2011)

Research Sources

Encyclopedias and Handbooks: BYA, CA (214), CANR (167)

Bibliographies: FF, OM

Biographies and Interviews

Hall, Melissa Mia. "Cold (and Bloody) Catering." *Publishers Weekly* 251.37 (September 13, 2004): 61.

Leonard, Beatrice. "Diane Mott Davidson Interview." (webcast) *Travelers with Disabilities Having Fun.* August 6, 2009. http://www.youtube.com/watch?v=0bnNZ35sIoY (accessed November 1, 2010).

Peters, Barbara. "Diane Mott Davidson Interview." (webcast—6 parts). *Poisoned Pen.* n.d. http://www.poisonedpen.com/interviews/diane-mott-davidson. Also available at http://www.youtube.com/watch?v=WZrrF9IxIPg (accessed November 1, 2010).

Criticism and Reader's Guides

Davis, J. Madison. "Crime & Mystery." *World Literature Today* 83.1 (2009): 9–12.

"Diane Mott Davidson." *MostlyFiction.* January 16, 2005. http://www.mostlyfiction.com/sleuths/davidson.htm. (accessed November 1, 2010).

Schoenfeld, Bethe. "Women Writers Writing about Women Detectives in Twenty-First Century America." *Journal of Popular Culture* 41.5 (2008): 836–53.

Web Site

Official Web site: http://www.harpercollins.com/authors/25347/Diane_Mott_Davidson/index.aspx (accessed November 1, 2010).

If You Like Diane Mott Davidson

Davidson's novels feature a caterer who solves crimes while running her business, tending to her son, and dealing with her abusive ex-husband. Her novels have a cooking theme and feature recipes.

Then You Might Like

Susan Wittig Albert

Albert's China Bayles series is about an ex-lawyer who now runs a shop that specializes in herbs and herbal concoctions. The theme of balancing personal and professional lives is one that can also be found in Davidson's books. The China Bayles books are set in the Texas hill country and have a strong sense of place. Titles include *Thyme of Death* and *Rosemary Remembered.*

Laura Childs

Another business owner solving crimes as an amateur detective is Theodosia Browning, owner of a tea shop in Charleston, South Carolina. The tea shop series also features recipes, and Theodosia does her share of catering. This is another series with a strong sense of place in its depiction of the Charleston setting. Titles include *Death by Darjeeling* and *Gunpowder Green.*

Joanne Fluke

The Hannah Swenson mysteries revolve around the proprietor of a cookie shop in Minnesota. With two boyfriends and a propensity to eat her products, Swenson is an entertaining heroine. With seventeen titles and counting, the series begins with *Chocolate Chip Cookie Murder.*

Kerry Greenwood

Greenwood's series about Corinna Chapman, set in Melbourne, Australia, features a baker surrounded by a cast of quirky characters. A lady of a certain size, Corinna and her boyfriend, Daniel, are a joy to know as they solve crimes, cook, and eat. *Earthly Delights,* followed by *Heavenly Pleasures,* begins the series.

Katherine Hall Page

Page's protagonist is Faith Fairchild, a caterer who is married to a minister and has two children. Faith's business leads her into various crime-related situations, and the books spice the mysteries with food details and recipes. Titles include *The Body in the Belfry* and *The Body in the Kelp.*

Elkins, Aaron, 1935–

And that deep, round dent in the helmet... that was interesting. It looked as if it had been caused by a hammerlike weapon, or perhaps a nearly spent musket ball that hadn't had the oomph left to penetrate the metal. Either way, it would likely have left a sizeable dent in the skull beneath it too, so it might well be that he was looking at evidence of the cause of death.

—*Unnatural Selection,* 2006

Biographical Sketch

Born in Brooklyn, Aaron Elkins graduated from Hunter College with a B.A. in 1956. He received M.A. degrees from both the University of Arizona and California State University, Los Angeles, and then a doctorate in education from Berkeley in 1976. He has had a varied career as a college and university instructor and lecturer in both anthropology and business and has held various positions in business and government. While teaching anthropology for the University of Maryland's Overseas Division, he spent two years in Europe teaching at various NATO bases—an experience he later put to good stead as he created the various locales used in his mysteries. He has been married twice and has two children by his first marriage. In 1972, he married Charlotte Trangmar, a writer, who coauthored the Lee Ofsted series with him.

Elkins's primary series features Gideon Oliver, a forensic anthropologist. His interest in art is reflected in the Chris Norgren series about a retired museum curator, as well as in his stand-alone novel, *Loot,* about stolen art during World War II. His novels have been well received critically and are popular with readers.

Categories: Amateur Detective, Forensic

Awards

Agatha Award for Best Short Story ("Nice Gorilla," *Malice Domestic 1—*
    with Charlotte Elkins)
Edgar Award for Best Novel (*Old Bones,* 1998)
Nero Award (*Old Scores,* 1994)

Major Works

Gideon Oliver series: *Fellowship of Fear* (1982), *The Dark Place* (1983),
    Murder in the Queen's Armes (1985), *Old Bones* (1987), *Curses!* (1989),
    Icy Clutches (1990), *Make No Bones* (1991), *Dead Men's Hearts* (1994),
    Twenty Blue Devils (1997), *Skeleton Dance* (2000), *Good Blood* (2004),
    Where There's a Will (2005), *Unnatural Selection* (2006), *Little Tiny
    Teeth* (2007), *Uneasy Relations* (2008), *Skull Duggery* (2009)
Chris Norgren series: *A Deceptive Clarity* (1987), *A Glancing Light* (1991),
    Old Scores (1993)
Lee Ofsted series (with Charlotte Elkins): *A Wicked Slice* (1989), *Rotten Lies*
    (1995), *Nasty Breaks* (1997), *Where Have All the Birdies Gone?* (2004),
    On the Fringe (2005)
Nonseries novels: *Loot* (1999), *Turncoat* (2002)

Research Sources

Encyclopedias and Handbooks: CA (126, 233), CANR (121, 173), EMM, MCF, STJ, WWW

Bibliographies: FF, OM

Biographies and Interviews

Peters, Barbara. "Aaron Elkins." (videocast—6 parts) *Poisoned Pen.* http://www.poisonedpen.com/interviews/aaron-elkins (accessed November 1, 2010).

Swaim, Don. "Aaron Elkins." (audiocast) *Wired for Books.* http://wiredforbooks.org/aaronelkins/ (accessed November 1, 2010).

Criticism and Reader's Guides

Elkins, Aaron. "Have Contract, Will Travel." *Armchair Detective: A Quarterly Journal Devoted to the Appreciation of Mystery, Detective, and Suspense Fiction* 27.2 (1994): 200–205.

Schultze, Sydney. "Gideon Oliver, Skeleton Detective of America." *Clues: A Journal of Detection* 13.1 (1992): 81–89.

Web Sites

Official Web site: http://www.aaronelkins.com/ (accessed November 1, 2010).

"Lee Ofsted." http://www.leeofsted.com A Web site about the Lee Ofsted series of mysteries (accessed November 1, 2010).

Evanovich, Janet, 1943–

> *People are like that, too. Sometimes you just can't tell what's on the inside from looking at the outside. Sometimes people are a big surprise, just like the salt cake. Sometimes the surprise turns out to be good. And sometimes the surprise turns out to be bad.*

> —*Twelve Sharp*, 2006

Biographical Sketch

Janet Evanovich was raised in South River, New Jersey. She majored in fine arts at Douglass College and later married Peter Evanovich while he was obtaining a Ph.D. in mathematics from Rutgers University. The couple had two children, a boy and a girl. Wanting to expand her horizons beyond the confines of family life she turned to writing. She wrote during the day while her children were in school and after they went to bed, but ten years passed before she received her first contract for a book, and at one point she burned all of her rejection letters. Her first few books were romances, some written under the name of Steffie Hall, but she wanted to write books with more action and adventure and so turned to the crime field. She credits the movie *Midnight Run* with inspiring her to make her main character a bounty hunter.

Evanovich's books are humorous and filled with colorful characterizations and snappy dialog. Her immensely popular Stephanie Plum series is set in New Jersey, obviously familiar territory, and the strongly realized setting is part of the books' attraction. Romance also plays a part in the books with an intriguing romantic triangle set up among Plum, Joe Morelli (a cop with whom she has a past), and Ranger, her bounty-hunting mentor. Although Evanovich has written other works, her Plum series remains by far her most popular, fueled by the humor, action, setting, and romance.

Categories: Amateur Detective, Humorous

Awards

Crime Writers Association (UK): Silver Dagger (*Three to Get Deadly,* 1997); Last Laugh Dagger (*Two for the Dough,* 1996)
Dilys Award (*One for the Money,* 1995; *Three to Get Deadly,* 1998)
Lefty Award (*Three to Get Deadly,* 1998)
Quill Award (*Eleven on Top,* 2005; *Twelve Sharp,* 2006)
Independent Mystery Booksellers Association, 100 Favorite Mysteries of the Century (*One for the Money,* 1994)

Major Works

Stephanie Plum series: *One for the Money* (1994), *Two for the Dough* (1996), *Three to Get Deadly* (1997), *Four to Score* (1998), *High Five* (1999), *Hot Six* (2000), *Seven Up* (2001), *Hard Eight* (2002), *To the Nines* (2003), *Ten Big Ones* (2004), *Eleven on Top* (2005), *Twelve Sharp* (2006). *Lean Mean Thirteen* (2007), *Fearless Fourteen* (2008), *Finger Lickin' Fifteen* (2009), *Sizzling Sixteen* (2010)
Stephanie Plum Holiday novels: *Visions of Sugar Plums* (2002), *Plum Lovin'* (2007), *Plum Lucky* (2008), *Plum Spooky* (2009)
Alexandra Barnaby series: *Metro Girl* (2004), *Motor Mouth* (2006), *Trouble-maker* (graphic novel with Alex Evanovich, art by Joelle Jones, 2010)
Nonfiction: *How I Write: Secrets of a Bestselling Author* (with Ina Yaloff and Alex Evanovich, 2006)

Research Sources

Encyclopedias and Handbooks: 100, CA (167), CANR (115, 162, 190), EMM, GWM, MCF, WWW

"Janet Evanovich." *Encyclopedia of World Biography.* 2005. http://www.nota blebiographies.com/newsmakers2/2005-A-Fi/Evanovich-Janet.html (accessed November 1, 2010).

Bibliographies: FF, OM

Biographies and Interviews

Christensen, Kate. "Jonesin' for an Escape? 'Money' Hits the Spot." (audio-cast) *All Things Considered, NPR.* June 8, 2009. http://www.npr.org/tem plates/story/story.php?storyId=105027843 (accessed November 1, 2010).
Clarson, Jennifer. "Janet Does It by the Numbers." *Book* (Summit, NJ) 22 (May–June 2002): 18–19.
Evanovich, Janet. "10 Questions for Janet Evanovich." *Time.com.* June 22, 2009. http://www.time.com/time/magazine/article/0,9171,1904152,00. html (accessed November 1, 2010).
Hayward, Mike. "Janet Evanovich Discusses *Twelve Sharp* and Much Else with Mike Hayward." *BookBrowse.com.* 2006. http://www.bookbrowse. com/author_interviews/full/index.cfm?author_number=232 (accessed November 1, 2010).
James, Pamela. "Three to Get Deadly: An Interview with Janet Evanovich, Creator of the Stephanie Plum Novels." *Armchair Detective: A Quarterly Journal Devoted to the Appreciation of Mystery, Detective, and Suspense Fiction* 30.1 (1997): 50–52.
"Janet Evanovich." *Twbooks.co.uk.* November 14, 2006. http://www.twbooks. co.uk/authors/janetevanovich.html (accessed November 1, 2010).
Muller, Adrian. "Interview with Janet Evanovich." *Deadly Women: The Woman Mystery Reader's Indispensable Companion.* Ed. Jan Grape et al. New York: Carroll & Graf, 1998. 227–31.
Muller, Adrian. "Janet Evanovich." *Speaking of Murder, vol. 2: Interviews with the Masters of Mystery and Suspense.* Ed. Ed Gorman and Martin H. Greenberg. New York: Berkley Prime Crime, 1999. 38–43.
Plagens, Peter. "Standing in the Line of Fire." *Newsweek* 144.1 (July 5, 2004), 56. http://www.newsweek.com/id/54334 (accessed November 1, 2010).
Schneider, Maria. "The WD Interview: Janet Evanovich." *Writer's Digest* 87.1 (2007): 76–80.
Tanenhaus, Sam, et al. "Arts: A Conversation with Janet Evanovich." (videocast) *New York Times.* July 20, 2009.http://www.youtube.com/ watch?v=KX7-34-14Xs (accessed November 1, 2010).
Tierney, Bruce. "Janet Evanovich: Mystery Maven Keeps Readers Coming Back for More." *BookPage.com.* n.d. http://www.bookpage.com/0007bp/ janet_evanovich.html (accessed November 1, 2010).
Ward, Jean Marie. "Janet Evanovich: Delivering a Plum Good Read." *Crescent Blues* 9.1 (2006). http://www.crescentblues.com/7_9issue/int_ evanovich.shtml (accessed November 1, 2010).

White, Claire E. "A Conversation with Janet Evanovich." *Writers Write.* January 1999. http://www.writerswrite.com/journal/jan99/evanovch.htm (accessed November 1, 2010).

Wyatt, Edward. "For This Author, Writing Is Only the Beginning." *New York Times.* June 22, 2005. http://www.nytimes.com/2005/06/22/books/22jane. html (accessed November 1, 2010).

Criticism and Reader's Guides

Allen, Tracy. "Mystery and the Romance Reader." *Collection Management* 29.3/4 (2004): 161–78.

Frizzoni, Brigitte. "Adonis Revisited: Erotic Representations of the Male Body in Women's Crime Fiction." *Folklore: Electronic Journal of Folklore* 43 (2009): 27–42. http://folklore.ee/folklore/vol43/frizzoni.pdf (accessed November 1, 2010).

Papinchak, Robert Allen. "Janet Evanovich: It's All in the Family." *The Writer* 115.8 (August 2002): 34.

Turnbull, Sue. "'Nice Dress, Take It Off': Crime, Romance and the Pleasure of the Text." *International Journal of Cultural Studies* 5.1 (March 2002): 67–82.

Wilson, Leah, ed. *Perfectly Plum: An Unauthorized Celebration of the Life, Loves and Other Disasters of Stephanie Plum, Trenton Bounty Hunter.* Dallas, TX: BenBella, 2007.

Web Site

Official Web site: http://www.evanovich.com/ (accessed November 1, 2010).

If You Like Janet Evanovich

Janet Evanovich's books are humorous mysteries featuring a female sleuth with an unusual occupation. Her protagonist Stephanie Plum is surrounded by well-drawn zany characters, many of whom are family members. Dialog is snappy, and the setting lends interest.

Then You Might Like

Nancy Bartholomew

The Sierra Lavotini series features a stripper who gets involved with mysteries. Like Stephanie, Sierra is surrounded by quirky characters, some of which are somewhat shady. She is assisted by her policeman boyfriend and her uncle who is in the Jersey syndicate, among others. The Florida setting also adds to the books. Titles include *Miracle Strip, Drag Strip,* and *Strip Poker*.

Joan Hess

Hess writes two series that might appeal to readers of Evanovich. The Claire Malloy series features a bookstore owner with a teenage daughter who insists on getting involved in Claire's amateur sleuthing. The series begins with *The Murder at the Murder at the Mimosa Inn,* and there are sixteen more titles. The Arly Hanks series recounts the cases of a small-town female sheriff. Filled with offbeat humor and set in Arkansas, the series begins with *Malice in Maggody*.

Susan Kandel

Kandel's heroine, Cece Caruso, writes biographies of mystery authors, and each of the books in the series revolves around a famous writer. Cece is feisty and funny, and the series gives a strong sense of southern California, where it is set. *I Dreamed I Married Perry Mason* is the first title, followed by *Not a Girl Detective.*

Claire Matturo

Matturo's sleuth is lawyer Lilly Belle Rose Cleary. The humor in the books that feature Cleary comes as much from the quirks of the character herself as from the oddball lawyers in the firm where she works. Again, the setting plays a role in the books. Among the titles are *Skinny Dipping, Wildcat Wine,* and *Bone Valley.*

Sarah Strohmeyer

Bubbles Yablonsky is a former beautician who occasionally works as a journalist. She describes herself as a Polish-Lithuanian Barbie doll and solves mysteries with brains, spunk, and considerable humor. Titles include *Bubbles Unbound* and *Bubbles Betrothed.*

Francis, Dick, 1920–2010

It was now impossible to see much further than from one fence to the next, and the silent surrounding whiteness seemed to shut us, and the isolated string of riders, into a private lonely limbo. Speed was the only reality. Winning post, crowds, stands and stewards, left behind in the mist, lay again invisibly ahead, but on the long deserted mile and a half circuit it was quite difficult to believe they were really there.

—Dead Cert, 1962

Biographical Sketch

Dick Francis, jockey turned author, was born in Wales (sources vary on location), the son of a professional steeplechase rider and stable manager. With horses so important in his family's life, it is not surprising that he grew up to become a jockey, and a very good one, winning more than three hundred and fifty National Hunt races. He was also a pilot in the Royal Air Force during World War II, flying fighters and bombers. Mary, his future wife, came into his life shortly after the war, and they were married in 1947, later having two sons. Francis returned to racing and was championship jockey in 1953–54. In 1956, he was riding a horse that belonged to the Queen Mother in the Grand National when, with a win virtually certain, the horse mysteriously collapsed fifty yards from the finish line. No cause for the collapse was ever found. In 1957, Francis retired from racing after a serious fall and turned to writing, penning an autobiography and working as racing correspondent for the *Sunday Express* of London. His first novel was published in 1962. Francis published more than forty books before his death, at eighty-nine, at his home in the Cayman Islands and was named Commander of the British Empire (CBE) in 2000.

Each of Francis's novels revolves around horse racing in some way. Most are stand-alones; only seven form part of one of his two series. His books have received numerous awards, and he is the only author to win the Edgar Award for Best Novel three times. In addition to the racing setting, his stories are noted for their strong characterizations and graphic violence.

Categories: Amateur Detective, English Setting

Awards

Agatha Malice Domestic Award for Lifetime Achievement (2000)
Gold Dagger Award (*Whip Hand,* 1979)
Diamond Dagger for Lifetime Achievement (1989)
Edgar Award for Best Novel (*Forfeit,* 1970; *Whip Hand,* 1981; *Come to Grief,* 1996)
Grand Master Award for Lifetime Achievement (1996)

Major Works

Sid Halley series: *Odds Against* (1965), *Whip Hand* (1979), *Come to Grief* (1995), *Win, Place, or Show* (collection of short stories, 2004), *Under Orders* (2006)
Kit Fielding series: *Break In* (1985), *Bolt* (1986)
Nonseries novels: *Dead Cert* (1962), *Nerve* (1964), *For Kicks* (1965), *Flying Finish* (1966), *Blood Sport* (1967), *Forfeit* (1968), *Enquiry* (1969), *Rat Race* (1970), *Bonecrack* (1971), *Smokescreen* (1972), *Slayride* (1973), *Knockdown* (1974), *High Stakes* (1975), *In the Frame* (1976), *Risk* (1977), *Trial Run* (1978), *Reflex* (1980), *Twice Shy* (1981), *Banker* (1982), *The Danger* (1983), *Proof* (1984), *Hot Money* (1987), *The Edge* (1988), *Straight* (1989), *Longshot* (1990), *Comeback* (1991), *Driving Force* (1992), *Decider* (1993), *Wild Horses* (1994), *To the Hilt* (1996), *10 Lb. Penalty* (1997), *Second Wind* (1999), *Shattered* (2000)

Novels with Felix Francis: *Dead Heat* (2007), *Silks* (2008), *Even Money* (2009), *Crossfire* (2010)
Short-story collection: *Field of Thirteen* (1998)
Nonfiction: *The Sport of Queens* (1957)—autobiography about racing years

Research Sources

Encyclopedias and Handbooks: 100, BEA, BEB, CA (5–8R), CANR, (9, 42, 68, 100, 141, 179), CLC (2, 22, 42, 102), EMM, MCF, OCC, STJ, WWW

Bibliographies: FF, OM

Biographies and Interviews

"Audio Interviews with Dick Francis." (audiocasts) *Wired for Books.* http://wiredforbooks.org/dickfrancis—Links to five audio interviews held at various times. (accessed November 1, 2010).

"Authors and Creators: Dick Francis." *Thrilling Detective.* n.d. http://www.thrillingdetective.com/trivia/francis.html (accessed November 1, 2010).

Carr, John C. "Dick Francis." *The Craft of Crime: Conversations with Crime Writers.* Boston: Houghton Mifflin, 1983. 202–26.

"Dick Francis." (obituary) *Telegraph.co.uk.* February 14, 2010. http://www.telegraph.co.uk/news/obituaries/culture-obituaries/books-obituaries/7237004/Dick-Francis.html (accessed November 1, 2010).

"Dick Francis and Felix Francis." (videocast) *PanMacmillan.* August 7, 2008. http://www.youtube.com/watch?v=4Fmb6dX1msc (accessed November 1, 2010).

"Dick Francis on the Writer's Life." *Bill Thompson's Eye on Books.* n.d. http://eyeonbooks.com/icp.php?authID=633 (accessed November 1, 2010).

Johnson, Rachel. "Our Favourite Thriller Author Dick Francis Is Back in the Saddle." *Timesonline.co.uk.* August 31, 2008. http://entertainment.timesonline.co.uk/tol/arts_and_entertainment/books/article4639752.ece (accessed November 1, 2010).

Nikkhah, Roya. "Dick Francis Interview for Even Money." *Telegraph.co.uk.* September 1, 2009. http://www.telegraph.co.uk/culture/books/authorinterviews/6121481/Dick-Francis-interview-for-Even-Money.html (accessed November 1, 2010).

Osborne, Lynda. "Dick Francis: Sportsman and Author." *Suite101.* November 14, 2009. http://horseracing.suite101.com/article.cfm/dick_francis_sportsman_and_author (accessed November 1, 2010).

Stasio, Marilyn. "Dick Francis, Jockey and Writer, Dies at 89." *New York Times.* February 14, 2010. http://www.nytimes.com/2010/02/15/books/15francis.html (accessed November 1, 2010).

Criticism and Reader's Guides

Bishop, Paul. "The Sport of Sleuths." *Armchair Detective: A Quarterly Journal Devoted to the Appreciation of Mystery, Detective, and Suspense Fiction* 17.2 (1984): 144–49.

Davis, J. Madison. "Women in Dick Francis." *Clues: A Journal of Detection* 11.1 (1990): 95–105.

DeKoven, Marianne. "Longshot: Crime Fiction as Postmodernism." *Lit: Literature Interpretation Theory* 4.3 (1993). 185–94.

Gould, Charles E., Jr. "The Reigning Phoenix." *Armchair Detective: A Quarterly Journal Devoted to the Appreciation of Mystery, Detective, and Suspense Fiction* 17.4 (1984): 407–10.

Knepper, Marty S. "Dick Francis." *Twelve Englishmen of Mystery*. Ed. Earl F. Bargainnier. Bowling Green, OH: Popular Press, 1984. 223–48.

Lewis, Lou. "'Silver Blaze': The Dick Francis Connection." *Baker Street Journal: An Irregular Quarterly of Sherlockiana* 54.2 (2004): 34–37.

Macdonald, Gina. "Dick Francis." *British Mystery and Thriller Writers since 1940: First Series*. Ed. Bernard Benstock and Thomas F. Staley. Detroit, MI: Gale, 1989. 136–55.

Nelles, William, and Fiona Kelleghan. "Dick Francis." *100 Masters of Mystery and Detection, vol. 1*. Ed. Fiona Kelleghan. Pasadena, CA: Salem Press, 2001. 253–57.

Schaffer, Rachel. "Dead Funny: The Lighter Side of Dick Francis." *Armchair Detective: A Quarterly Journal Devoted to the Appreciation of Mystery, Detective, and Suspense Fiction*. 26.2 (Spring 1993): 76–81.

Schaffer, Rachel. "Dick Francis." *Mystery and Suspense Writers: The Literature of Crime, Detection and Espionage, I*. Ed. Robin W. Winks and Maureen Corrigan. New York: Scribner's Sons, 1998. 383–98.

Schaffer, Rachel. "Dick Francis's Six-Gun Mystique." *Clues: A Journal of Detection* 21.2 (2000): 17–26.

Schaffer, Rachel. "The Pain: Trials by Fire in the Novels of Dick Francis." *Armchair Detective: A Quarterly Journal Devoted to the Appreciation of Mystery, Detective, and Suspense Fiction* 27.3 (1994): 348–57.

Stanton, Michael N. "Dick Francis: The Worth of Human Love." *Armchair Detective: A Quarterly Journal Devoted to the Appreciation of Mystery, Detective, and Suspense Fiction* 15.2 (1982): 137–43.

Sugden, Stephen. *A Dick Francis Companion: Characters, Horses, Plots, Settings and Themes*. Jefferson, NC: McFarland, 2008.

Wagner, Elaine. "The Theme of Parental Rejection in the Novels of Dick Francis." *Clues: A Journal of Detection* 18.1 (1997): 7–13.

Wilhelm, Albert E. "Fathers and Sons in Dick Francis' 'Proof.'" *Critique: Studies in Contemporary Fiction* 32.3 (1991): 169–78.

Wilhelm, Albert E. "Finding the True Self: Rites of Passage in Dick Francis's 'Flying Finish.'" *Clues: A Journal of Detection* 9.2 (1988): 1–8.

Zalewski, James W., and Lawrence B. Rosenfield. "Rules for the Game of Life: The Mysteries of Robert B. Parker and Dick Francis." *Clues: A Journal of Detection* 5.2 (1984): 72–81.

Web Sites

Official Web site: http://www.dickfrancis.com/ (accessed November 1, 2010).

"DickFrancisBooks." http://www.dickfrancisbooks.com/ A fan site that includes a list of books, a page of links to resources, and a page of "fun stuff." Not updated since 2008 (accessed November 1, 2010).

"Dick Francis." http://wejosephson.home.mindspring.com/dfrancis.htm A fan site that includes an overview of Francis's life and work and a list of books with plot synopses and reviews. Not updated since 2007 (accessed November 1, 2010).

George, Elizabeth, 1949–

He'd come out for this walk unprepared and uncaring that he was unprepared. He'd known only that he had to walk or he had to remain home and sleep, and if he remained at home and slept, he'd come to realize that eventually he would will himself not to awaken again.

—Careless in Red, 2008

Biographical Sketch

Susan Elizabeth George was born in Warren, Ohio, but her family soon moved to California. By the age of twelve, she had already written a novel inspired by teen sleuth Nancy Drew. George graduated from the University of California at Riverside and received an M.A. degree from California State University at Fullerton. She made her first trip to England in 1966 in connection with a Shakespeare seminar and immediately felt at home there. She taught English in California schools for more than thirteen years but left when she sold her first novel. In addition to authoring her novels, she has also been a writing instructor at several institutions of higher learning. George is married to Tom McCabe (a second marriage); she continues to travel to England frequently.

George's popular Inspector Lynley series revolves around an aristocratic Scotland Yard policeman and his working-class partner, Sergeant Barbara Havers. It has been noted that her novels depict English life so well that they deceive readers on both sides of the Atlantic into believing the author is herself English.

Categories: English Setting, Police Procedural

Awards

Agatha Award for Best First Novel (*A Great Deliverance,* 1988)
Anthony Award for Best First Novel (*A Great Deliverance,* 1989)

Major Works

Inspector Lynley series: *A Great Deliverance* (1988), *Payment in Blood* (1989),
    Well-Schooled in Murder (1990), *A Suitable Vengeance* (1991), *For the
    Sake of Elena* (1992), *Missing Joseph* (1993), *Playing for the Ashes* (1994),
    In the Presence of the Enemy (1996), *Deception on His Mind* (1997), *In
    Pursuit of the Proper Sinner* (1999), *A Traitor to Memory* (2001), *With
    No One as Witness* (2005), *What Came Before He Shot Her* (2006), *Care-
    less in Red* (2008), *This Body of Death* (2010)
Nonseries novel: *A Place of Hiding* (2003)
Short-story collections: *The Evidence Exposed* (1999), *I, Richard: Stories of
    Suspense* (2002)
Nonfiction: *Write Away: One Novelist's Approach to Fiction and the Writing
    Life* (2004)

Research Sources

*Encyclopedias and Handbooks: BYA, CA (137), CANR (62, 112,
162), GWM, EMM, MCF, STJ, WWW*

Bibliographies: FF, OM

Biographies and Interviews

"Author Elizabeth George." *PBS.* n.d. http://www.pbs.org/wgbh/mystery/
    lynley/george.html (accessed November 1, 2010).
Dillon-Parkin, Crow. "Elizabeth George." *Speaking of Murder: Interviews
    with the Masters of Mystery and Suspense.* Ed. Ed Gorman and Martin
    H. Greenberg. New York: Berkley Prime Crime, 1998. 65–72.
Dillon-Parkin, Crow. "Interview with Elizabeth George." *Deadly Women:
    The Woman Mystery Reader's Indispensable Companion.* Ed. Jan Grape
    et al. New York: Carroll & Graf, 1998. 199–204.
"Elizabeth George." (videocast) No producer given. October 21, 2008. http://
    www.youtube.com/watch?v=o1NpOu51q-I (accessed November 1, 2010).
"Elizabeth George, Bestselling Author, Talks to Authorlink." (video-
    cast) *AuthorLink.* June 25, 2008. http://www.youtube.com/watch?
    v=OXZGd3iDEsM (accessed November 1, 2010).
Espinoza, Galina, Cynthia Wang, and Kwala Mandel. "English Lessons."
    People 58.9 (August 26, 2002): 107. http://www.people.com/people/
    archive/article/0,,20137845,00.html (accessed November 1, 2010).

George, Elizabeth. "A Novel by Any Other Name." *The Writer* 107.1 (January 1994): 11.

Julian, K. "The Anglo File." *Book* (Summit, NJ) 29 (July–August 2003): 22.

Macdonald, Jay. "The Other Side of the Story." *Book Page*. n.d. http://www.bookpage.com/0611bp/elizabeth_george.html (accessed November 1, 2010).

"Mystery! Inspector Lynley." *Washington Post*. June 27, 2005. http://www.washingtonpost.com/wp-dyn/content/discussion/2005/06/23/DI2005062301410.html (accessed November 1, 2010).

Nolan, Tom. "A Writer Seeks Her Inspiration across the Pond." *Wall Street Journal—Eastern Edition* (September 10, 2001): A16.

Picker, Leonard. "Not Writing What You Know." *Publishers Weekly* 255.12 (March 24, 2008): 56. http://www.publishersweekly.com/pw/by-topic/1-legacy/16-all-book-reviews/article/9518-not-writing-what-you-know-.html (accessed November 1, 2010).

Pohl, Kathy. "Demystifying the Writing Process." *The Writer* 120.6 (June 2007): 20–22.

"Powell's Q&A: Elizabeth George." *Powell's Books*. n.d. http://www.powells.com/ink/elizabethgeorge.html (accessed November 1, 2010).

See, Lisa. "Elizabeth George: An American in Scotland Yard." *Publishers Weekly* 243.11 (March 11, 1996): 38.

Woodsum, Jo Ann. "Elizabeth George on Novel Writing." *Suite101*. September 12, 2009. http://resourcesforwriters.suite101.com/article.cfm/elizabeth_george_on_novel_writing (accessed November 1, 2010).

Criticism and Reader's Guides

Koppelman, Kate. "Deliver Us to Evil: Religion as Abject Other in Elizabeth George's *A Great Deliverance*." *Race and Religion in the Postcolonial British Detective Story: Ten Essays*. Ed. Julie H. Kim. Jefferson, NC: McFarland, 2005. 96–118.

Libretti, Tim. "Detecting Empire from Inside-Out and Outside-In: The Politics of Detection in the Fiction of Elizabeth George and Lucha Corpi." *Race and Religion in the Postcolonial British Detective Story: Ten Essays*. Ed. Julie H. Kim. Jefferson, NC: McFarland, 2005. 71–95.

Malmgren, Carl D. "Truth, Justice, the American Way: Martha Grimes and Elizabeth George." *Clues: A Journal of Detection* 21.2 (Fall-Winter, 2000): 47–56.

Stenger, Karl L. "Elizabeth George." *American Mystery and Detective Writers* (*Dictionary of Literary Biography* 306). Ed. George Parker Anderson. Detroit, MI: Thomson Gale, 2005. 132–43.

Web Site

Official Web site: http://www.elizabethgeorgeonline.com/ (accessed November 1, 2010).

Gerritsen, Tess, 1953–

He fled down the hallway, running in blind panic, lost in a maze of corridors. Where was he? Why did nothing seem familiar? Then, straight ahead, he saw the window, and beyond it, the swirling snow. Snow. That cold, white lace would purify him, would cleanse this blood from his hands.

—Life Support, 1997

Biographical Sketch

Born in San Diego, Tess Tom attended Stanford University, where she received a B.A. She went on to receive an M.D. degree, in 1979, from the University of California, San Francisco. She married a fellow physician, Jacob Gerritsen, and has two children. Gerritsen practiced medicine in Honolulu for ten years, but ,while on maternity leave, she began to write fiction, and her first novel was published in 1987. She started writing full time in 1989 and published eight more romantic suspense novels, including *Never Say Die,* which won some romance awards. She then switched to writing medical thrillers; her novel *Harvest* propelled her onto the best-seller list for the first time. She is the recipient of a Rita Award for best romantic suspense novel, for *The Surgeon.*

Gerritsen's series about detective Jane Rizzoli and medical examiner Maura Isles combine police procedural detail, medical knowledge, and suspense in page-turning thrillers, while her stand-alone medical thrillers are based on such themes as genetics and bioterrorism. The novels have generally been well reviewed, and she is a regular on best-seller lists. The Rizzoli and Isles series is the basis for a new television series that debuted in the summer of 2010.

Categories: Medical, Thriller

Awards

Nero Award (*Vanish,* 2006)

Major Works

Jane Rizzoli and Maura Isles series: *The Surgeon* (2001), *The Apprentice* (2002), *The Sinner* (2003), *Body Double* (2004), *Vanish* (2005) *The Mephisto Club* (2006), *The Keepsake* (2008), *Ice Cold* (2010)

Nonseries novels: *Whistleblower* (1992), *Never Say Die* (1992), *Harvest* (1996), *Life Support* (1997), *Bloodstream* (1998), *Gravity* (1999), *The Bone Garden* (2007)

Research Sources

Encyclopedias and Handbooks: CA (159), CANR (116, 155, 197)

Bibliographies: FF, OM

Biographies and Interviews

Anable, Steve. "I'm No Angel." *Publishers Weekly* 253.31 (August 7, 2006): 28. http://www.publishersweekly.com/pw/by-topic/1-legacy/16-all-book-reviews/article/10352-i-m-no-angel-.html (accessed November 1, 2010).

Bolton, Kathleen. "Author Interview: Tess Gerritsen." *Writer Unboxed.* January 18, 2008. http://writerunboxed.com/2008/01/18/author-interview-tess-gerritsen-part-one/ (accessed November 1, 2010).

Dunn, Adam, and Jeff Zaleski. "Thriller Writer Utilizes Hands-On Experience." *Publishers Weekly* 250.28 (July 14, 2003): 56.

"Gossip Lady with Thriller Author Tess Gerritsen." (videocast) *Gossip Lady: Seacoastonline.* October 22, 2008. http://www.youtube.com/watch?v=Obgxft-TXPE (accessed November 1, 2010).

Holden, Rob. "Author Tess Gerritsen." *ReadersRoom Coffee Chats.* September 15, 2006. http://www.readersroom.com/2006/09/author-tess-gerritsen.html (accessed November 1, 2010).

Karm, Ali. "Interview." *Shots: the Crime and Mystery Magazine.* September 2002. http://www.shotsmag.co.uk/SHOTS%2017/Tess%20Gerritsen/gerritsen.htm (accessed November 1, 2010).

Liaguno, Vince A. "Tess Gerritsen: The Accidental Novelist." *Dark Scribe Magazine.* October 10, 2008. http://www.darkscribemagazine.com/feature-interviews/tess-gerritsen-the-accidental-novelist.html (accessed November 1, 2010).

Peters, Barbara. "Tess Gerritsen." (videocast—7 parts) *Poisoned Pen.* October 4, 2008. http://www.youtube.com/watch?v=EuFtjiKwvmg (accessed November 1, 2010).

Smiley, Tavis. "Tess Gerritsen." (audiocast) *PBS.* November 9, 2006. http://www.pbs.org/kcet/tavissmiley/archive/200611/20061109_gerritsen.html (accessed November 1, 2010).

"Tess Gerritsen." *Bookreporter.com.* September 12, 2008. http://www.bookreporter.com/authors/au-gerritsen-tess.asp (accessed November 1, 2010).

"Tess Gerritsen and Dennis Lehane in Discussion." (videocast—3 parts) *Transworldvideos.* February 27, 2009. http://www.youtube.com/watch?v=0wYb26oShcg (accessed November 1, 2010).

"Tess Gerritsen Talks Medical Thrillers." *Writer's Forensics Blog.* May 29, 2009. http://writersforensicsblog.wordpress.com/2009/05/29/tess-gerritsen-talks-medical-thrillers/ (accessed November 1, 2010).

White, Claire E. "A Conversation with Tess Gerritsen." *Writers Write.* October–November 2001. http://www.writerswrite.com/journal/nov01/gerritsen.htm (accessed November 1, 2010).

Criticism and Reader's Guides

Ephron, Hallie. "Chilled to the Bone." *Writer* 121.9 (September 2008): 18–21.
"The Mephisto Club." (reading guide) *Reading Group Guides.* n.d. http://www.readinggroupguides.com/guides3/mephisto_club1.asp (accessed November 1, 2010).

Web Site

Official Web site: http://www.tessgerritsen.com/ (accessed November 1, 2010).

Grafton, Sue, 1940–

My name is Kinsey Millhone. I'm a private investigator, licensed by the state of California. I'm thirty-two years old, twice divorced, no kids. The day before yesterday I killed someone and the fact weighs heavily on my mind.

—A Is for Alibi, 1982

Biographical Sketch

Sue Grafton was born in Louisville, Kentucky, to parents who were both offspring of Presbyterian missionaries. She attended the University of Louisville, where she received a B.A. in 1961. She has been married three times and has three children from her first two marriages; her third husband is Steven F. Humphrey, a professor of philosophy, whom she married in 1978. Grafton has been a hospital admissions clerk, a cashier, and a clerical/medical secretary, as well as a lecturer at various institutions of higher learning and writers' conferences. She has written a number of television scripts, both alone and with her husband.

Grafton was one of the early authors to write about a strong female private investigator. Her series character, Kinsey Millhone, has continued to grow and change throughout the series, which has contributed to the continuing popularity of Grafton's novels. She has won a number of awards and has received lifetime achievement awards from two major crime authors' associations in the United States and the United Kingdom.

Categories: Hard-Boiled, Private Detective

Awards

Anthony Award for Best Novel (*B Is for Burglar,* 1986; *C Is for Corpse,* 1987; *G Is for Gumshoe,* 1991)

Anthony Award for Best Short Story ("The Parker Shotgun," *Mean Streets,* 1987)

Diamond Dagger for Lifetime Achievement (2008)

Edgar Grand Master Award for Lifetime Achievement (2009)

Macavity Award for Best Short Story ("The Parker Shotgun," *Mean Streets,* 1987)

Shamus Award for Best PI Novel (*B Is for Burglar,* 1986; *G Is for Gumshoe,* 1991; *K Is for Killer,* 1995).

Major Works

The Kinsey Millhone series: *A Is for Alibi* (1982), *B Is for Burglar* (1985), *C Is for Corpse* (1986), *D Is for Deadbeat* (1987), *E Is for Evidence* (1988), *F Is for Fugitive* (1989), *G Is for Gumshoe* (1990), *H Is for Homicide* (1991), *I Is for Innocent* (1992), *J Is for Judgment* (1993), *K Is for Killer* (1994), *L Is for Lawless* (1995), *M Is for Malice* (1996), *N Is for Noose* (1998), *O Is for Outlaw* (1999), *P Is for Peril* (2001), *Q Is for Quarry* (2002), *R Is for Ricochet* (2004), *S Is for Silence* (2005), *T Is for Trespass* (2007), *U Is for Undertow* (2009)

Short-story collections: *Kinsey and Me* (1992)

Nonfiction: *Writing Mysteries: A Handbook* (editor, 1992, 2nd ed., 2002)

Research Sources

Encyclopedias and Handbooks: 100, BYA, CA (108), CANR (31, 55, 111, 134, 195), CLC (163), EMM, GWM, MCF, OCC, STJ, WWW

Bibliographies: FF, OM

Biographies and Interviews

Herbert, Rosemary. "Sue Grafton." *The Fatal Art of Entertainment: Interviews with Mystery Writers.* New York: G. K. Hall, 1994. 28–53.

Kaminsky, Stuart, and Laurie Roberts. "Sue Grafton." *Behind the Mystery: Top Mystery Writers Interviewed.* Cohasset, MA: Hot House, 2005. 2–13.

Peters, Barbara. "Sue Grafton Interview." (videocast—6 parts) *Poisoned Pen.* n.d. http://www.poisonedpen.com/interviews/sue-grafton-interview (accessed November 1, 2010).

Picker, Leonard. "I Is for Interview." *Publishers Weekly* 254.40 (October 8, 2007): 39.

"Q&A: Sue Grafton." *Kirkus Reviews*. 73.11 (June 1, 2005): S8.

Richards, Linda. "G Is for Grafton." *January Magazine*. 1997. http://www.januarymagazine.com/grafton.html (accessed November 1, 2010).

Silet, Charles L. P. "Sue Grafton." *Speaking of Murder: Interviews with the Masters of Mystery and Suspense*. Ed. Ed Gorman and Martin H. Greenberg. New York: Berkley Prime Crime, 1998. 205–22.

"Sue Grafton." *Writer Magazine*. March 19, 2002. http://www.writermag.com/wrt/default.aspx?c=a&id=418 (accessed November 1, 2010).

"Sue Grafton Talks about 'U Is for Undertow' and More." (videocast) *Borders Media*. October 18, 2009. http://www.youtube.com/watch?v=xrGn_60Kdx0 (accessed November 1, 2010).

White, Claire E. "A Conversation with Sue Grafton." *Writers Write*. October 1999. http://www.writerswrite.com/journal/oct99/grafton.htm (accessed November 1, 2010).

Criticism and Reader's Guides

Blade, Jenny Elizabeth. "Grafton's Progression from the Hard-Boiled Tradition." *Clues: A Journal of Detection* 19.2 (1998): 69–77.

Brandt, Kate, and Paula Lichtenberg. "On the Case with V. I. and Kinsey." *Hot Wire: The Journal of Women's Music and Culture* 10.1 (1994): 48–50.

Christianson, Scott. "Talkin' Trash and Kickin' Butt: Sue Grafton's Hard-Boiled Feminism." *Feminism in Women's Detective Fiction*. Ed. Glenwood Irons. Toronto: University of Toronto Press, 1995. 127–47.

Cook, Lisa A. "The Female Private Detective: Kinsey Millhone—America's New Hero." *The Image of the Hero in Literature, Media, and Society*. Ed. Will Wright and Steven Kaplan. Pueblo: Colorado State University, 2004. 135–40.

DeWeese, Bev. "Why We Love Kinsey Millhone." *Deadly Women: The Woman Mystery Reader's Indispensable Companion*. Ed. Jan Grape, et al. New York: Carroll & Graf, 1998. 221–25.

DuBose, Martha Hailey. "Sue Grafton: An 'Ornery' Original." *Women of Mystery: The Lives and Works of Notable Women Crime Novelists*. New York: St. Martin's Minotaur, 2000. 386–92.

Freier, Mary P. "Information Ethics in the Detective Novel." *Clues: A Journal of Detection* 24.1 (2005): 18–26.

Gray, W. Russel. "Flow Gently, Sweet Grafton: 'M' Is for Metaphysical (or at Least Metaphor) in 'C Is for Corpse.'" *Clues: A Journal of Detection* 20.1 (1999): 63–69.

Hubbell, Gary. "All You Have Left in the End: Conclusions and the Series Character in Sue Grafton's 'Alphabet Series.'" *Clues: A Journal of Detection* 18.1 (1997): 15–23.

Johnson, Patricia E. "Sex and Betrayal in the Fiction of Sue Grafton and Sara Paretsky." *Journal of Popular Culture* 27.4 (Spring 1994): 97–106.

Jones, Louise Conley. "Feminism and the P. I. Code: Or, 'Is a Hard-Boiled Warshawski Unsuitable to Be Called a Feminist?'" *Clues: A Journal of Detection* 16.1 (1995): 77–87.

Kay, Carol McGinnis. "Sue Grafton." *American Hard-Boiled Crime Writers (Dictionary of Literary Biography* 226). Ed. George Parker Anderson and Julie B. Anderson. Detroit, MI: Gale, 2000. 175–87.

Matheson, Sue. "Food Is Never Just Something to Eat: Sue Grafton's Culinary Critique of Mainstream America." *Journal of Popular Culture* 41.5 (2008): 809–22.

Rabinowitz, Peter J. "'Reader, I Blew Him Away': Convention and Transgression in Sue Grafton." *Famous Last Words: Changes in Gender and Narrative Closure.* Ed. Alison Booth. Charlottesville: University Press of Virginia, 1993. 326–44.

Reddy, Maureen T. "The Feminist Counter-Tradition in Crime: Cross, Grafton, Paretsky, and Wilson." *The Cunning Craft: Original Essays on Detective Fiction and Contemporary Literary Theory.* Ed. Ronald G. Walker and June M. Frazer. Macomb: Western Illinois University Press, 1990. 174–87.

Reynolds, Moira Davison. "Sue Grafton." *Women Authors of Detective Series: Twenty-One American and British Writers, 1900–2000.* Jefferson, NC: McFarland, 2001. 132–38.

Schaffer, Rachel. "Armed (with Wit) and Dangerous: Sue Grafton's Sense of Black Humor." *Armchair Detective: A Quarterly Journal Devoted to the Appreciation of Mystery, Detective, and Suspense Fiction* 30.3 (1997): 316–22.

Shuker-Haines, Timothy, and Martha M. Umphrey. "Gender (De)Mystified: Resistance and Recuperation in Hard-Boiled Female Detective Fiction." *The Detective in American Fiction, Film, and Television.* Ed. Jerome H. Delamater and Ruth Prigozy. Westport, CT: Greenwood, 1998. 71–82.

Svoboda, Frederic. "Hard-Boiled Feminist Detectives and Their Families: Reimaging a Form." *Gender in Popular Culture: Images of Men and Women in Literature, Visual Media, and Material Culture.* Ed. Peter C. Rollins and Susan W. Rollins. Cleveland, OH: Ridgemont, 1995. 247–72.

Swanson, Jean. "Sue Grafton." *Mystery and Suspense Writers: The Literature of Crime, Detection, and Espionage, I.* Ed. Robin W. Winks and Maureen Corrigan. New York: Scribner's, 1998. 439–48.

Taylor, Bruce. "G Is for (Sue) Grafton." *Armchair Detective: A Quarterly Journal Devoted to the Appreciation of Mystery, Detective, and Suspense Fiction* 22.1 (1989): 4–13.

Walton, Priscilla L. "'E' Is for En/Gendering Readings: Sue Grafton's Kinsey Millhone." *Women Times Three: Writers, Detectives, Readers.* Ed. Kathleen Gregory Klein. Bowling Green, OH: Popular Press, 1995. 101–15.

Wilson, Ann. "The Female Dick and the Crisis of Heterosexuality." *Feminism in Women's Detective Fiction.* Ed. Glenwood Irons. Toronto: University of Toronto Press, 1995. 148–56.

Web Site

Official Web site: http://www.suegrafton.com/ (accessed November 1, 2010).

Grisham, John, 1955–

> It's [Professor Smoot's] opinion that all students enter law school with a
> certain amount of idealism and desire to serve the public, but after three
> years of brutal competition we care for nothing but the right job with the
> right firm where we can make partner in seven years and earn big bucks.
> He's right about this.

> —*The Rainmaker*, 1995

Biographical Sketch

The son of a construction worker and a housewife, Grisham was born in
Jonesboro, Arkansas. Because of his father's work, the family moved several
times before settling in Southaven, Mississippi. Grisham was always a reader,
but he also loved baseball and had dreams of becoming a pro. When he realized that wasn't going to happen, he transferred to Mississippi State University, where he majored in accounting and then went on to get a J.D. from
the University of Mississippi. He set up practice in Southaven and was later
elected to the Mississippi legislature as a representative, a post in which he
served for seven years. During this time, he was working on his first novel. Rejected by a number of publishers, it was bought by a small firm that printed
only a few thousand copies. But Grisham hit it big with his second novel, *The
Firm,* which was the best-selling book of 1991. He currently lives in Charlottesville, Virginia, and is a full-time writer.

The majority of Grisham's novels are legal thrillers. They usually pit an
unknown lawyer against a large law firm or other overwhelming opponent.
His books have been translated into twenty-nine languages, and the copies in
print number in the hundreds of millions worldwide. Critics have praised the
suspenseful writing and the fast pace of the books.

Categories: Legal, Thriller

Major Works

Novels: *A Time to Kill* (1989), *The Firm* (1991), *The Pelican Brief* (1992),
The Client (1993), *The Chamber* (1994), *The Rainmaker* (1995), *The Run-
away Jury* (1996), *The Partner* (1997), *The Street Lawyer* (1998), *The
Testament* (1999), *The Brethren* (1999), *The Summons* (2002), *The King*

of Torts (2003), *The Last Juror* (2004), *The Broker* (2005), *The Appeal* (2008), *The Associate* (2009), *The Confession* (2010)
Short-story collection: *Ford County* (2009)
Nonfiction: *The Innocent Man: Murder and Injustice in a Small Town* (2006)

Research Sources

Encyclopedias and Handbooks: 100, BEA, BEB, CA (138), CANR (47, 69, 114, 133), CLC (84, 273), EMM, MCF, STJ, WWW

Bibliographies: FF, OM

Biographies and Interviews

"10 Questions." *Time* 171.5 (January 24, 2008): 6. http://www.time.com/time/magazine/article/0,9171,1706764,00.html (accessed November 1, 2010).

Duffy, Martha. "Grisham's Law." *Time* 145.19 (1995): 87.

Ferranti, Jennifer. "Grisham's Law." *Saturday Evening Post* 269.2 (March 1997): 42–43, 81–82.

Garner, Dwight. "Mississippi Churning." *Salon.com.* March 1997. http://www.salon.com/march97/grisham970312.html (accessed November 1, 2010).

"Grisham's 'Appeal' Tackles Down-and-Dirty Politics." (audiocast) *Weekend All Things Considered, NPR.* January 27, 2008. http://www.npr.org/templates/story/story.php?storyId=18402286 (accessed November 1, 2010).

Grossman, Lev. "Grisham's New Pitch." *Time* 168.16 (October 9, 2006): 68–70. http://www.time.com/time/magazine/article/0,9171,1543958,00.html (accessed November 1, 2010).

Hosie, Sean. "John Grisham." *Mississippi Writers and Musicians.* January 2008. http://www.mswritersandmusicians.com/writers/john-grisham.html (accessed November 1, 2010).

"John Grisham." *Academy of Achievement.* February 4, 2009. http://www.achievement.org/autodoc/page/gri0bio-1 (accessed November 1, 2010).

"John Grisham." *BookReporter.com.* May 1997. http://www.bookreporter.com/authors/au-grisham-john.asp (accessed November 1, 2010).

"John Grisham." *Mississippi Writer's Page.* January 2005. http://www.olemiss.edu/mwp/dir/grisham_john/index.html (accessed November 1, 2010).

"John Grisham: 2009 National Book Festival." (videocast) *Library of Congress.* September 26, 2009. http://www.loc.gov/today/cyberlc/feature_wdesc.php?rec=4722. Also available at http://www.youtube.com/watch?v=-Iu_DMLKQPs (accessed November 1, 2010).

"John Grisham: 2009 National Book Festival Welcome." (videocast) *Book TV, C-Span 2.* September 30, 2009. http://www.youtube.com/watch?v=krr683y5WDA (accessed November 1, 2010).

"John Grisham: 2009 Virginia Festival of the Book." (videocast) *Book TV,*
  C-Span2. http://www.booktv.org/Watch/10374/2009+Virginia+Festival+
  of+the+Book+John+Grisham.aspx (accessed November 1, 2010).
"John Grisham Room." *Mississippi State Library.* September 22, 2009. http://
  library.msstate.edu/grishamroom/index.asp (accessed November 1,
  2010). Includes information about Grisham.
Lauer, Matt. "John Grisham." (videocast) *MSNBC.com.* November 9, 2009.
  http://www.msnbc.msn.com/id/21134540/vp/33600917#33600917 (accessed November 1, 2010).
"Meet the Writers: John Grisham." (videocast) *Barnes and Noble.* April 4,
  2008. http://www.youtube.com/watch?v=V8S7C-hdKR4 (accessed November 1, 2010).
Summer, Bob. "Grisham's Southern Loyalists." *Publishers Weekly* 250.9
  (March 3, 2003): 33.
Williams, Geoff. "A Brutal Crime, a Passion for Justice." *Biography* 1.1 (1997):
  68+.
Zaleski, Jeff. "The Grisham Business." *Publishers Weekly* 245.3 (1998):
  248–51.

Criticism and Reader's Guides

Black, Joel. "Grisham's Demons." *College Literature* 25.1 (1998): 35–40.
Breen, Jon L. "The Legal Crime Novel." *Mystery and Suspense Writers: The
  Literature of Crime, Detection, and Espionage, II.* Ed. Robin W. Winks
  and Maureen Corrigan. New York: Scribners, 1998. 1103–15.
Cauthen, Cramer R., and Donald G. Alpin III. "The Gift Refused: The
  Southern Lawyer in *To Kill a Mockingbird, The Client,* and *Cape Fear.*"
  Studies in Popular Culture 19.2 (1996): 257–75.
Conniff, Ruth. "Justice for Sale." *Progressive* 72.6 (2008): 10–11.
Corn, David. "Populism: The Thriller." *Nation* 274.13 (2002): 31–33.
Diggs, Terry K. "Through a Glass Darkly." *ABA Journal* 82.10 (1996): 72–74,
  76.
Goodnight, G. Thomas. "The Firm, the Park and the University: Fear and
  Trembling on the Postmodern Trail." *Quarterly Journal of Speech* 81.3
  (1995): 267–90.
Heffernan, Nick. "Law Crimes: The Legal Fictions of John Grisham and
  Scott Turow." *Criminal Proceedings: The Contemporary American Crime
  Novel.* Ed. Peter Messent London: Pluto Press, 1997. 187–213.
"The Innocent Man." (reading guides) *Reading Group Guides.* n.d. http://
  www.readinggroupguides.com/guides3/innocent_man1.asp (accessed
  November 1, 2010); *BookBrowse.com.* n.d. http://www.bookbrowse.com/
  reading_guides/detail/index.cfm?book_number=1915 (accessed Novem-
  ber 1, 2010).
"John Grisham." *Enotes.com.* n.d. http://www.enotes.com/contemporary-
  literary-criticism/grisham-john (accessed November 1, 2010).

Nickelson, Katie. "Lawyers as Tainted Heroes in John Grisham's Novels." *The Image of the Hero in Literature, Media, and Society.* Ed. Will Wright and Steven Kaplan. Pueblo: Colorado State University, 2004. 539–41.

Robson, Peter. "Adapting the Modern Law Novel: Filming John Grisham." *Journal of Law & Society* 28.1 (2001): 147–63.

Rubin, Jennifer. "John Grisham's Law: The Social and Economic Impact of a Pop Novelist." *Commentary* 127.6 (2009): 56–60.

Runyon, Randolph Paul. "John Grisham: Obsessive Imagery." *Southern Writers at Century's End.* Ed. Jeffrey J. Folks and James A. Perkins. Lexington: University Press of Kentucky, 1997. 44–59.

Swirski, Peter, and Faye Wong. "Briefcases for Hire: American Hardboiled to Legal Fiction." *Journal of American Culture* 29.3 (2006): 307–20.

Web Site

Official Web site: http://www.jgrisham.com/ (accessed November 1, 2010).

If You Like John Grisham

Grisham's hallmark is the fast-paced legal thriller in which plotting and suspense are the paramount elements.

Then You Might Like

William Bernhardt

Bernhardt's series of legal and political thrillers stars Ben Kincaid. As in Grisham's novels, the crux of the action revolves around lawyers and legislators. Kincaid is a Tulsa attorney who also spends time in Washington, D.C., when he is appointed to fill an unexpired congressional vacancy. The political backdrop adds to the legal focus of the series. The Kincaid series begins with *Primary Justice,* followed by *Blind Justice.*

Stephen W. Frey

The action moves to Wall Street in Frey's financial thrillers. Frey is another author whose suspense-filled plotting about movers and shakers who just may be on the wrong side of the law makes for a compelling read. Frey's first two novels were *The Takeover* and *The Vulture Fund.*

Steve Martini

Martini's primary series stars Paul Madriani, who loses his job at a major legal firm in the first book in the series. Martini writes strong courtroom scenes, and his books have thrilling plots that take place both inside and outside the courtroom. *Compelling Evidence* and *Prime Witness* begin the series.

Brad Meltzer

Meltzer's novels are stand-alones, but his legal thrillers are well regarded and popular. *The Tenth Justice* revolves around an ethical error made by the law clerk of a Supreme Court justice. In trying to undo the damage, the novice lawyer gets himself into ever deeper peril. *Dead Even* pits two married lawyers against each other in a case because of which each is threatened with death if he or she should lose the case. Other titles include *The First Counsel* and *The Millionaires*.

Richard North Patterson

Patterson's novels are set in a variety of milieus, from the courtroom to big business to government. Like Grisham, Patterson has a legal background, which lends verisimilitude to his novels. The Kerry Kilcannon series is about a politician who becomes president, while the Christopher Paget series follows a lawyer who works for the Economic Crimes Commission. Titles to try include *The Lasko Tangent, No Safe Place,* and the stand-alone novel *The Final Judgment.*

Harris, Charlaine, 1951–

> *Ever since vampires came out of the coffin (as they laughingly put it) four years ago, I'd hoped one would come to Bon Temps. We had all the other minorities in our little town—why not the newest, the legally recognized undead? But rural northern Louisiana wasn't too tempting to vampires, apparently; on the other hand, New Orleans was a real center for them— the whole Anne Rice thing, right?*

> —*Dead Until Dark*, 2001

Biographical Sketch

Charlaine Harris was born in Tunica, Mississippi. Her father, Robert, was a high school principal, and her mother, Jean, was a librarian. She received a B.A. in English from Southwestern (now Rhodes) College, in Memphis, in 1973 and held several different jobs before becoming a professional writer. She married Hal Schulz, a chemical engineer, in 1978 after her first marriage ended in divorce; the couple has three children and lives in Arkansas near Texarkana. Harris took a creative writing class led by Shannon Ravenel (who now runs Algonquin Press); Ravenel was impressed enough with Harris's manuscript for the class to recommend it to Houghton Mifflin, leading to the publication of *Sweet and Deadly* in 1980. Another stand-alone mystery followed before Harris started the Aurora Teagarden series, cozy mysteries about a sleuthing librarian. She also started the Lily Bard series, much darker stories about a cleaning lady in Shakespeare, Arkansas, who had suffered a terrible attack in the past, leaving her physically and emotionally scarred. Although modestly successful, these two series didn't bring the level of sales that Harris wanted, so she rethought her career and turned to writing the cross-genre Southern Vampires series about a telepathic waitress and various vampires, werewolves, and so forth. Not falling strictly into the crime, romance, or supernatural genres but, rather, a blend of all three, these novels quickly became very popular, helping to start the current trend of cross-over paranormal mystery-romance works. Harris's latest series, about Harper Connelly, depicts a woman who, because she was struck by lightning as a teenager, can find dead bodies. All of her series are set in the South.

Harris's series run the gamut from the cozy, lightly humorous Teagarden novels to the much darker and more serious Bard and Connelly series. The Southern Vampire books feature suspenseful plots mixed with dark humor and have been adapted into the *True Blood* television series on HBO.

Categories: Amateur Detective, Paranormal

Awards

Anthony Award for Best Paperback Original (*Dead until Dark,* 2002)

Major Works

Aurora Teagarden series: *Real Murders* (1990), *A Bone to Pick* (1992), *Three Bedrooms, One Corpse* (1994), *The Julius House* (1995), *Dead over Heels* (1996), *A Fool and His Honey* (1999), *Last Scene Alive* (2002), *Poppy Done to Death* (2003)

Harper Connelly series: *Grave Sight* (2005), *Grave Surprise* (2006), *An Ice Cold Grave* (2007), *Grave Secret* (2009)

Lily Bard series: *Shakespeare's Landlord* (1996), *Shakespeare's Champion* (1997), *Shakespeare's Christmas* (1998), *Shakespeare's Trollop* (2000), *Shakespeare's Counselor* (2001)

Southern Vampires (Sookie Stackhouse) series: *Dead until Dark* (2001), *Living Dead in Dallas* (2002), *Club Dead* (2003), *Dead to the World* (2004), *Dead as a Doornail* (2005), *Definitely Dead* (2006), *All Together Dead* (2007), *From Dead to Worse* (2008), *Dead and Gone* (2009), *A Touch of Dead* (2009), *Dead in the Family* (2010)

Nonseries novels: *Sweet and Deadly* (1981), *A Secret Rage* (1984)

Research Sources

Encyclopedias and Handbooks: BYA, CA (105), CANR (99, 155, 197), GWM

"Charlaine Harris." *Encyclopedia of Arkansas History and Culture*. May 30, 2009. http://www.encyclopediaofarkansas.net/encyclopedia/entry-detail. aspx?entryID=3281 (accessed November 1, 2010).

Bibliographies: FF, OM

Biographies and Interviews

"Charlaine Harris." *BooksnBytes*. n.d. http://www.booksnbytes.com/authors/ harris_charlaine.html (accessed November 1, 2010).

"Charlaine Harris." *Mississippi Writers and Musicians:* n.d. http://www. mswritersandmusicians.com/writers/charlaine-harris.html (accessed November 1, 2010).

"Charlaine Harris Interview by CNN." (videocast) *CNN.* October 20, 2009. http:// www.youtube.com/watch?v=n36EpjE23B8 (accessed November 1, 2010).

"Charlaine Harris: Putting the Bite on Cozy Mysteries." *Crescent Blues* 4.4 (2001). http://www.crescentblues.com/4_4issue/int_charlaine_harris. shtml (accessed November 1, 2010).

"Exclusive: We Chat with Charlaine Harris." (text and audiocast) *True-Blood. net.* May 15, 2009. http://true-blood.net/2009/05/15/exclusive-we-chat-with-charlaine-harris/ (accessed November 1, 2010).

Hall, Melissa Mia. "The Gift of Lightning." *Publishers Weekly* 254.32 (August 13, 2007): 38. http://www.publishersweekly.com/pw/by-topic/new-titles/ adult-announcements/article/4579-the-gift-of-lightning-.html (accessed November 1, 2010).

Hall, Robert L. "Cozies with Teeth: An Interview with Charlaine Harris." *Southern Scribe* (2004): http://www.southernscribe.com/zine/authors/ Harris_Charlaine.htm (accessed November 1, 2010).

Howlett-West, Stephanie. "Mistress of the Southern Vampire Romantic Mystery." *Publishers Weekly* 251.14 (May 4, 2004): 45.

"Interview, Chat and Contest with Charlaine Harris." *Bitten by Books.* October 22, 2009. http://bittenbybooks.com/?p=12124 (accessed November 1, 2010).

Jamneck, Lynne. "Interview with Charlaine Harris." *Suite101.* February 16, 2009. http://writing-genre-fiction.suite101.com/article.cfm/charlaine_ harris (accessed November 1, 2010).

McCune, Alisa. "A Conversation with Charlaine Harris." *SF Site* (April 2004): http://www.sfsite.com/05a/ch175.htm (accessed November 1, 2010).

Peters, Barbara. "Charlaine Harris Interview." (videocast—6 parts): *Poisoned Pen.* n.d. http://www.youtube.com/watch?v=qtOh6l7XbUo (accessed November 1, 2010).

"Project Paranormal: A Backstage Pass to the Worlds of Charlaine Harris." (videocast—7 parts) *Penguin*. n.d. http://us.penguingroup.com/static/pages/publishersoffice/screeningroom/0909/projectparanormal/charlaine_harris.html#vmix_media_id=6421628 (accessed November 1, 2010).

Rich, Motoko. "Vampire-Loving Barmaid Hits Jackpot for Author." *New York Times*. May 20, 2009. http://www.nytimes.com/2009/05/20/books/20sook.html (accessed November 1, 2010).

Shepard, Martha Hunter. "Charlaine Harris: Dead-on Author." *Rhodes Magazine* 14.3 (Fall 2007). http://www.rhodes.edu/155_9930.asp (accessed November 1, 2010).

Trachtenberg, Jeffrey. "Charlaine Harris' Vampire Empire." *Wall Street Journal*. May 5, 2009. http://online.wsj.com/article/SB124120839635478289.html (accessed November 1, 2010).

Criticism and Reader's Guides

Bakerman, Jane S. "Water on Stone: Long-Term Friendships in Jane Smiley's *Duplicate Keys* and Charlaine Harris' *A Secret Rage*." *Clues: A Journal of Detection* 10.2 (1989): 49–63.

Web Site

Official Web site: http://www.charlaineharris.com/ (accessed November 1, 2010).

Hart, Carolyn, 1936–

She approached cautiously, a veteran of many losing skirmishes with her gorgeous but iron-willed cat. The choice of Agatha to honor Agatha Christie had perhaps been a mistake, since the celebrated Queen of Crime had been known as a kindly person. Maybe she should have named Agatha, gender aside, for Mickey Spillane.

—Laughed 'Til He Died, 2010

Biographical Sketch

Born in Oklahoma City, Carolyn Gimpel Hart received her B.A. from the University of Oklahoma-Norman, where she met her husband, Phil, on a student trip to Europe. She worked as a newspaper reporter and newsletter editor before becoming a freelance writer in 1961 and also taught journalism at the University of Oklahoma for three years.

Hart's early mysteries were stand-alones, but her later writing has mostly been done in the series format, with her longest and best-known series being the Death on Demand series, set in and around a bookstore in Broward's Rock, South Carolina. Her crime fiction falls mainly into the cozy category, and she has received numerous awards, including a Pulitzer Prize nomination for fiction in 2003 for *Letters from Home,* an acclaimed stand-alone novel set during World War II.

Categories: Amateur Detective, Cozy

Awards

Agatha Award for Best Novel (*Something Wicked,* 1988; *Dead Man's Island,* 1993; *Letter from Home,* 2003)
Agatha Malice Domestic Award for Lifetime Achievement (2007)
Anthony Award for Best Paperback Original (*Something Wicked,* 1989; *Honeymoon with Murder,* 1990)
Macavity Award for Best Novel (*A Little Class on Murder,* 1990)
Macavity Award for Best Short Story ("Henrie O's Holiday, *Crime on Her Mind,* 1993)

Major Works

Death on Demand series: *Death on Demand* (1987), *Design for Murder* (1988), *Something Wicked* (1988), *Honeymoon with Murder* (1989), *A Little Class on Murder* (1989), *Deadly Valentine* (1990), *The Christie Caper* (1991), *Southern Ghost* (1992), *Mint Julep Murder* (1995), *Yankee Doodle Dead* (1998), *White Elephant Dead* (1999), *Sugarplum Dead* (2000), *April Fool Dead* (2002), *Engaged to Die* (2003), *Murder Walks the Plank* (2004), *Death of the Party* (2005), *Dead Days of Summer* (2006), *Death Walked In* (2008), *Dare to Die* (2009), *Laughed 'Til He Died* (2010)
Henrie O. series: *Dead Man's Island* (1993), *Scandal in Fair Haven* (1994), *Death in Lovers' Lane* (1997), *Death in Paradise* (1998), *Death on the River Walk* (1999), *Resort to Murder* (2001), *Set Sail for Murder* (2007)
Bailey Ruth Raeburn series: *Ghost at Work* (2008), *Merry, Merry Ghost* (2009), *Ghost in Trouble* (2010)
Nonseries novels: *Flee from the Past* (1975), *A Settling of Accounts* (1976), *Escape from Paris* (1982), *The Rich Die Young* (1983), *Death by Surprise* (1983), *Castle Rock* (1983), *Skulduggery* (1984), *Brave Hearts* (1987), *Letters from Home* (2003)
Short-story collections: *Crimes of the Heart* (editor, 1995), *Crime on Her Mind* (1999), *Secrets and Other Stories of Suspense* (2002)

Research Sources

Encyclopedias and Handbooks: BYA, CA (13–16R), CANR (25, 41, 58, 126), GWM, EMM, MCF, STJ, WWW

Bibliographies: FF, OM

Biographies and Interviews

Andrews, Donna. "Carolyn Hart: Justice on Demand." *Crescent Blues* 2:4.1 (1999). http://www.crescentblues.com/2_4issue/hart.shtml (accessed November 1, 2010).

Bruss, Angi. "Carolyn Hart on 'Dare to Die.'" (videocast) *The Oklahoman.* n.d. http://feeds.newsok.tv/services/player/bcpid1766638491?bclid=0&bctid=18500726001 (accessed November 1, 2010).

Carl, JoAnna. "Carolyn Hart at Home." *Mystery Fanfare.* April 2, 2009. http://mysteryreadersinc.blogspot.com/2009/04/carolyn-hart-at-homeinterviewed-by.html (accessed November 1, 2010).

"Carolyn Hart: National Book Festival, 2007." (videocast) *Library of Congress.* September 29, 2007. http://www.loc.gov/today/cyberlc/feature_wdesc.php?rec=4151 (accessed November 1, 2010).

Miller, Teresa. "Carolyn Hart." (videocast) *Writing Out Loud* n.d. http://ra.okstate.edu/osu_tulsa/WritingOutLoud/CarolynHart/video.htm (accessed November 1, 2010).

Moreau, Emrys. "Carolyn Hart." *Oklahoma Center for Poets and Writers.* n.d. http://poetsandwriters.okstate.edu/OKauthor/hart.html (accessed November 1, 2010).

"The Raven's Eye Is on Carolyn Hart." *The Raven Croaks.* October 17, 2009. http://theravencroaks.blogspot.com/2009/10/ravens-eye-is-on-carolyn-hart.html (accessed November 1, 2010).

Rosenthal, David. "Carolyn Hart on Good vs. Evil." *Read Street: The Baltimore Sun.* October 7, 2008. http://weblogs.baltimoresun.com/entertainment/books/blog/2008/10/carolyn_hart_on_good_vs_evil.html (accessed November 1, 2010).

Silet, Charles L. P. "Carolyn G. Hart." *Speaking of Murder: Interviews with the Masters of Mystery and Suspense.* Ed. Ed Gorman and Martin H. Greenberg. New York: Berkley Prime Crime, 1998. 87–102.

Wall, Judith. "Hart of the Mystery." *Sooner Magazine.* Winter 2007. http://www.oufoundation.org/sm/winter07/story2.asp?ID=225 (accessed November 1, 2010).

Williams, B. J. "Read about It Author Interview: Carolyn Hart." (videocast) *Metropolitan Library System, Oklahoma City.* November 19, 2009. http://www.youtube.com/watch?v=aMBn9Tdauks (accessed November 1, 2010).

Criticism and Reader's Guides

Hart, Carolyn. "Plotting a Mystery Novel." *Writer* 110.8 (1997): 7–10.

Hart, Carolyn. "The Secrets of Death on Demand." *Ed Gorman Blog.* February 20, 2010. http://newimprovedgorman.blogspot.com/2010/02/secrets-of-death-on-demand-by-carolyn.html (accessed November 1, 2010).

Hart, Carolyn. "Why I Write…" *Publishers Weekly* 256.18 (May 4, 2009): 25.

Hart, Carolyn G. "It's No Mystery." *The Writer* 106.8 (1993): 20–23.

Meyers, Joe. "The Comforting/Disturbing World of Carolyn Hart." *Joe's View.* May 13, 2009. http://blog.ctnews.com/meyers/2009/05/13/the-comfortingdisturbing-world-of-carolyn-hart/ (accessed November 1, 2010).

Web Site

Official Web site: http://www.carolynhart.com/ (accessed November 1, 2010).

Hiaasen, Carl, 1953–

Nobody could have guessed what actually had killed Sparky Harper. It was supple and green and exactly five and one-quarter inches long. Dr. Allen found it lodged in the trachea. At first he thought it was a large chunk of food, but it wasn't.

It was a toy rubber alligator. It had cost seventy-nine cents at a tourist shop along the Tamiami Trail. The price tag was still glued to its corrugated tail.

—Tourist Season, 1986

Biographical Sketch

Carl Hiaasen was born in Fort Lauderdale, Florida. He attended Emory University and graduated from the University of Florida in 1974 with a B.S. He has worked as a newspaper reporter and columnist for the *Miami Herald* since 1976 and has been a finalist for the Pulitzer Prize twice. He is an environmentalist, and many of his books revolve around environmental issues and themes. In 2002, he published his first children's book, *Hoot,* which received a Newbery Honor designation, and has since published two more juvenile works. Two of his books (*Strip Tease* and *Hoot*) have been made into movies. He has three children and still lives in Florida with his second wife, Fenia.

Hiaasen's novels are satirical mysteries that delve into the greed, plunder, and social ills that afflict his native state. Both his heroes and his villains are quirky, with a penchant for imaginative forms of violence. His mysteries are popular with critics and readers alike.

Categories: Amateur Detective, Caper

Major Works

Novels: *Tourist Season* (1986), *Double Whammy* (1987), *Skin Tight* (1989), *Native Tongue* (1991), *Strip Tease* (1993), *Stormy Weather* (1995), *Naked Came the Manatee* (1996), *Lucky You* (1997), *Sick Puppy* (2000), *Basket Case* (2002), *Skinny Dip* (2004), *Nature Girl* (2006), *Star Island* (2010)

Novels with William D. Montalbano: *Powder Burn* (1981), *Trap Line* (1982), *A Death in China* (1984)

Juvenile mystery novels: *Hoot* (2002), *Flush* (2005), *Scat* (2009).

Research Sources

Encyclopedias and Handbooks: 100, CA (105), CANR (22, 45, 65, 113, 133, 168), CLC (238), EMM, MCF, STJ, WWW

"Carl Hiaasen." *Encyclopedia of World Biography.* 2007. http://www.notablebi ographies.com/newsmakers2/2007-Co-Lh/Hiaasen-Carl.html. (accessed April 26, 2010).

Bibliographies: FF

Biographies and Interviews

Bowman, David. "Carl Hiaasen." *Salon.* January 31, 2000. http://www.salon. com/people/lunch/2000/01/31/hiaasen/ (accessed November 1, 2010).

"Carl Hiaasen." *Bookreporter.com.* July 2004. http://www.bookreporter.com/ authors/au-hiaasen-carl.asp (accessed November 1, 2010).

Cochran, Stacey. "Carl Hiaasen." (videocast) *The Artist's Craft: Raleigh Television Network.* February 3, 2009. http://www.youtube.com/watch?v=S-NCWaQR4yA (accessed November 1, 2010).

Frostrup, Mariella. "Interview with Carl Hiaasen." (audiocast) *BBC-4.* October 31, 2004. http://www.bbc.co.uk/radio4/arts/openbook/open book_20041031.shtml (accessed November 1, 2010).

Kroft, Steve. "Florida: A Paradise of Scandals." (videocast) *CBS 60 Minutes.* June 4, 2006. http://www.cbsnews.com/stories/2005/04/15/60minutes/ main688458_page3.shtml (accessed November 1, 2010).

MacDonald, Jay Lee. "Carl Hiaasen Takes a Bite out of Crimes against the Environment." *BookPage.* n.d. http://www.bookpage.com/0001bp/carl_ hiaasen.html (accessed November 1, 2010).

Richards, Linda. "January Interview with Carl Hiaasen." *January Maga-zine*. January 2002. http://januarymagazine.com/profiles/hiaasen.html (accessed November 1, 2010).

Silet, Charles L. P. "Carl Hiaasen." *Speaking of Murder, vol. 2: Interviews with the Masters of Mystery and Suspense*. Ed. Ed Gorman and Martin H. Greenberg. New York: Berkley Prime Crime, 1999. 66–77.

Welch, Dave. "A Kinder, Gentler Carl Hiaasen, Still Pissing People Off." *Powells Books*. September 29, 2005. http://www.powells.com/authors/hiaasen.html (accessed November 1, 2010).

Criticism and Reader's Guides

Brannon, Julie Sloan. "The Rules Are Different Here: South Florida Noir and the Grotesque." *Crime Fiction and Film in the Sunshine State: Florida Noir*. Ed. Steve Glassman and Maurice O'Sullivan. Bowling Green, OH: Popular Press, 1997. 47–64.

Geherin, David. "Carl Hiaasen: South Florida." *Scene of the Crime: The Importance of Place in Crime and Mystery Fiction*. Jefferson, NC: Mc-Farland, 2008. 109–21.

Herman, Luc, and Bart Vervaeck. "Narrative Interest as Cultural Negotia-tion." *Narrative* 17.1 (January 2009): 111–29.

Jordan, Peter. "Carl Hiaasen's Environmental Thrillers: Crime Fiction in Search of Green Peace." *Studies in Popular Culture* 13.1 (1990): 61–71.

Phillips, Dana. "Is Nature Necessary?" *The Ecocriticism Reader: Landmarks in Literary Ecology*. Ed. Cheryll Glotfelty and Harold Fromm. Athens: University of Georgia Press, 1996. 204–22.

Web Sites

Official Web site: http://www.carlhiaasen.com/index.shtml (accessed Novem-ber 1, 2010).

Miami Herald: http://www.miamiherald.com/424—Web page with links to author's newspaper columns (accessed November 1, 2010).

Hillerman, Tony, 1925–2008

George had asked too many questions, and since George was a friend he had given more answers than he should have given. No matter how badly he wanted to be a Zuñi, to join the Fire God's own Badger Clan, George was still a Navajo. He had not been initiated, had not felt the darkness of the mask slip over his head, and seen through the eyes of the kachina spirit.

—Dance Hall of the Dead, 1973

Biographical Sketch

Tony Hillerman was born in Sacred Heart, Oklahoma, and grew up in rural Oklahoma; his parents farmed and ran a store. He served in the U.S. Army during World War II and was awarded the Silver Star, Bronze Star, and Purple Heart. He attended Oklahoma State University and then the University of Oklahoma, where he received a B.A. in 1946. He later earned an M.A. degree from the University of New Mexico in 1966. Hillerman worked as a newspaper reporter for various publications in west Texas, Oklahoma, and New Mexico, as well as for United Press International. He was a university professor at the University of New Mexico from 1965 to 1980 and was named professor emeritus of journalism in 1985. Hillerman married Marie Unzner in 1948, and the couple had six children. He died in 2008 of pulmonary failure.

Hillerman's crime novels broke new territory with their Native American protagonists, Joe Leaphorn and Jim Chee of the Navajo nation. Setting was supremely important in the novels, and they conveyed a palpable sense of the arid Four Corners region of the Southwest. Hillerman's accomplishments in the crime fiction field earned many awards, including the Special Friend of Dineh Award, Navajo Tribal Council, in 1987, and two honorary doctorates, from the University of New Mexico (1990) and from Arizona State University (1991). The books were also very popular with the reading public.

Categories: Diverse Characters, Police Procedural

Awards

Agatha Malice Domestic Award for Lifetime Achievement (2002)
Anthony Award for Best Novel (*Skinwalkers,* 1988)
Anthony Award for Lifetime Achievement (1994)
Edgar Award for Best Novel (*Dance Hall of the Dead,* 1974)
Grandmaster Award for Lifetime Achievement (1991)
Macavity Award for Best Novel (*A Thief of Time,* 1989)
Nero Award (*Coyote Waits,* 1991)

Major Works

The Navajo series (featuring Joe Leaphorn and/or Jim Chee): *The Blessing Way* (1970), *Dance Hall of the Dead* (1973), *Listening Woman* (1978), *People of Darkness* (1980), *The Dark Wind* (1982), *The Ghostway* (1984), *Skinwalkers* (1986), *A Thief of Time* (1988), *Talking God* (1989), *Coyote Waits* (1990), *Sacred Clowns* (1993), *The Fallen Man* (1996), *The First Eagle* (1998), *Hunting Badger* (1999), *The Wailing Wind* (2002), *The Sinister Pig* (2003), *Skeleton Man* (2004), *The Shape Shifter* (2006)

Nonseries novels: *The Fly on the Wall* (1971), *Finding Moon* (1995)
Nonfiction: *Talking Mysteries: A Conversation with Tony Hillerman* (with
Ernie Bulow, 1991), *Hillerman Country: A Journey through the Southwest
with Tony Hillerman* (1991), *The Perfect Murder: Five Great Mystery Writ-
ers Create the Perfect Crime* (with others, 1991), *Seldom Disappointed: A
Memoir* (2001)

Research Sources

*Encyclopedias and Handbooks: 100, BEA, BEB, CA (29–32R),
CANR (21, 42, 65, 97, 134), CLC (62, 170), EMM, MCF, OCC,
STJ, WWW*

Bibliographies: FF, OM

Biographies and Interviews

Bates, Judy, and Jeff Zaleski. "Politics and the Reservation." *Publishers
Weekly* 250.15 (April 14, 2003): 52.
Britton, Vickie. "Biography and Works of Tony Hillerman." *Suite101.* De-
cember 4, 2008. http://murder-mysteries.suite101.com/article.cfm/biogra
phytony_hillerman (accessed November 1, 2010).
Grape, Jan. "Tony Hillerman." *Speaking of Murder: Interviews with the Mas-
ters of Mystery and Suspense.* Ed. Ed Gorman and Martin H. Green-
berg. New York: Berkley Prime Crime, 1998. 143–52.
Hamm, Ron. "Ron Hamm Interview with Tony Hillerman for Clues." *Clues:
A Journal of Detection* 21.2 (2000): 27–35.
Herbert, Rosemary. "Tony Hillerman." *The Fatal Art of Entertainment: Inter-
views with Mystery Writers.* New York: G. K. Hall, 1994. 84–111.
Hill, Hamlin. "Interview with Tony Hillerman." *South Central Review* 12.1
(1995): 31–42.
Hillerman, Tony. "Mystery, Country Boys, and the Big Reservation." *Collo-
quium on Crime: Eleven Renowned Mystery Writers Discuss Their Work.*
Ed. Robin W. Winks. New York: Scribner's, 1986. 127–47.
Hillerman, Tony. *Seldom Disappointed: A Memoir.* New York: HarperCollins, 2001.
"In Memory of Tony Hillerman: A 2008 Interview." *HistoryNet.* October 28,
2008. http://www.historynet.com/in-memory-of-tony-hillerman-a-2008-
interview.htm/print (accessed November 1, 2010).
Kaminsky, Stuart, and Laurie Roberts. "Tony Hillerman." *Behind the Mystery: Top Mystery Writers Interviewed.* Cohasset, MA: Hot House, 2005.
120–31.
Materassi, Mario. "The Case of Tony Hillerman: An Interview." *Journal of
the Southwest* 50.4 (2008): 447+.

Kehe, Marjorie. "In Appreciation of Tony Hillerman." *Christian Science Monitor*. October 27, 2008. http://www.csmonitor.com/Books/chapter-and-verse/2008/1027/in-appreciation-of-tony-hillerman (accessed November 1, 2010).

Sobol, John. *Tony Hillerman: A Public Life*. Toronto: ECW Press, 1994.

Swaim, Don. "Audio Interview with Tony Hillerman." (audiocast) *Wired for Books*. July 14, 1988. http://wiredforbooks.org/tonyhillerman/ (accessed November 1, 2010).

"Tony Hillerman." *Monroe Library*. May 5, 2005. http://monroe.lib.mi.us/Documents/Book_Clubs/Tony%20Hillerman%20Bio.pdf (accessed November 1, 2010).

"Tony Hillerman: Bookfest 02." (videocast—2 parts) *Library of Congress*. October 12, 2002. http://www.loc.gov/today/cyberlc/feature_wdesc.php?rec=3487; http://www.loc.gov/today/cyberlc/feature_wdesc.php?rec=3488 (accessed November 1, 2010).

"Tony Hillerman Dies at 83." *Confessions of an Idiosyncratic Mind*. October 27, 2008. http://www.sarahweinman.com/confessions/2008/10/tony-hillerman.html—Links to a number of tributes to Hillerman (accessed November 1, 2010).

Zibart, Rosemary. "Sitting Down and Setting Out with Tony Hillerman" *BookPage*. n.d. http://www.bookpage.com/9809bp/tony_hillerman.html (accessed November 1, 2010).

Criticism and Reader's Guides

Bakerman, Jane S. "Tony Hillerman's Joe Leaphorn and Jim Chee." *Cops and Constables: American and British Fictional Policemen*. Ed. Earl F. Bargainnier and George N. Dove. Bowling Green, OH: Popular Press, 1986. 98–112.

Browne, Ray B. "The Ethnic Detective: Arthur W. Upfield, Tony Hillerman, and Beyond." *Mystery and Suspense Writers: The Literature of Crime, Detection, and Espionage, III*. Ed. Robin W. Winks and Maureen Corrigan. New York: Scribner's, 1998. 1029–46.

Chapman, G. Clarke. "Tony Hillerman's Fiction: Crime and Common Grace." *Christianity and Literature* 48.4 (1999): 473–86.

Davis, J. Madison. "The Bag Lady's Novels: Tony Hillerman and the Craft of Writing." *World Literature Today* 83.2 (2009): 9–11.

Donaldson, John K. "Native American Sleuths: Following in the Footsteps of the Indian Guides." *Telling the Stories: Essays on American Indian Literatures and Cultures*. Ed. Elizabeth Hoffman Nelson and Malcolm A. Nelson. New York: Peter Lang, 2001. 109–29.

Erisman, Fred. *Tony Hillerman*. Boise, Idaho: Boise State University, 1989.

Geherin, David. "Tony Hillerman: The American Southwest." *Scene of the Crime: The Importance of Place in Crime and Mystery Fiction.* Jefferson, NC: McFarland, 2008. 35–48.

Goeller, Alison D. "The Mystery of Identity: The Private Eye (I) in the Detective Fiction of Walter Mosley and Tony Hillerman." *Sleuthing Ethnicity: The Detective in Multiethnic Crime Fiction.* Ed. Dorothea Fischer-Hornung and Monika Mueller. Madison, NJ: Fairleigh Dickinson University Press, 2003. 175–86.

Greenberg, Martin Harry, ed. *The Tony Hillerman Companion: A Comprehensive Guide to His Life and Work.* New York: HarperCollins, 1994.

Hillerman, Tony, and Ernie Bulow. *Talking Mysteries: A Conversation with Tony Hillerman.* Albuquerque: University of New Mexico Press, 1991.

Lachman, Marvin S. "Tony Hillerman." *American Mystery and Detective Writers* (*Dictionary of Literary Biography* 306). Ed. George Parker Anderson. Detroit, MI: Thomson Gale, 2005. 162–73.

Michaud, Marc. "Mythology as Memory in Tony Hillerman's Novels." *Questions of Identity in Detective Fiction.* Ed. Linda Martz and Anita Higgle. Newcastle upon Tyne, England: Cambridge Scholars, 2007. 95–101.

O'Sullivan, Maurice J. "Tony Hillerman and the Navajo Way." *Crime Fiction and Film in the Southwest: Bad Boys and Bad Girls in the Badlands.* Ed. Steve Glassman and Maurice O'Sullivan. Bowling Green, OH: Popular Press, 2001. 163–76. http://web65.rollins.edu/~mosullivan/documents/Hillman%20Article%20(optimized%20copy).pdf (accessed November 1, 2010).

Perricone, Mike. "The Joe Leaphorn Mysteries." *Suite101.* 2009. http://mysterycrimefiction.suite101.com/article.cfm/the_joe_leaphorn_mysteries_by_tony_hillerman. (accessed November 1, 2010).

Pierson, James C. "Anthropologists as Detectives and Detectives as Anthropologists." *Murder 101: Essays on the Teaching of Detective Fiction.* Ed. Edward J. Reilly. Jefferson, NC: McFarland, 2009. 166–77.

Reilly, John M. *Tony Hillerman: A Critical Companion.* Westport, CT: Greenwood, 1996.

Web Sites

"Welcome to Hillerman Country" (fansite): http://www.umsl.edu/~smueller/— Includes biography, book list, bibliography of critical sources, awards, etc. Well-organized site (accessed November 1, 2010).

"Tony Hillerman's Jim Chee and Joe Leaphorn Mysteries": http://www.dancingbadger.com/tony_hillerman.htm—Annotated bibliography of the mysteries (accessed November 1, 2010).

Hunter, Evan—see McBain, Ed

James, P. D. (Phyllis Dorothy James White), 1920–

And then, about thirty yards ahead, I saw what looked like a black bundle lying at the foot of the cliff. I hurried up to it and found a cassock, neatly folded, and beside it a brown cloak, also carefully folded. Within a few feet the cliff had slithered and tumbled and now lay in great clumps of compacted sand, tufts of grass, and tones. I knew at once what must have happened.

—*Death in Holy Orders,* 2001

Biographical Sketch

Phyllis Dorothy James was born in Oxford. She attended the Cambridge High School for Girls, but there is no report of her having matriculated at a university. She married Ernest Conner Bantry White in 1941, and they had two daughters. During World War II, she served as a Red Cross nurse and worked at the Ministry of Food. After the war, she was administrative assistant for the North West Regional Hospital Board and then worked in various departments of the British Civil Service before becoming a full-time writer in 1979. She has served as a magistrate and on the board of governors of the BBC. She received the Order of the British Empire in 1983 and was created a Life Peer of the United Kingdom in 1991; her title is Baroness James of Holland Park. She lives in London and Oxford.

James's novels carry on some of the traditions from the golden age in that they have a puzzle plot and genteel characters. However, her characters are more fully realized, and she delves into their emotions and motivations in a way that was uncommon for earlier crime novelists. Her stories are told in a leisurely and literate manner but nevertheless come to grips with moral and social issues. Critics have a high regard for her writing, and readers enjoy her compassionate yet clear-eyed view of her characters and stories.

Categories: Police Procedural, Private Detective

Awards

Silver Dagger Award for runner-up for best novel (*A Shroud for a Nightingale,* 1971; *The Black Tower,* 1975; *A Taste for Death,* 1986)
Diamond Dagger Award for Lifetime Achievement (1987)
Grand Master Award for Lifetime Achievement (1999)
Macavity Award for Best Novel (*A Taste for Death,* 1987)

Major Works

Adam Dalgleish series: *Cover Her Face* (1966), *A Mind to Murder* (1967), *Unnatural Causes* (1967), *A Shroud for a Nightingale* (1971), *The Black Tower* (1975), *Death of an Expert Witness* (1977), *A Taste for Death*

(1985), *Devices and Desires* (1989), *Original Sin* (1995), *A Certain Justice* (1997), *Death in Holy Orders* (2001), *The Murder Room* (2003), *The Lighthouse* (2005), *The Private Patient* (2008)

Cordelia Gray series: *An Unsuitable Job for a Woman* (1972), *The Skull Beneath the Skin* (1982)

Nonseries novels: *Innocent Blood* (1980), *The Children of Men* (1992)

Nonfiction: *Time to Be in Earnest: A Fragment of an Autobiography* (2000), *Talking about Detective Fiction* (2009)

Research Sources

Encyclopedias and Handbooks: 100, BEA, BEB, BYA, CA (21–24R), CANR (17, 43, 65, 112, 201), CLC (18, 46, 122, 226), EMM, GWM, MCF, OCC, STJ, WWW

Bibliographies: FF, OM

Biographies and Interviews

Frumkes, Lewis Burke. "A conversation with . . . P. D. James." *The Writer* June 1998: 17+.

Herbert, Rosemary. "P. D. James." *The Fatal Art of Entertainment: Interviews with Mystery Writers*. New York: G. K. Hall, 1994. 54–83.

James, P. D. *Time to Be in Earnest: A Fragment of Autobiography.* Knopf, 2000.

"The Murder Room: P. D. James." *Mystery*, *PBS.org.* n.d. http://www.pbs.org/wgbh/mystery/murderroom/james.html. (accessed November 1, 2010)

"P. D. James, Talking and Writing 'Detective Fiction.'" (audiocast) *Morning Edition, NPR.* December 22, 2009. http://www.npr.org/templates/story/story.php?storyId=121721631 (accessed November 1, 2010).

Page, Benedicte. "With Benefit of Hindsight: Crime Writer P. D. James Talks about Producing Bestsellers in Her Eighties." *The Bookseller* (May 2, 2003): 29.

Picker, Leonard. "Not an Action Hero: PW Talks with P. D. James." *Publishers Weekly* 252.45 (November 14, 2005): 47.

Reese, Jennifer. "P. D. James: The Art of Murder." *Salon.com.* February 26, 1998. http://www.salon.com/books/int/1998/02/cov_si_26int.html (accessed November 1, 2010).

Rose, Charlie. "A Conversation with P. D. James." (videocast) *Charlie Rose.* May 19, 2000. http://www.charlierose.com/view/interview/3684 (accessed November 1, 2010).

Salwak, Dale. "An Interview with P. D. James." *Clues: A Journal of Detection* 6.1 (1985): 31–50.

Swaim, Don. "Audio Interviews with P.D. James." (audiocasts—3) *Wired for Books.* October 27, 1986, February 11, 1990, February 29 [*sic*], 1993. http://wiredforbooks.org/pdjames/ (accessed November 1 2010).

Criticism and Reader's Guides

Adcock, Patrick, et al. "P. D. James." *100 Masters of Mystery and Detection, vol. 1.* Ed. Fional Kelleghan. Pasadena, CA: Salem Press, 2001. 359–66.

Bakerman, Jane S. "Cordelia Gray: Apprentice and Archetype." *Clues: A Journal of Detection* 5.1 (1984): 101–14.

Benstock, Bernard. "The Clinical World of P. D. James." *Twentieth-Century Women Novelists.* Ed. Thomas F. Staley. Totowa, NJ: Barnes & Noble, 1982. 104–29.

Coale, Samuel. "Carnage and Conversion: The Art of P. D. James." *Clues: A Journal of Detection* 20.1 (1999): 1–14.

DuBose, Martha Hailey. "P. D. James: An Artful Kind of Order." *Women of Mystery: The Lives and Works of Notable Women Crime Novelists.* New York: St. Martin's Minotaur, 2000. 340–61.

Gidez, Richard B. *P. D. James.* Boston: Twayne, 1986.

Harkness, Bruce. "P. D. James." *Art in Crime Writing: Essays on Detective Fiction.* Ed. Bernard Benstock. New York: St. Martin's, 1983. 119–41.

Jones, Marnie, and Barbara Barker. "'An Unsuitable Job' for Anyone: The 'Filthy Trade' in P. D. James." *Theory and Practice of Classic Detective Fiction.* Ed. Jerome Delamater and Ruth Prigozy. Westport, CT: Greenwood, 1997. 137–48.

Joyner, Nancy Carol. "P. D. James." *10 Women of Mystery.* Ed. Earl F. Bargainnier. Bowling Green, OH: Popular Press, 1981. 106–23.

Kotker, Joan G. "The Re-Imagining of Cordelia Gray." *Women Times Three: Writers, Detectives, Readers.* Ed. Kathleen Gregory Klein. Bowling Green, OH: Popular Press, 1995. 53–64.

Kotker, Joan G. "P. D. James's Adam Dalgliesh Series." *In the Beginning: First Novels in Mystery Series.* Ed. Mary Jean DeMarr. Bowling Green, OH: Popular Press, 1995. 139–53.

Macdonald, Andrew F. "P. D. James." *British Mystery and Thriller Writers since 1960 (Dictionary of Literary Biography* 276). Ed. Gina Macdonald. Detroit, MI: Thomson Gale, 2003. 217–28.

Maxfield, James F. "The Unfinished Detective: The Work of P. D. James." *Critique: Studies in Contemporary Fiction* 28.4 (1987): 211–23.

Nelson, Eric. "P. D. James and the Dissociation of Sensibility." *British Women Writing Fiction.* Ed. Abby H. P. Werlock. Tuscaloosa: University of Alabama Press, 2000. 59–69.

Oates, Joyce Carol. "Inside the Locked Room: P. D. James." *Where I've Been, and Where I'm Going: Essays, Reviews, and Prose.* New York: Plume Books, 1999. 191–202.

"P. D. James." *Novelguide.com.* 1998. http://www.novelguide.com/a/discover/ewb_08/ewb_08_03274.html (accessed November 1, 2010).

Porter, Dennis. "Detection and Ethics: The Case of P. D. James." *The Sleuth and the Scholar: Origins, Evolution, and Current Trends in Detective*

Fiction. Ed. Barbara A. Rader and Howard G. Zettler. Westport, CT: Greenwood, 1988. 11–18.

Porter, Dennis. "P. D. James." *Mystery and Suspense Writers: The Literature of Crime, Detection, and Espionage, I*. Ed. Robin W. Winks and Maureen Corrigan. New York: Scribner's, 1998. 541–57.

Priestman, Martin. "P. D. James and the Distinguished Thing." *On Modern British Fiction*. Ed. Zachary Leader. New York: Oxford University Press, 2002. 234–57.

Prono, Luca. "P. D. James." *Contemporary Writers*. 2004. http://www.contemporarywriters.com/authors/?p=auth193 (accessed November 1, 2010).

Reynolds, Moira Davison. "Phyllis Dorothy James White (P. D. James)." *Women Authors of Detective Series: Twenty-One American and British Writers, 1900–2000*. Jefferson, NC: McFarland, 2001. 84–90.

Rowland, Susan. *From Agatha Christie to Ruth Rendell: British Women Writers in Detective and Crime Fiction*. New York: Palgrave, 2001.

Rowland, Susan. "The Horror of Modernity and the Utopian Sublime: Gothic Villainy in P. D. James and Ruth Rendell." *The Devil Himself: Villainy in Detective Fiction and Film*. Ed. Stacy Gillis and Philippa Gates. Westport, CT: Greenwood, 2002. 135–46.

Siebenheller, Norma. *P. D. James*. New York: Ungar, 1981.

Vanacker, Sabine. "The Family Plot in Recent Novels by P. D. James and Reginald Hill." *Critical Survey* 20.1 (2008): 17–28.

Web Site

Official Web site: http://www.randomhouse.com/features/pdjames/index.html (accessed November 1, 2010).

Jance, J. A., 1944–

Stepping up to the corpse, Audrey Cummings squatted beside the sodden body, gazing at the dead man respectfully but curiously, with the watchful, no-nonsense demeanor that, in the gruesome world of medical examiners, must pass for bedside manner.

—*Name Withheld*, 1995

Biographical Sketch

Judith Ann Jance was born in Watertown, South Dakota, and graduated from high school in Bisbee, Arizona. She attended the University of Arizona, where she received a B.A. in 1966 and an M. Ed. in library science in 1970. She was an English teacher for two years and then a librarian in the Indian Oasis Schools in Sells, Arizona, for five years. Her first marriage, to Jerry

Joseph Teale Jance, ended in divorce, and he later died of chronic alcoholism. She worked in the insurance industry for 10 years before becoming a writer. She married William Allan Schilb in 1985 and has one child from each marriage, as well as three stepchildren. She divides her time between Seattle and Tucson.

Jance states that even the disagreeable things in life are useful to a writer (official Web site) and has used her insights from being married to an alcoholic in the Beaumont series and the trials of being a single, working mother in the Joanna Brady series. Her experiences in working on a Native American reservation are reflected in the Walker series. Her books feature strong characters and exciting plots, and they have been popular with readers and critics alike. Jance received an honorary doctorate from the University of Arizona in 2000 in recognition of her work.

Categories: Amateur Detective, Police Procedural

Major Works

J. P. Beaumont series: *Until Proven Guilty* (1985), *Injustice for All* (1986), *Trial by Fury* (1987), *Improbable Cause* (1987), *A More Perfect Union* (1988), *Dismissed with Prejudice* (1989), *Minor in Possession* (1990), *Payment in Kind* (1991), *Without Due Process* (1992), *Failure to Appear* (1993), *Lying in Wait* (1994), *Name Withheld* (1995), *Breach of Duty* (1999), *Birds of Prey* (2001), *Long Time Gone* (2005), *Justice Denied* (2007), *Fire and Ice* (also features Brady, 2009)

Joanna Brady series: *Desert Heat* (1993), *Tombstone Courage* (1994), *Shoot/ Don't Shoot* (1995), *Dead to Rights* (1997), *Skeleton Canyon* (1997), *Rattlesnake Crossing* (1998), *Outlaw Mountain* (1999), *Devil's Claw* (2000), *Paradise Lost* (2001), *Dead Wrong* (2001), *Partner in Crime* (also features Beaumont, 2002), *Exit Wounds* (2003), *Damage Control* (2008)

Ali Reynolds series: *Edge of Evil* (2006), *Web of Evil* (2007), *Hand of Evil* (2007), *Cruel Intent* (2008), *Trial by Fire* (2009), *Fatal Error* (2011)

Sheriff Brandon Walker series: *Hour of the Hunter* (1991), *Kiss of the Bees* (2000), *The Day of the Dead* (2004), *Queen of the Night* (2010)

Research Sources

Encyclopedias and Handbooks: 100, BYA, CA (118), CANR (61, 105, 155, 185), EMM, GWM, MCF, STJ, WWW

Bibliographies: FF, OM

Biographies and Interviews

"Authors@Google: J. A. Jance." (videocast) *AtGoogleTalks*. July 25, 2008. http://www.youtube.com/watch?v=vKbY4X6fbTo (accessed November 1, 2010).

Cochran, Stacey. "The Artist's Craft: J. A. Jance." (videocast) *Raleigh Television Network.* August 2, 2008. http://www.youtube.com/watch?v=ek9BAP69ryM (accessed November 1, 2010).

Friesinger, Alison. "R-Rated Thrillers, PG-13 Mysteries." *Publishers Weekly* 251.15 (April 12, 2004): 35.

Goldberg, Rylla. "J. A. Jance." *Mystery Scene* 51 (1996): 28–30. Also in *Speaking of Murder, vol. 2: Interviews with the Masters of Mystery and Suspense.* Ed. Ed Gorman and Martin H. Greenberg. New York: Berkley Prime Crime, 1999. 44–49.

"J. A. Jance." *MysteryNet.* n.d. http://www.mysterynet.com/jance/author.shtml (accessed November 1, 2010).

"J. A. Jance: Book Fest 07." (videocast) *Library of Congress.* September 24, 2007. http://www.loc.gov/today/cyberlc/feature_wdesc.php?rec=4144 (accessed November 1, 2010).

Jance, J. A. "An Essay." *Book Browse.* n.d. http://www.bookbrowse.com/author_interviews/full/index.cfm/author_number/927/JA-Jance (accessed November 1, 2010).

Jance, J. A. "The Long Slide Home." *The Writer* 117.1 (January 2004): 17–20.

Jones, Louise. "*PW* Talks With J. A. Jance." *Publishers Weekly* 249.29 (July 22, 2002): 162.

Jones, Louise. "Stranger on a Train: *PW* Talks with J.A. Jance." *Publishers Weekly* 252.25 (June 20, 2005): 61.

Richards, Linda. "J. A. Jance." *January Magazine.* February 2001. http://januarymagazine.com/profiles/jajance.html (accessed November 1, 2010).

Criticism and Reader's Guides

"Cruel Intent." (reading guide) *Simon and Schuster.* n.d. http://books.simonandschuster.com/Cruel-Intent/J-A-Jance/9781416566359/reading_group_guide (accessed November 1, 2010).

Rye, Marilyn. "Changing Gender Conventions and the Detective Formula: J. A. Jance's Beaumont and Brady Series." *Journal of Popular Culture* 37.1 (2003): 105–19.

"Trial by Fire." (reading guide) *Simon and Schuster.* n.d. http://books.simonandschuster.com/Trial-by-Fire/J-A-Jance/9781416563808/reading_group_guide (accessed November 1, 2010).

Web Sites

Official Web site: http://www.jajance.com/jajance.com/Welcome.html (accessed November 1, 2010).

Jance's blog: http://blog.seattlepi.com/jajance/ (accessed November 1, 2010).

"J. A. Jance": http://ofearna.us/books/jance.html—Includes jacket illustrations of books in series and a short essay by author (accessed November 1, 2010).

King, Laurie R., 1952–

"It was on her hand, the mud. Her left hand, and the right boot." I stopped, disbelieving, and looked at Holmes. His grey eyes were positively dancing. "She replenished the mud, to keep the path obvious. This whole episode—it was deliberately staged. She wants you to know that she was there, and she put the Baker Street mud on her shoe to thumb her nose at you."

—*The Beekeeper's Apprentice*, 1994

Biographical Sketch

Born in Oakland, California, Laurie R. King attended the University of California, Santa Cruz, where she received a B.A. in 1977 before pursuing an advanced degree in religious studies at Graduate Theological Union. While working as a manager of Kaldi's Fine Coffees and Teas, she visited a former professor and found common interests and good conversation, which led to marriage. She and Noel Q. King had two children. She started writing when her youngest entered preschool, but it was several years before her first novel was published. The Kings have homes in California and England.

King's two major series are quite different. One, set in modern San Francisco, has a lesbian police inspector as its main protagonist. The other takes place during the early years of the twentieth century and introduces a young American girl into Sherlock Holmes's life and heart. Both have been popular with readers and critics alike. Many of her books have religious themes, reflecting her education and interest in that area. Titles from both series have won awards, along with one stand-alone novel, *Folly*. The Independent Mystery Booksellers Association named *The Beekeeper's Apprentice* as one of the best one hundred mysteries of the century.

Categories: Diverse Characters, Historical, Police Procedural

Awards

John Creasey Dagger (*A Grave Talent*, 1995)
Edgar Award, Best First Novel by an American (*A Grave Talent*, 1994)
Macavity Award for Best Novel (*Folly*, 2002)
Nero Award (*A Monstrous Regiment of Women*, 1996)

Major Works

Kate Martinelli series: *A Grave Talent* (1993), *To Play the Fool* (1995), *With Child* (1996), *Night Work* (2000), *The Art of Detection* (2006)

Mary Russell/Sherlock Holmes series: *The Beekeeper's Apprentice; or, On the Segregation of the Queen* (1994), *A Monstrous Regiment of Women* (1995), *A Letter of Mary* (1997), *The Moor* (1998), *O, Jerusalem* (1999), *Justice Hall* (2002), *The Game* (2004), *Locked Rooms* (2005), *The Language of Bees* (2009), *The God of the Hive* (2010)

Nonseries novels: *A Darker Place* (1999), *Folly* (2001), *Keeping Watch* (2003), *Touchstone* (2007)

Research Sources

Encyclopedias and Handbooks: BYA, CA (140, 207), CANR (63, 105, 164), EMM, GWM. MCF, STJ

Bibliographies: FF, OM

Biographies and Interviews

"Book Talk with Laurie R. King." (videocast) *Gav TV*. December 8, 2009. http://blip.tv/file/2949299. (accessed November 1, 2010).

James, Dean. "Laurie King." *Mystery Scene* 48 (1995): 20–21, 50. Also in *Speaking of Murder, vol. 2: Interviews with the Masters of Mystery and Suspense*. Ed. Ed Gorman and Martin H. Greenberg. New York: Berkley Prime Crime, 1999. 173–83.

King, Laurie R. "Autobiography." *Laurie R. King Official Web site*. 2007. http://www.laurierking.com/author/bios/autobiography: A lengthy autobiographical essay published in *Contemporary Authors, vol. 207* (accessed November 1, 2010).

"Laurie R. King." *Bookreporter.com*. June 24, 2005. http://www.bookre porter.com/authors/au-king-laurie.asp (accessed November 1, 2010).

Lo, Malinda. "Interview with Laurie R. King." *AfterEllen*. September 27, 2004. http://www.afterellen.com/archive/ellen/People/interviews/92004/laurieking.html (accessed November 1, 2010).

Peters, Barbara. "Laurie R. King." (videocast—6 parts) *Poisoned Pen*. n.d. http://www.poisonedpen.com/interviews/laurie-r-king (accessed November 1, 2010).

Silet, Charles L. P. "An Interview with Laurie R. King." *Armchair Detective: A Quarterly Journal Devoted to the Appreciation of Mystery, Detective, and Suspense Fiction* 30.1 (1997): 10–15.

Criticism and Reader's Guides

Emrys, A. B. "Under Cover of Wartime: Disguised Murder in Works by Rennie Airth, Laurie R. King, Martha Grimes, and Anthony Horowitz." *Clues: A Journal of Detection* 25.4 (2007): 53–63.

Johnsen, Rosemary. "Historical Mysteries in the Literature Classroom." *Murder 101: Essays on the Teaching of Detective Fiction*. Ed. Edward J. Reilly. Jefferson, NC: McFarland, 2009. 106–14.

King, Laurie R. "Guest Post: Laurie R. King on Historical Fiction." *A Work in Progress*. March 11, 2009. http://danitorres.typepad.com/work inprogress/2009/03/laurie-kings-post.html: Includes links to other posts on King's blog tour in 2009 (accessed November 1, 2010).

Loftus, David. "*The Language of Bees* by Laurie R. King." *California Literary Review*. August 20, 2009. http://calitreview.com/4543 (accessed November 1, 2010).

Markowitz, Judith A. "The Art of Detection." Lambda Book Report 14.3 (Fall 2006): 11.

Peters, Timothy B. "Laurie King's Twist." *Publishers Weekly* 253.24 (2006): 24–25.

Preussner, Alanna. "The Nouveau Sherlock Holmes: Rewriting History and Implying Audience." *Publications of the Missouri Philological Association* 27 (2002): 92–102.

Taylor, Rhonda Harris. "'It's about Who Controls the Information': Mystery Antagonists and Information Literacy." *Clues: A Journal of Detection* 24.1 (2005): 7–17.

Web Sites

Official Web site: http://www.laurieking.com/ (accessed November 1, 2010).

Dammit, Holmes (fan site): http://community.livejournal.com/dammit_ holmes/: A LiveJournal community devoted to the Mary Russell/ Sherlock Holmes series. (accessed November 1, 2010).

Facebook site: http://www.facebook.com/laurieking (accessed November 1, 2010).

The Mary Russell Holmes Page (fan site): http://www.rj-anderson.com/ russell/: Includes brief information. Most useful for a list of links to other related sites (accessed November 1, 2010).

Lehane, Dennis, 1965–

Jimmy and Sean would play in the backyard, sometimes with Dave Boyle, a kid with girl's wrists and weak eyes who was always telling jokes he'd learned from his uncles. From the other side of the kitchen window screen, they would hear the hiss of the beer can pull-tabs, bursts of hard, sudden laughter, and the heavy snap of Zippos as Mr. Devine and Mr. Marcus lit their Luckys.

—Mystic River, 2001

Biographical Sketch

Dennis Lehane was born and raised in Dorchester, Massachusetts; his father, Michael, was a foreman and his mother, Ann, a cafeteria worker. He received a

B.A.S. from Eckerd College in 1988 and an M.F.A. from Florida International University in 1993. He worked as a counselor for mentally handicapped and emotionally disturbed children, a college instructor in English, a truck loader, a waiter, a bookstore worker, and a hotel chauffeur before his writing career took off. He is married to Sheila Lehane.

Lehane's first novels were about Patrick Kenzie and Angela Gennaro, a pair of cynical private detectives who grew up together. With the publication of *Mystic River,* he is considered to have broken out of the traditional crime novel mold, although his later novels still involve crime and violence. He has received critical acclaim and awards for his books, and several have been made into movies, most notably *Mystic River* and *Shutter Island.* His recent novel, *The Given Day,* is a vast historical epic about Boston during the early part of the twentieth century and is an even greater departure from his traditional crime fiction roots. His novels evoke a strong sense of place in their depiction of Boston.

Categories: Hard-Boiled, Private Detective

Awards

Anthony Award for Best Novel (*Mystic River,* 2002)
Barry Award for Best Novel (*Gone, Baby Gone,* 1999; *Mystic River,* 2002)
Nero Award (*Sacred,* 1998)
Shamus Award for Best First PI Novel *(A Drink before the War,* 1995)

Major Works

Patrick Kenzie and Angela Gennaro series: *A Drink before the War* (1994), *Darkness, Take My Hand* (1996), *Sacred* (1997), *Gone, Baby, Gone* (1998), *Prayers for Rain* (1999), *Moonlight Mile* (2010)
Nonseries novels: *Mystic River* (2001), *Shutter Island* (2003), *The Given Day* (2008), *Shutter Island Graphic Novel* (2010)
Short-story collections: *Coronado Island* (2006)

Research Sources

Encyclopedias and Handbooks: CA (154), CANR (72, 112, 136, 168), EMM, MCF, WWW

Bibliographies: FF, OM

Biographies and Interviews

Abram, Len. "Dennis Lehane." *The Drood Review.* January-February 2002. http://www.droodreview.com/features/lehane.htm (accessed November 1, 2010).

Anable, Stephen. "Lose the Fedora: PW Talks with Dennis Lehane." *Publishers Weekly* 256.38 (2009): 42.

Brockes, Emma. "A Life in Writing: Dennis Lehane." *The Guardian.co.uk.* January 24, 2009. http://www.guardian.co.uk/culture/2009/jan/24/dennis-lehane (accessed November 1, 2010).

"Dennis Lehane." *Bookreporter.com.* March 2001. http://www.bookreporter.com/authors/au-lehane-dennis.asp (accessed November 1, 2010).

"Dennis Lehane." *The Writer* 115.8 (2002): 66. http://www.writermag.com/en/Articles/2002/06/Dennis%20Lehane.aspx (accessed November 1, 2010).

"Dennis Lehane's 'Prayers for Rain.'" *Mysterynet.* 1999. http://www.mysterynet.com/lehane/author.shtml (accessed November 1, 2010).

Dunn, Adam. "A Good Place to Die." *Book* (March 2001): 52–56.

"Hookers, Guns and Money." *Atlantic Unbound.* May 5, 2004. http://www.theatlantic.com/magazine/archive/2004/05/hookers-guns-and-money/3125/ (accessed November 1, 2010).

Miller, Lynn I. "Dennis Lehane and George Pelecanos: Hard-Boiled Buddies." *Crescent Blues* 2.4 (1999). http://www.crescentblues.com/2_4issue/lehpel.shtml (accessed November 1, 2010).

Nawotka, Edward. "Boston's Uncommon Bestseller: Dennis Lehane." *Publishers Weekly* 250.15 (April 14, 2003): 39–40, 42.

Peters, Barbara. "Dennis Lehane." (videocast—6 parts) *The Poisoned Pen.* October 1, 2007. http://www.poisonedpen.com/interviews/dennis-lehane. Also available at http://www.youtube.com/watch?v=HACK68KMiMk (accessed November 1, 2010).

Richards, Linda. "Dennis Lehane." *January Magazine.* March 2001. http://januarymagazine.com/profiles/lehane.html (accessed November 1, 2010).

"Tess Gerritsen and Dennis Lehane in Discussion." (videocast—3 parts) *Transworldvideos.* February 27, 2009. http://www.youtube.com/watch?v=0wYb26oShcg (accessed November 1, 2010).

Welch, Dave. "Dennis Lehane Meets the Bronte Sisters." *Powells Books.* May 28, 2003. http://www.powells.com/authors/lehane.html (accessed November 1, 2010).

Criticism and Reader's Guides

Jones, Malcolm. "Mean Street Makeover." *Newsweek* 137.8 (2001): 58–59. http://www.newsweek.com/id/80531 (accessed November 1, 2010).

Lehane, Dennis. "Questions of Character." *Writer* 113.1 (2000): 7+.

"Reading Guide: *The Given Day.*" *HarperCollins Publishers.* n.d. http://www.harpercollins.com/author/microsite/readingguide.aspx?authorID=17394&isbn13=9780688163181&displayType=readingGuide (accessed November 1, 2010).

"*Shutter Island* (discussion guide)." *LitLovers.* n.d. http://www.litlovers.com/
    guide_shutter_island.html (accessed November 1, 2010).

Tom, Mary Lee. "*Mystic River*: A Reading and Discussion Guide." May 13
    2004. http://www.massbook.org/reading_guides/mystic_river_guide.pdf
    (accessed November 1, 2010).

Web Site

Official Web site: http://www.dennislehanebooks.com/ (accessed November
    2010).

Leonard, Elmore, 1925–

*Frank went into the used-car office, called the Detroit police, and gave
them a description of the car. He didn't do it right away. He took his time,
thinking the guy must be a real farmer to try and steal a car off a lot that
was all lit up. The guy had been very cool about it, though. Slow-talking,
relaxed, with the trace of a Southern accent.*

—*Swag*, 1976

Biographical Sketch

Elmore Leonard, also known as Dutch, was born in New Orleans, the son
of Elmore John (an automobile executive) and Flora Emilia Leonard. He
attended the University of Detroit, where he received a Bachelor of Philosophy degree. He worked in advertising and briefly had his own agency. He
was divorced from his first wife, married Joan Shepard in 1979, and, after
her death, married Christine Kent. He has five children. Leonard started out
writing westerns and was very successful in that genre, with one of his novels
Hombre, being named one of the twenty-five best western novels of all time
by the Western Writers of America. With the decline in popularity of the
western, he turned his hand to crime fiction and has been equally successful
in that genre. A number of his books have been adapted for movies or television series.

Often regarded as a successor to Raymond Chandler and Dashiell Hammett, Leonard populates his books with street-wise, often morally ambivalent
characters in darkly humorous situations. He is particularly praised for his
smart dialog, and he himself says that he lets his characters do the talking to
tell the story. Leonard's novels transcend the crime fiction genre with their
commentary on society, and he is one of the few successful crime authors
who do not rely on series characters. He is regarded as one of the outstanding
novelists of our time.

Categories: Caper, Hard-Boiled

Awards

Diamond Dagger for Lifetime Achievement (2006)
Edgar Award for Best Novel (*LaBrava,* 1984)
Edgar Grand Master Award for Lifetime Achievement (1992)

Major Works

Novels: *The Big Bounce* (1969), *The Moonshine War* (1969), *Mr. Majestyk* (1974), *Fifty-two Pickup* (1974), *Swag* (1976), *Unknown Man No. 89* (1977), *The Hunted* (1977), *The Switch* (1978), *City Primeval: High Noon in Detroit* (1980), *Gold Coast* (1985), *Split Images* (1978), *Cat Chaser* (1982), *Stick* (1983), *LaBrava* (1983), *Glitz* (1985), *Bandits* (1987), *Touch* (1987), *Freaky Deaky* (1988), *Killshot* (1989), *Get Shorty* (1990), *Maximum Bob* (1991), *Rum Punch* (1992), *Pronto* (1993), *Riding the Rap* (1995), *Out of Sight* (1996), *Cuba Libre* (1998), *Be Cool* (sequel to *Get Shorty,* 1999), *Pagan Babies* (2000), *Tishomingo Blues* (2002), *Mr. Paradise* (2004), *The Hot Kid* (2005), *Up in Honey's Room* (2007), *Djibouti* (2010)
Nonfiction: *Elmore Leonard's Ten Rules of Writing* (2007)

Research Sources

Encyclopedias and Handbooks: 100, BEA, BEB, CA (81–84), CANR (2, 28, 53, 76, 96, 133, 176), CLC (28, 34, 71, 12, 222), EMM, ICF, OCC, STJ, WWW

Bibliographies: FF

Biographies and Interviews

Amis, Martin. "Martin Amis Interviews Elmore Leonard." (pdf) *Writers Bloc.* January 23, 1998. www.martinamisweb.com/interviews_files/amis_int_leonard.pdf (accessed November 1, 2010).
Ashbrook, Tom. "Leonard Elmore." (audiocast) *On Point with Tom Ashmore, NPR.* May 29, 2009. http://www.onpointradio.org/2009/05/elmore-leonard (accessed November 1, 2010).
Bolton, Chris. "Elmore Leonard Hits the *Road.*" *Powells Books.* May 18, 2009. http://www.powells.com/blog/?p=6360 (accessed November 1, 2010).
Brookman, Rob. "Dark Genius: Elmore Leonard Doesn't Like Mysteries—But He Does Have a Thing for Bad Behavior." *Book* (March-April 2002): 28–30.
Challen, Paul. *Get Dutch.* Toronto: ECW Press, 2000.
"Elmore Leonard." *Bookreporter.com.* September 8, 2000. http://www.bookreporter.com/authors/au-leonard-elmore.asp (accessed November 1, 2010).

"Elmore Leonard Interview: From the F. Scott Fitzgerald Literary Conference." (vidoecast—4 parts) *Montgomery College.* December 12, 2008. http://www.youtube.com/watch?v=I9QbTQpiDsM (accessed November 1, 2010).

"Elmore Leonard: Novelist and Screenwriter." *New York State Writers Institute.* September 9, 2001. http://www.albany.edu/writers-inst/webpages4/archives/leonardelmore.html (accessed November 1, 2010).

Kaminsky, Stuart, and Laurie Roberts. "Elmore Leonard." *Behind the Mystery: Top Mystery Writers Interviewed.* Cohasset, MA: Hot House, 2005. 14–27.

Marling, William. "Elmore Leonard, Detective Novelist." *Detnovel.com.* n.d. http://www.detnovel.com/Leonard.html (accessed November 1, 2010).

Naylor, Brian. "Elmore Leonard's Characters Talk or Die." (audiocast) *Weekend Edition, NPR.* February 8, 2004. http://www.npr.org/templates/story/story.php?storyId=1651959 (accessed November 1, 2010).

Newman, Rick. "Q&A with Novelist Elmore Leonard." *US News and World Report.* October 22, 2007. http://www.usnews.com/news/articles/2007/10/22/a-qa-with-novelist-elmore-leonard.html (accessed November 1, 2010).

Rose, Charlie. "A Conversation with author Elmore Leonard." (videocast) *Charlie Rose.* May 27, 2009. http://www.charlierose.com/view/interview/10334 (accessed November 1, 2010).

Swaim, Don. "Elmore Leonard Interviews with Don Swaim." (audiocasts) *Wired for Books.* November 20, 1985; September 21, 1987. http://wiredforbooks.org/elmoreleonard/ (accessed November 1, 2010).

Taylor, Keith. "Bad Guys Are More Fun: An Interview with Elmore Leonard." *Witness* 14.2 (2000): 126–41.

"10 Questions for Elmore Leonard." *Time.* June 12, 2005. http://www.time.com/time/magazine/article/0,9171,1071265,00.html (accessed November 1, 2010).

Zaleski, Jeff. "Dutch in Detroit." *Publishers Weekly* (January 21, 2002): 52–53, 56–58.

Criticism and Reader's Guides

Amis, Martin. "Maintaining on Elmore Leonard." *The War against Cliché.* New York: Hyperion, 2001. 225–28.

Atwood, Margaret. "Tishomingo Blues by Elmore Leonard." *Writing with Intent: Essays, Reviews, Personal Prose, 1983-2005.* New York: Carroll & Graf, 2005.

Devlin, James E. *Elmore Leonard.* New York: Twayne, 1999.

Elder, Sean. "Elmore Leonard." *Salon.com.* September 28, 1999. http://archive.salon.com/people/bc/1999/09/28/leonard/ (accessed November 1, 2010).

Geherin, David. *Elmore Leonard.* New York: Continuum, 1989.

Gorman, Edward, Robert Skinner, and Robert Gleason. "Elmore Leonard." *Mystery and Suspense Writers: The Literature of Crime, Detection, and Espionage, I.* Ed. Robin W. Winks and Maureen Corrigan. New York: Scribner's, 1998. 589–603.

Grella, George. "Film in Fiction: The Real and the Reel in Elmore Leonard." *The Detective in American Fiction, Film, and Television.* Ed. Jerome H. Delamater and Ruth Prigozy. Westport, CT: Greenwood, 1998. 35–44.

Hynes, Joseph. "'High Noon in Detroit': Elmore Leonard's Career." *Journal of Popular Culture* 25.3 (1991): 181–87.

Leonard, Elmore. "Writers on Writing: Easy on the Adverbs, Exclamation Points and Especially Hooptedoodle." *New York Times.* July 16, 2001. http://www.nytimes.com/2001/07/16/arts/writers-writing-easy-adverbs-exclamation-points-especially-hooptedoodle.html?pagewanted=1 (accessed November 1, 2010).

Lillios, Anna. "Paradise Noir: Land of Gold, Moon, and Pixie Dust." *Crime Fiction and Film in the Sunshine State: Florida Noir.* Ed. Steve Glassman and Maurice O'Sullivan. Bowling Green, OH: Popular Press, 1997. 103–18.

Most, Glenn W. "Elmore Leonard: Splitting Images." *The Sleuth and the Scholar: Origins, Evolution, and Current Trends in Detective Fiction.* Westport, CT: Greenwood, 1988. 101–10. Also in *Western Humanities Review* 41.1 (1987): 78–86.

Rhodes, Chip. "Elmore Leonard: Realism after the End of Ideology." *Politics, Desire, and the Hollywood Novel.* Iowa City: University of Iowa Press, 2008. 139–63.

Sandels, Robert. "Common Criminals and Ordinary Heroes." *Armchair Detective* 22.1 (Winter 1989): 14–20.

Whalan, Mark. "The Literary Detective in Postmodernity." *Paradoxa: Studies in World Literary Genres* 4.9 (1998): 119–33.

Yearley, Clifton K. "Elmore Leonard." *100 Masters of Mystery and Detection, vol. 2.* Ed. Fiona Kelleghan. Pasadena, CA: Salem Press, 2001. 390–95.

Zackel, Frederick William. "Elmore Leonard." *American Hard-Boiled Crime Writers (Dictionary of Literary Biography* 226). Ed. George Parker Anderson and Julie B. Anderson. Detroit, MI: Thomson Gale, 2000. 223–46.

Web Site

Official Web site: http://www.elmoreleonard.com/ (accessed November 1, 2010).

Lippman, Laura, 1959–

Tess inhaled—deeply, happily, nostalgically. Food was only part of the draw here. Sour Beef Day was a scene, and the Monaghan-Weinstein clans had always been in the thick of it. Politicians paid their respects, in memory of the power Uncle Donald, her mother's brother, had once wielded behind the scenes. Shadier types shook Spike's hand, whispering things better not overheard.

—*The Sugar House,* 2000

Biographical Sketch

Lippman was born in Atlanta, Georgia, but her family moved north when she was two—first to Washington, D.C., and then to Baltimore, where she grew up. Her father was a journalist, and her mother was a librarian. With journalism in her blood, so to speak, she studied the subject at Northwestern University's Medill School of Journalism. After graduating, she worked as a reporter for the *Waco Herald-Tribune,* the *San Antonio Light,* and the *Baltimore Evening Sun* (later the *Baltimore Sun*). Her first seven novels were published while she was working at the *Sun.* She left journalism in 2001 and currently divides her time between New Orleans and Baltimore.

Lippman's series protagonist, Tess Monaghan, is a former reporter who becomes a private investigator after being downsized out of a job. The author describes her as having a rough exterior but a much softer interior than Lippman herself (*Contemporary Authors* online version). Her stand-alone novels have also been critically recognized. Lippman's Baltimore-based books give a realistic sense of the city, and she has received the Baltimore Mayor's Award for Literary Excellence. Lippman has won numerous awards from virtually every mystery and crime fiction organization, and her books have been published in at least five other countries.

Categories: Police Procedural, Private Detective

Awards

Agatha Award for Best Novel (*Butcher's Hill,* 1998)

Anthony Award for Best Novel (*Every Secret Thing,* 2004; *No Good Deeds,* 2007; *What the Dead Know,* 2008)

Anthony Award for Best Paperback Original (*Butcher's Hill,* 1999; *In Big Trouble,* 2000)

Anthony Award for Best Short Story ("Hardly Knew Her," *Dead Man's Hand,* 2008)

Barry Award for Best Novel (*Every Secret Thing,* 2004; *What the Dead Know,* 2008)

Edgar Award for Best Paperback Original (*Charm City,* 1998)
Macavity Award for Best Novel (*What the Dead Know,* 2008)
Nero Award (*Sugar House,* 2001)
Shamus Award for Best Paperback Original PI Novel (*Charm City,* 1998; *Big Trouble,* 2000)

Major Works

Tess Monaghan series: *Baltimore Blues* (1997), *Charm City* (1997), *Butcher's Hill* (1998), *In Big Trouble* (1999), *The Sugar House* (2000), *In a Strange City* (2001), *The Last Place* (2002), *By a Spider's Thread* (2004), *No Good Deeds* (2006), *Another Thing to Fall* (2008)
Nonseries novels: *Every Secret Thing* (2003), *To the Power of Three* (2005), *What the Dead Know* (2007), *Life Sentences* (2009), *I'd Know You Anywhere* (2010)
Short-story collections: *Hardly Knew Her* (2008)

Research Sources

Encyclopedias and Handbooks: CA (207), CANR (147, 190), GWM, MCF

Bibliographies: FF, OM

Biographies and Interviews

Adams, Noah. "Laura Lippman's Baltimore: Loving a Flawed Place." (audiocast) *Morning Edition, NPR.* August 23, 2007. http://www.npr.org/templates/story/story.php?storyId=13871677 (accessed November 1, 2010).
Cochran, Tracy. "The Baltimore Beat." *Publishers Weekly* 251.27 (July 5, 2004): 29–30, 32.
Fox, Suzanne. "Topical Crimes." *Publishers Weekly* 253.23 (June 5, 2006): 30.
"Interview with Laura Lippman." *Readers Read.* n.d. http://www.reader sread.com/features/lauralippman.htm (accessed November 1, 2010).
Koryta, Michael. "Laura Lippman: Bouchercon 2008." (videocast) *Stacey Cochran Productions.* October 20, 2008. http://www.youtube.com/watch?v=THt6DHiSOlM (accessed November 1, 2010).
"Laura Lippman." *Book Browse.* October 10, 2003. http://www.bookbrowse.com/biographies/index.cfm/author_number/832/Laura-Lippman (accessed November 1, 2010).
"Laura Lippman." *Bookreporter.com.* September 5, 2003. http://www.bookreporter.com/authors/au-lippman-laura.asp#view030905 (accessed November 1, 2010).
Lippman, Laura. "Laura Lippman Shows Off Her Mysterious Baltimore." (videocast) *VisitMyBaltimore.* September 29, 2008. http://www.youtube.com/watch?v=gbFyRmC-xDE (accessed November 1, 2010).

McCallum-Smith, Susan. "Web Extra: A Conversation with Laura Lippman." *Urbanite.* April 2009. http://www.urbanitebaltimore.com/sub.cfm?issueID=71&sectionID=4&articleID=1202 (accessed November 1, 2010).

"Meet the Author Series: Laura Lippman." (videocast) *Northeastern University.* March 12, 2009. http://www.youtube.com/watch?v=aslD_FpDv8U (accessed November 1, 2010).

Nelson, Sara. "Lady Baltimore." *Publishers Weekly* 255.6 (February 11, 2008): 46.

Peters, Barbara. "Laura Lippman Interview." (videocast—6 parts) *Poisoned Pen.* November 11, 2008. http://www.youtube.com/watch?v=XkbywwmGQcQ (accessed November 1, 2010).

Skurnick, Lizzie. "Secrets and Ties." *Baltimore City Paper.* August 20, 2003. http://www.citypaper.com/news/story.asp?id=3325 (accessed November 1, 2010).

Criticism and Reader's Guides

Clements, William M. "Some Literary Redactions of 'The Devil in the Dance Hall.'" *ANQ: A Quarterly Journal of Short Articles, Notes, and Reviews* 21.4 (2008): 51–59.

Lippman, Laura. "The Writer's Life: Laura Lippman; Knowing When to Say When." *Washington Post.* August 16, 2009.

Lippman, Laura. "Tess Monaghan." *The Lineup: The World's Greatest Crime Writers Tell the Inside Story of Their Greatest Detectives.* Ed. Otto Penzler. New York: Little, Brown, 2009. 239–54.

"Reading Guide: Life Sentences." *HarperCollins.* n.d. http://www.harpercollins.com/author/microsite/readingguide.aspx?authorID=17461&isbn13=9780061128899&displayType=readingGuide (accessed November 1, 2010).

"Reading Guide: What the Dead Know." *HarperCollins.* n.d. http://www.harpercollins.com/author/microsite/readingguide.aspx?authorID=17461&isbn13=9780061128851&displayType=readingGuide (accessed November 1, 2010).

Web Sites

Official Web site: http://www.lauralippman.com/index.html (accessed November 1, 2010).

Facebook site: http://www.facebook.com/lauralippman?v=app_10531514314 (accessed November 1, 2010).

Lovesey, Peter, 1936–

Yes, by George! If Brighton in September lived up to its reputation he would need the bag. The signs were promising enough. As the train had steamed into the terminus the crowds on the platform were three and four deep. Third class passengers, every one; there was no doubt of that. Each group carrying its own luggage and every face lobster-red from the sun.

—Mad Hatter's Holiday, 1973

Biographical Sketch

Born in Whitton, Middlesex, Lovesey was the son of a bank official. On his official Web site, he recounts how the family's house was destroyed by a bomb during World War II, with all of the family miraculously surviving—he himself was at school when it happened. After the war, he developed an interest in sports, specifically track, and attended the London Olympics and other meets. He was an indifferent athlete but has retained his interest—all of his nonfiction is about track and field, and his first mystery novel was inspired by the sport, as well. He graduated with honors from the University of Reading and joined the Royal Air Force, where he served as an education officer and then as a flying officer. He married Jacqueline Ruth Lewis in 1959, and they had two children. After leaving the Air Force, he was a lecturer and then an administrator in two institutions of higher education before becoming a full-time writer. In addition to writing books and short stories, he has also written screenplays with his wife for the *Cribb* television series based on his books; he also served as story consultant for the television series *Rosemary and Thyme*.

Lovesey's books have won numerous awards and have been translated into twenty-two languages. He has written two historical and two modern series; they feature both police detectives and an amateur detective in the form of the Prince of Wales. He has been praised for his strong characterization, vivid historical details, and polished plotting.

Categories: Historical, Police Procedural

Awards

Agatha Malice Domestic Lifetime Achievement Award (2008)
Anthony Award for Best Novel (*The Last Detective,* 1992)
Barry Award for Best Novel (*Bloodhounds,* 1997)
Gold Dagger Award (*The False Inspector Dew,* 1982)
Silver Dagger Award (*Waxwork,* 1978; *The Summons,* 1995; *Bloodhounds,* 1996)
Diamond Dagger for Lifetime Achievement (2000)
Macavity Award for Best Novel (*Bloodhounds,* 1997; *The House Sitter,* 2004)

Major Works

Sergeant Cribb series: *Wobble to Death* (1970), *The Detective Wore Silk Drawers* (1971), *Abracadaver* (1972), *Mad Hatter's Holiday: A Novel of*

Murder in Victorian Brighton (1973), *Invitation to a Dynamite Party* (U.S. title: *The Tick of Death*, 1974), *A Case of Spirits* (1975), *Swing, Swing Together* (1976), *Waxwork* (1978)

Albert Edward, Prince of Wales, series: *Bertie and the Tinman* (1988), *Bertie and the Seven Bodies* (1990), *Bertie and the Crime of Passion* (1993)

Peter Diamond series: *The Last Detective* (1991), *Diamond Solitaire* (1992), *The Summons* (1995), *Bloodhounds* (1996), *Upon a Dark Night* (1997), *Do Not Exceed the Stated Dose* (short stories, 1998), *The Vault* (2000), *Diamond Dust* (2002), *The House Sitter* (2003), *The Secret Hangman* (2007), *Skeleton Hill* (2009)

Inspector Hen Mallin series: *The Circle* (2005), *The Headhunters* (2008)

Nonseries novels: *The False Inspector Dew* (1982), *Keystone* (1983), *Rough Cider* (1986), *On the Edge* (1989), *The Reaper* (2001)

Short-story collections: *Butchers and Other Stories of Crime* (1985), *The Staring Man and Other Stories* (1989), *The Crime of Miss Oyster Brown and Other Stories* (1994), *The Sedgemoor Strangler, and Other Stories of Crime* (1994), *Murder on the Short List* (2009)

Research Sources

Encyclopedias and Handbooks: CA (41–44R), CANR (28, 59, 99, 170), EMM, MCF, STJ, WWW

Bibliographies: FF, OM

Biographies and Interviews

Carr, John C. "Peter Lovesey." *The Craft of Crime: Conversations with Crime Writers*. Boston: Houghton Mifflin, 1983: 258–88.

Chernow, Annie. "Peter Lovesey: Interview." *Crime Spree Magazine.* July-August 2007. http://peterlovesey.com/peter-lovesey-interview-by-annie-chernow (accessed November 1 2010).

Edwards, Martin. "Peter Lovesey." *TW Books.* 1996. http://www.twbooks. co.uk/crimescene/ploveseyme.html (originally appeared in *Deadly Pleasures Magazine*, Summer 1996) (accessed November 1, 2010).

Guili, Andrew. "Peter Lovesey." *Strand Magazine* 7 (2001). http://www. strandmag.com/htm/strandmag_lovesey.htm (accessed November 1, 2010).

"Men of Mystery: Peter Lovesey and James Benn." (audiocast) *Westport Public Library.* October 25, 2009. http://www.westportlibrary.org/events/podcasts/index.html (scroll down) (accessed November 1, 2010).

Muller, Adrian. "Peter Lovesey." *Speaking of Murder*. Ed. Ed Gorman and Martin H. Greenberg. New York: Berkley Prime Crime, 1998. 73–85. http://peterlovesey.com/peter-lovesey-speaking-of-murder (accessed November 1, 2010).

Perry, Anne. "At Home Online: Peter Lovesey." *Mystery Readers International*. n.d. http://www.mysteryreaders.org/athomelovesey.html (accessed November 1,2010).

Picker, Leonard. "An Up-to-Date Victorian." *Publishers Weekly* 252.13 (March 28, 2005): 60.

Criticism and Reader's Guides

Bedell, Jeanne F. "Peter Lovesey's Sergeant Cribb and Constable Thackeray." *Cops and Constables: American and British Fictional Policemen*. Ed. Earl F. Bargainnier and George N. Dove. Bowling Green, OH: Popular Press, 1986. 170–82.

Hurt, James. "How Unlike the Home Life of Our Own Dear Queen: The Detective Fiction of Peter Lovesey." *Art in Crime Writing: Essays on Detective Fiction*. Ed. Bernard Benstock. New York: St. Martin's, 1983. 142–58.

Hurt, James. "Peter Lovesey." *British Mystery and Thriller Writers since 1940: First Series*. Ed. Bernard Benstock and Thomas F. Staley. Detroit, MI: Gale, 1989. 256–74.

Miller, Stephen. "At the End of His Rope." *January Magazine*. September 2007. http://januarymagazine.com/crfiction/secrethangman.html (accessed November 1, 2010).

Moules, Joan M. "He Started with a Wobble: Peter Lovesey, Crime Writer." *Writer's Forum*. May 2005. http://peterlovesey.com/he-started-with-a-wobble (accessed November 1, 2010).

Web Site

Official Web site: http://peterlovesey.com/ (accessed November 1, 2010).

Maron, Margaret

> *Czarnecki, who was boogie-ing on back up to Teaneck, New Jersey, got lucky. His outlandish hair, his satanic earring, and his smartass sweatshirt afforded so many opportunities to zing me, that Hobart finally let the kid off with a ninety-day suspended and a two-fifty fine.*
>
> *Did I mention that Harrison Hobart's seat is up for election?*
> *Or that I'm one of the candidates?*
>
> —*The Bootlegger's Daughter,*1992

Biographical Sketch

Margaret Maron was born in Greensboro, North Carolina, and raised on a tobacco farm. She attended two years of college after high school and met her husband during a summer job at the Pentagon. They lived in Italy, then in Brooklyn, and had one son. Eventually, they moved back to the family farm, where they now live.

Maron started her writing with short stories and poetry (mostly bad, she says on her Web site) before turning to crime novels featuring police detective Sigrid Harald. After several novels in the Harald series, Maron started a new series about Deborah Knott, a district court judge and the youngest of twelve children, eleven of them male. Her first novel in that series, *Bootlegger's Daughter,* was the first to win four major crime fiction awards for the same book—the Agatha, Anthony, Edgar, and Macavity awards for best novel. Maron's two female protagonists are quite different: the Harald books portray a working detective, while Knott is a southern charmer and politician. Maron is also a prolific short-story writer.

Categories: Legal, Police Procedural

Awards

Agatha Award for Best Novel (*Bootlegger's Daughter,* 1992; *Up Jumps the Devil,* 1996; *Storm Track,* 2000)

Agatha Award for Best Short Story ("Deborah's Judgment," *A Woman's Eye,* ed. Sara Paretsky, 1991), ("The Dog That Didn't Bark," *Ellery Queen Mystery Magazine,* December 2002, 2002)

Anthony Award for Best Novel (*Bootlegger's Daughter,* 1993)

Edgar Award for Best Novel (*Bootlegger's Daughter,* 1993)

Macavity Award for Best Novel (*Bootlegger's Daughter,* 1993)

Macavity Award for Best Short Story ("Deborah's Judgment," *A Woman's Eye,* ed. Sara Paretsky, 1992)

Major Works

Sigrid Harald series: *One Coffee With* (1981), *Death of a Butterfly* (1984), *Death in Blue Folders* (1985), *The Right Jack* (1987), *Baby Doll Games* (1988), *Corpus Christmas* (1988), *Past Imperfect* (1991), *Fugitive Colors* (1995)

Deborah Knott series: *Bootlegger's Daughter* (1992), *Southern Discomfort* (1993), *Shooting at Loons* (1994), *Up Jumps the Devil* (1996), *Killer Market* (1997), *Shoveling Smoke: Selected Mystery Stories* (short stories, 1997), *Home Fires* (1999), *Storm Track* (2000), *Uncommon Clay* (2001), *Slow Dollar* (2002), *High Country Fall* (2004), *Rituals of the Season* (2005), *Winter's Child* (2006), *Hard Row* (2007), *Death's Half Acre* (2008), *Sand Sharks* (2009), *Christmas Mourning* (2010)

Nonseries novels: *Bloody Kin* (1985), *Last Lessons of Summer* (2003)

Short-story collection: *Suitable for Hanging: Selected Stories* (2004)

Research Sources

Encyclopedias and Handbooks: BYA, CA (172), CANR (44, 50, 66, 152, 191), GWM, EMM, MCF, STJ, WWW

Bibliographies: FF, OM

Biographies and Interviews

Carroll, Mary. "The Booklist Interview: Margaret Maron." *Booklist.* 97.17 (May 1, 2001): 1604–5.

Koch, Pat. "*PW* Talks with Margaret Maron." *Publishers Weekly.* 248.15 (April 9, 2001): 54.

Silet, Charles L. P. "Knotty Problems: Interview with Margaret Maron." *Armchair Detective: A Quarterly Journal Devoted to the Appreciation of Mystery, Detective, and Suspense Fiction* 30.3 (1997): 308–15.

Silet, Charles L. P. "Margaret Maron." *Speaking of Murder, vol. 2: Interviews with the Masters of Mystery and Suspense.* Ed. Ed Gorman and Martin H. Greenberg. New York: Berkley Prime Crime, 1999. 102–14.

Taylor, Art. "Margaret Maron Author Interview." *MysteryNet.* n.d. http://www.mysterynet.com/books/testimony/homefires/ (accessed November 1, 2010).

Taylor, Art. "Margaret Maron Talks about Sand Sharks." *Art and Literature: Southern Lit Mysteries and Thrillers, the Literary Blog of Metro Magazine.* September 8, 2009. http://artandliterature.wordpress.com/2009/09/08/margaret-maron-talks-about-sand-sharks/ (accessed November 1, 2010).

Criticism and Reader's Guides

Buchanan, Harriette C. "Sigrid's Saga: Text, Subtext, and Supertext in Margaret Maron's Sigrid Harald Novels." *Clues: A Journal of Detection* 17.2 (1996): 33–42.

Taylor, Art. "Blood Kin and Bloody Kin: Villainy and Family in the Works of Margaret Maron." *Armchair Detective: A Quarterly Journal Devoted to the Appreciation of Mystery, Detective, and Suspense Fiction* 27.1 (1994): 20–25.

Town, Caren J. "'The Same Old Same Old': Gender and Race in Margaret Maron's Deborah Knott Series." *Clues: A Journal of Detection* 25.3 (2007): 57–71.

Web Sites

Official Web site: http://www.margaretmaron.com/ (accessed November 1, 2010).

Facebook site: http://www.facebook.com/pages/Margaret-Maron/290105072 569?ref=search&sid=100000605920094.989877134.1 (accessed November 1, 2010).

Marsh, Ngaio, 1895–1982

He tried to remember if he had ever before been quite so pointedly snubbed by a total stranger. Only, he reflected, by persons he was obliged to interview in the execution of his duties as an officer of Scotland Yard. On those occasions he persisted. On this, an apologetic exit seemed to be clearly indicated.

—Artists in Crime, 1938

Biographical Sketch

Edith Ngaio (pronounced Ny-o) Marsh was the only child of Henry Edmund and Rose Elizabeth Marsh. "Ngaio" is a Maori word for a type of flowering tree in New Zealand. She attended St. Margaret's College and, later, the University of Canterbury in New Zealand, where she studied art. While at St. Margaret's, she developed the love of Shakespeare and theater that would be her life's passion. The young man with whom she might have formed a lasting relationship was killed in World War I, and Ngaio never married. In 1928, she went to England, where she had friends from New Zealand. While there, she began to write detective stories and left a manuscript with an agent when she went home to care for her dying mother. The manuscript was published as *A Man Lay Dead,* and her writing career was launched. She would continue to publish crime novels for almost fifty years. However, her true love was the theater, and she spent a good deal of her time producing and directing plays in New Zealand. She was honored with the Order of the British Empire in 1948 and named Dame Commander, Order of the British Empire in 1966, as much for her theater work as for her writing. She died in Christchurch in 1982.

Ngaio Marsh was one of the women considered the queens of the golden age of crime fiction in the 1920s, 1930s, and 1940s, although her career lasted far past that. Her novels feature a Scotland Yard detective and are a good portrayal of the gentleman policeman whom critics consider to have a depth of characterization missing in some of the other well-known detectives of the period. Inspector Alleyn marries an artist during the series, and Marsh was able to incorporate her love of art and theater into many of the books. Her works continue to be in print and are popular with readers who enjoy the interesting plots, gentle humor, well-drawn characters, and British ambience.

Categories: English Setting, Police Procedural

Awards

Edgar Grand Master Award for Lifetime Achievement (1978)

Major Works

Roderick Alleyn series: *A Man Lay Dead* (1934), *Enter a Murderer* (1935), *The Nursing-Home Murder* (with Henry Jellett, 1935), *Death in Ecstasy* (1936), *Vintage Murder* (1937), *Artists in Crime* (1938), *Death in a White Tie* (1938), *Overture to Death* (1939), *Death of a Peer* (1940), *Death at the Bar* (1940), *Death and the Dancing Footman* (1941), *Colour Scheme* (1943), *Died in the Wool* (1945), *Final Curtain* (1947), *A Wreath for Rivera* (1949), *Night at the Vulcan* (1951), *Spinsters in Jeopardy* (1955), *Scales of Justice* (1955), *Death of a Fool* (1956), *Singing in the Shrouds* (1958), *False Scent* (1960), *Hand in Glove* (1962), *Dead Water* (1963), *Killer Dolphin* (1966), *Clutch of Constables* (1968), *When in Rome* (1970), *Tied Up in Tinsel* (1972), *Black as He's Painted* (1975), *Last Ditch* (1977), *Grave Mistake* (1978), *Photo Finish* (1980), *Light Thickens* (1982)

Plays: *The Nursing-Home Murder* (with Henry Jellett, 1936), *Surfeit of Lampreys* (with Owen B. Howell, 1950), *False Scent* (with Eileen MacKay, 1961), *Murder Sails at Midnight* (1963)

Short-story collections: *The Collected Shorter Fiction of Ngaio Marsh* (U.K. title *Death on the Air and Other Stories*, 1989), *Alleyn and Others* (1992)

Nonfiction: *Black Beech and Honeydew* (1965, rev. ed. 1981)

Research Sources

Encyclopedias and Handbooks: CA (9–12R), CANR (6, 58), CLC (7, 53), EMM, MCF, OCC, STJ, WWW

"Ngaio Marsh." *Dictionary of New Zealand Biography*: 1998. http://www.dnzb.govt.nz/dnzb/. (accessed November 1, 2010). You will need to search to find entry on Marsh.

Bibliographies: FF

Biographies and Interviews

Harding, Bruce. "Ngaio Marsh, 1895–1982." *Kotare, 2007, Special Issue–Essays in New Zealand Literary Biography, Series One: Women Prose Writers to World War I.* http://www.nzetc.org/tm/scholarly/tei-Whi071Kota-t1-g1-t10.html—Includes lengthy biographical essay with critical components (accessed November 1, 2010).

Lewis, Margaret. *Ngaio Marsh: A Life.* London: Chatto & Windus, 1991. Reprinted by Poisoned Pen Press, 1998.

Marsh, Ngaio. *Black Beech and Honeydew: An Autobiography.* Boston: Little Brown, 1965.

"Ngaio Marsh." *Books and Writers.* n.d. http://www.kirjasto.sci.fi/nmarsh.htm (accessed November 1, 2010).

Criticism and Reader's Guides

Acheson, Carole. "Cultural Ambivalence: Ngaio Marsh's New Zealand Detective Fiction." *Journal of Popular Culture* 19.2 (1985): 159–74.

Bargainnier, Earl F. "Ngaio Marsh." *10 Women of Mystery*. Bowling Green, OH: Popular Press, 1981. 78–105.

Bloom, Harold, ed. *Modern Mystery Writers*. New York: Chelsea House, 1995. 124–38.

Dooley, Allan C., and Linda J. Dooley. "Rereading Ngaio Marsh." *Art in Crime Writing: Essays on Detective Fiction*. Ed. Bernard Benstock. New York: St. Martin's, 1983. 33–48.

DuBose, Martha Hailey. "Ngaio Marsh: The Secret Self." *Women of Mystery: The Lives and Works of Notable Women Crime Novelists*. New York: St. Martin's Minotaur, 2000. 225–61.

Grost, Mike. "Ngaio Marsh." *A Guide to Classic Mystery and Detection*. (fansite) n.d. http://mikegrost.com/ngmarsh.htm#Marsh (accessed November 1, 2010).

Harding, Bruce. "Ngaio Marsh." *Mystery and Suspense Writers: The Literature of Crime, Detection, and Espionage, II*. Ed. Robin W. Winks and Maureen Corrigan. New York: Scribner's, 1998. 665–77.

Lachman, Marvin S. "Ngaio Marsh." *British Mystery Writers, 1920–1939* (*Dictionary of Literary Biography* 77). Ed. Bernard Benstock and Thomas F. Staley. Detroit, MI: Gale, 1989. 198–213.

Mahoney, MaryKay. "Ngaio Marsh's Roderick Alleyn." *In the Beginning: First Novels in Mystery Series*. Ed. Mary Jean DeMarr. Bowling Green, OH: Popular Press, 1995. 69–76.

Mann, Jessica. "Ngaio Marsh." *Deadlier Than the Male: Why Are Respectable English Women So Good at Murder?* New York: Macmillan, 1981. 218–33.

"Marsh, Ngaio." *New Zealand Book Council*. 1998. http://www.bookcouncil.org.nz/writers/marshn.html#a1530 (accessed November 1, 2010).

Marsh, Ngaio. "Roderick Alleyn." *The Great Detectives*. Ed. Otto Penzler. Boston: Little, Brown, 1978. 3–8.

McDorman, Kathryne Slate. *Ngaio Marsh*. Boston: Twayne, 1991.

McDorman, Kathryne Slate. "Ngaio Marsh." *100 Masters of Mystery and Detection, vol. 2*. Ed. Fiona Kelleghan. Pasadena, CA: Salem Press, 2001. 460–66.

McDorman, Kathryne Slate. "Ngaio Marsh and the "Drug Scene" of Detective Fiction." Ed. Jane Lilienfeld and Jeffrey Oxford. *The Languages of Addiction*. New York: St. Martin's Press, 1999. 136–60.

Rahn, B. J., ed. *Ngaio Marsh: The Woman and Her Work*. Lanham, MD: Scarecrow Press, 1995.

Reynolds, Moira Davison. "Ngaio Marsh." *Women Authors of Detective Series: Twenty-One American and British Writers, 1900–2000*. Jefferson, NC: McFarland, 2001. 50–58.

Rowland, Susan. *From Agatha Christie to Ruth Rendell: British Women Writers in Detective and Crime Fiction.* New York: Palgrave, 2001.

"Three New Zealanders: Ngaio Marsh." (videocast) *NZOnScreen.* 1977. http://www.nzonscreen.com/title/three-new-zealanders-ngaio-marsh-1977 (accessed November 1, 2010).

Weinkauf, Mary S. *Murder Most Poetic: The Mystery Novels of Ngaio Marsh.* San Bernardino, CA: Brownstone Books, 1996.

Web Sites

"Dame Ngaio Marsh's Home." http://www.ngaio-marsh.org.nz/—Site about Marsh's home, with a link to an extensive bibliography of her works (accessed November 1, 2010).

"Ngaio Marsh: A Pathfinder." http://www.unc.edu/~belll/pathfinder/ngaio. html—Links and information about a number of sources, both critical and biographical (accessed November 1, 2010).

If You Like Ngaio Marsh

Roderick Alleyn, Marsh's protagonist, is a gentleman policeman at Scotland Yard. The Alleyn series falls into the cozy category, with puzzle plots, a policeman and his sergeant sidekick, and gentle humor.

Then You Might Like

Catherine Aird

Inspector C. D. Sloane and his assistant/nemesis, Sergeant Crosby, solve mysteries in the mythical county of Calleshire. Humorous and quirky, these cozy reads feature strong characterizations and good plotting. The series begins with *The Religious Body,* followed by *Henrietta Who?,* and continues with at least eighteen additional titles.

Graham, Caroline

Graham's Chief Inspector Barnaby series is another example of the small-village police procedural. Barnaby and Sergeant Troy investigate crimes in various small villages, with Barnaby providing the reasoning and aided by the brash Sergeant Troy. Start with *The Killings at Badger's Drift,* followed by *The Hollow Man.*

Martha Grimes

The title of each of Grimes's mysteries in the Richard Jury series is the name of a pub. Jury, a Scotland Yard detective, has the obligatory sidekick, but this one is an English gentleman, rather than a policeman. Jury is a rather broody hero, but his cases fit into the English police procedural tradition. *The Man With a Load of Mischief* begins the multivolume series.

Michael Innes

Innes, a pseudonym for John Innes Macintosh Stewart, was an Oxford don and a contemporary of Marsh. His best-known series features Inspector Appleby of Scotland Yard, another example of the gentleman policeman. The earlier novels especially have a rather antic sense of humor and delightfully quirky characters. The series begins with *Death at the President's Lodging,* followed by *Hamlet, Revenge!* and *Lament for a Maker* and almost thirty more titles.

Dorothy Simpson

Simpson's series features Inspector Luke Thanet (along with the obligatory sergeant sidekick) who does his detecting in the town of Sturrenden. The Thanet books portray a strong relationship between the inspector and his wife and children, as well as well-crafted plots. Start with *The Night She Died.*

Josephine Tey

Inspector Allen Grant is not the main character in all of Tey's novels, but he appears in most of them and takes the lead in some. He is brilliant and intuitive, traits regarded with some disfavor by his Scotland Yard superiors. Tey's mysteries are considered to be classics of plotting and style. Titles include *Daughter of Time* and *The Man in the Queue,* among others.

McBain, Ed (aka Evan Hunter), 1926–2005

The dead man was lying on his back, covered with a blanket, his eyes and his mouth open, his tongue protruding. Carella glanced at him again, a faint look of sorrow and pain momentarily knifing his eyes. In these moments, he felt particularly vulnerable, wondering as he often did if he was perhaps unsuited to a job that brought him into frequent contact with death.

—*The Last Dance,* 2000

Biographical Sketch

Evan Hunter was born in New York City as Salvatore Lombino (his name was legally changed to Evan Hunter in 1952). He attended Cooper Union and then went into the service during World War II, during which he served in the U.S. Navy. After leaving the service, he graduated from Hunter College with Phi Beta Kappa honors. He taught high school for a few months and then worked for a literary agency, at which time he started writing. His first successful publication was *The Blackboard Jungle,* about an idealistic teacher in a tough high school. He was married three times and had three children by his first wife. He died of cancer of the larynx.

Hunter was an incredibly prolific writer, with well over one hundred books to his credit, more than fifty in the 87th Precinct series alone. In addition he wrote screenplays for movies and television, most notably for Alfred Hitchcock's film *The Birds*. His best-known crime fiction was written under the Ed McBain pseudonym, and the 87th Precinct books are considered to have established the recognized conventions for the modern police procedural novel, with multiple story lines and a rotating cast of characters. Throughout the fifty years during which he published the series, the plots and characters remained fresh and appealing to readers. In recognition of his achievements in crime fiction, he was the first American author to receive the Diamond Dagger Award for Lifetime Achievement from the U.K. Crime Writers Association.

Categories: Legal, Police Procedural

Awards

Diamond Dagger for Lifetime Achievement (1998)
Edgar Grand Master Award for Lifetime Achievement (1986)

Major Works (selected)

87th Precinct series (as Ed McBain): *Cop Hater* (1956), *The Mugger* (1956), *The Pusher* (1956), *The Con Man* (1957), *Killer's Choice* (1957), *Killer's Payoff* (1958), *Lady Killer* (1958), *Killer's Wedge* (1958), *'Til Death* (1959), *King's Ransom* (1959), *Give the Boys a Great Big Hand* (1960), *The Heckler* (1960), *See Them Die* (1960), *Lady, Lady, I Did It!* (1961), *Like Love* (1962), *The Empty Hours* (1962), *Ten Plus One* (1963), *Ax* (1964), *He Who Hesitates* (1965), *Doll* (1965), *Eighty Million Eyes* (1966), *Fuzz* (1968), *Shotgun* (1969), *Jigsaw* (1970), *Hail, Hail, the Gang's All Here* (1971), *Sadie When She Died* (1972), *Let's Hear It for the Deaf Man* (1972), *Hail to the Chief* (1973), *Bread* (1974), *Blood Relatives* (1975), *So Long as You Both Shall Live* (1976), *Long Time No See* (1977), *Calypso* (1979), *Ghosts* (1980), *Heat* (1981), *Ice* (1983), *Lightning* (1984), *Eight Black Horses* (1985), *Poison* (1987), *Tricks* (1987), *Lullaby* (1989), *Vespers* (1990), *Widows* (1991), *Kiss* (1992), *Mischief* (1993), *And All Through the House* (1994), *Romance* (1995), *Nocturne* (1997), *The Big, Bad City* (1998), *The Last Dance* (2000), *Money, Money, Money* (2001), *Fat Ollie's Book* (2002), *The Frumious Bandersnatch* (2004), *Hark!* (2004), *Fiddlers* (2005)
Matthew Hope series (as Ed McBain): *Goldilocks* (1977), *Rumpelstiltskin* (1981), *Beauty and the Beast* (1982), *Jack and the Beanstalk* (1984), *Snow White and Rose Red* (1985), *Cinderella* (1986), *Puss in Boots* (1987), *The House That Jack Built* (1988), *Three Blind Mice* (1990), *Mary, Mary* (1992), *There Was a Little Girl* (1994), *Gladly the Cross-Eyed Bear* (1996), *The Last Best Hope* (1998)

Short-story collection: *The Best American Mystery Stories* (editor, 1999)
Nonfiction: *Me and Hitch* (1997), *Let's Talk: A Story of Cancer and Love* (memoir, 2005)

Research Sources

Encyclopedias and Handbooks: 100, BEA, CA (5–8R), CANR (5, 38, 62, 97, 149), CLC (11, 31), EMM, MCF, OCC, STJ, WWW

Bibliographies: FF

Biographies and Interviews

Carr, John C. "Ed McBain." *The Craft of Crime: Conversations with Crime Writers.* Boston: Houghton Mifflin, 1983. 1–23.

"Ed McBain (Evan Hunter)." *Bookreporter.com.* January 21, 2000. http://www.bookreporter.com/authors/au-mcbain-ed.asp (accessed November 1, 2010).

Forshaw, Barry. "Ed McBain." *Crime Time.* n.d. http://www.crimetime.co.uk/interviews/edmcbain.html (accessed November 1, 2010).

Grady, James. "How Ed McBain Made His Name." *Slate.* July 11, 2005. http://www.slate.com/id/2122426/ (accessed November 1, 2010).

Kaminsky, Stuart, and Laurie Roberts. "Evan Hunter/Ed McBain." *Behind the Mystery: Top Mystery Writers Interviewed.* Cohasset, MA: Hot House, 2005. 176–87.

Kimberley, Nick. "Obituary: Ed McBain." *Guardian.co.uk.* July 8, 2005. http://www.guardian.co.uk/news/2005/jul/08/guardianobituaries.booksobituaries (accessed November 1, 2010).

Kovach, Ronald. "Urban Legend." *The Writer* 115.3 (2002): 24–28.

Silet, Charles L. P. "Ed McBain." *Speaking of Murder: Interviews with the Masters of Mystery and Suspense.* Ed. Ed Gorman and Martin H. Greenberg. New York: Berkley Prime Crime, 1998. 43–54.

Silet, Charles L. P. "Writing for Hitchcock: An Interview with Ed McBain." *MysteryNet.* n.d. http://www.mysterynet.com/hitchcock/mcbain/ (accessed November 1, 2010).

Stotter, Mike. "Online Interview: Ed McBain." *Shots: The Magazine for Crime and Mystery.* n.d. http://www.shotsmag.co.uk/mcbain.htm (accessed November 1, 2010).

Walker, Fiona. "Tribute to Ed McBain." *Mystery Ink.* 2006. http://www.mysteryinkonline.com/2006/05/tribute_to_ed_m.html (accessed November 1, 2010).

Criticism and Reader's Guides

Dove, George N. *The Boys from Grover Avenue: Ed McBain's 87th Precinct Novels.* Bowling Green, OH: Popular Press, 1985.

Dove, George N. "Cop Hater: Gateway to the 87th Precinct." *In the Beginning: First Novels in Mystery Series.* Ed. Mary Jean DeMarr. Bowling Green, OH: Popular Press, 1995. 105–17.

Hamill, Pete. "The Poet of Pulp." *New Yorker* 75.41 (2000): 62–68, 70–71.

Kich, Martin. "Evan Hunter (Ed McBain)." *American Mystery and Detective Writers (Dictionary of Literary Biography* 306). Ed. George Parker Anderson. Detroit, MI: Gale, 2005. 183–95.

McBain, Ed. "The 87th Precinct." *The Great Detectives.* Ed. Otto Penzler. Boston: Little, Brown, 1978. 89–97.

MacDonald, Erin E. "Genre and Masculinity in Ed McBain's 87th Precinct Novels." *Journal of American & Comparative Cultures* 25.1/2 (2002): 47–50.

Miller, Dean A. "Evan Hunter." *Mystery and Suspense Writers: The Literature of Crime, Detection, and Espionage, I.* Ed. Robin W. Winks and Maureen Corrigan. New York: Scribner's, 1998. 517–16.

O'Sullivan, Maurice. "Fairy Tale Noir." *Crime Fiction and Film in the Sunshine State: Florida Noir.* Ed. Steve Glassman and Maurice O'Sullivan. Bowling Green, OH: Popular Press, 1997. 127–34.

Pierce, J. Kingston. "The Double Man: A Final Farewell to Novelist Ed McBain." *January Magazine.* October 2005. http://januarymagazine. com/features/mcbainintro.html (accessed November 1, 2010).

Yearley, Clifton K. "Ed McBain." *100 Masters of Mystery and Detection, vol. 2.* Ed. Fiona Kelleghan. Pasadena, CA: Salem Press, 2001. 424–30.

Web Site

Official Web site http://www.edmcbain.com/default.asp (accessed November 1, 2010).

McCall Smith, Alexander—see Smith, Alexander McCall

Mertz, Barbara—see Peters, Elizabeth

Michaels, Barbara—see Peters, Elizabeth

Mosley, Walter, 1952–

> *His skin was smooth and pale with just a few freckles. One lick of strawberry-blond hair escaped the band of his hat. He stopped in the doorway, filling it with his large frame, and surveyed the room with pale eyes; not a color I'd ever seen in a man's eyes. When he looked at me I felt a thrill of fear, but that went away quickly because I was used to white people by 1948.*

> —Devil in a Blue Dress, 1990

Biographical Sketch

Walter Mosley was born in Los Angeles and attended Goddard College and Johnson State College, where he received a B.A. in 1977. He did graduate work at City College of the City University of New York and achieved a M.A. and a Ph.D. He married Joy Kellman, but the couple later divorced. He has worked as a potter, a computer programmer, and an educator and founded the publishing degree program at City College.

Mosley's best-known work is the Easy Rawlins series, a gritty hard-boiled look at black city life after World War II. Easy isn't too particular about the jobs he takes or where the money comes from. Mosley has been compared to Chandler because of his depiction of Los Angeles and the hard side of life. Critical reception has been mixed, but Mosley has not been afraid to take risks in his writing, and his story telling is sound and thought-provoking. In a field where there are few African American writers, he has set a high standard.

Categories: Diverse Characters, Private Detective

Awards

John Creasey Dagger for previously unpublished authors (*Devil in a Blue Dress,* 1991)
Shamus Award for Best First PI Novel (*Devil in a Blue Dress,* 1991)
Nero Award *(Fear Itself,* 2004)

Major Works

Easy Rawlins series: *Devil in a Blue Dress* (1990), *A Red Death* (1991), *White Butterfly* (1992), *Black Betty* (1994), *A Little Yellow Dog* (1996), *Gone Fishin'* (1997), *Bad Boy Brawley Brown* (2002), *Six Easy Pieces: Easy Rawlins Stories* (2003), *Little Scarlet* (2004), *Cinnamon Kiss* (2005), *Blonde Faith* (2007)
Fearless Jones series: *Fearless Jones* (2001), *Fear Itself* (2003), *Fear of the Dark* (2006)
Leonid McGill series: *The Long Fall* (2009), *Known to Evil* (2010)
Nonseries novel: *The Last Days of Ptolemy Grey* (2010)
Nonfiction: *This Year You Write Your Novel* (2007)

Research Sources

Encyclopedias and Handbooks: 100, BEA, BEB, CA (142), CANR (57, 92, 136, 172), CLC (97, 184, 278), EMM, MCF, OCC, STJ, WWW

Bibliographies: FF, OM

Biographies and Interviews

"Author Interviews: Walter Mosley, Uneasy Street." Powells Books. n.d. http://www.powells.com/authors/mosley.html (accessed November 1, 2010).

"Easy Rawlins and the Unbearable Sadness of Being." (audiocast) *All Things Considered, NPR*. October 10, 2007. http://www.npr.org/templates/story/story.php?storyId=15151902 (accessed November 1, 2010).

Frumkes, Lewis Burke. "A Conversation with… Walter Mosley." *The Writer* 112.12 (December 1999): 20.

Gilmer, Marcus. "Interview: Walter Mosley." *Chicagoist.* April 6, 2009. http://chicagoist.com/2009/04/06/interview_walter_mosley.php (accessed November 1, 2010).

Hahn, Robert C. "The End of Easy?" *Publishers Weekly* 254.52 (December 31, 2007): 25.

Hill, Logan. "Free Radical." *New York Books*. September 18, 2005. http://nymag.com/nymetro/arts/books/14455/ (accessed November 1, 2010).

"Interview with Walter Mosley." *Readers Read.* n.d. http://www.readersread.com/features/mosley.htm (accessed November 1, 2010).

Knotts, Kristina L. "Walter Mosley (1952–)." *Contemporary African American Novelists: A Bio-Bibliographical Critical Sourcebook*. Ed. Emmanuel S. Nelson. Westport, CT: Greenwood, 1999. 350–54.

Mosley, Walter. "Stop Reading and Starting Writing." (audiocast) *Talk of the Nation, NPR*. April 17, 2007. http://www.npr.org/templates/story/story.php?storyId=9620861 (accessed November 1, 2010).

Mosley, Walter. "The Writing Life: Or the Novelist's Obligation to Employ Politics and Poetry." *Washington Post.* November 20, 2005. http://www.washingtonpost.com/wp-dyn/content/article/2005/11/17/AR2005111701424.html (accessed November 1, 2010).

Mosley, Walter, and Colson Whitehead. "Eavesdropping." *Book* (May 2001): 44.

Silet, Charles L. P. "Walter Mosley." *Speaking of Murder, vol. 2: Interviews with the Masters of Mystery and Suspense*. Ed. Ed Gorman and Martin H. Greenberg. New York: Berkley Prime Crime, 1999. 89–101.

"Walter Mosley." *BookBrowse.com*. September 1, 2007. http://www.bookbrowse.com/biographies/index.cfm?author_number=636 (accessed November 1, 2010).

"Walter Mosley." *Bookreporter.com*. July 2002. http://www.bookreporter.com/authors/au-mosley-walter.asp (accessed November 1, 2010).

"Walter Mosley: Book Fest 09." (webcast) *Library of Congress*. September 26, 2009. http://www.loc.gov/today/cyberlc/feature_wdesc.php?rec=4654 (accessed November 1, 2010).

Williams, Juan. "Walter Mosley: What Next" (audiocast) *Morning Edition, NPR*. March 17, 2003. http://www.npr.org/templates/story/story.php?storyId=1192760 (accessed November 1, 2010).

Criticism and Reader's Guides

Berger, Roger A. "'The Black Dick': Race, Sexuality, and Discourse in the L. A. Novels of Walter Mosley." *African American Review* 31.2 (1997): 281–94.

Bertens, Hans, and Theo D'haen. "'Other' Detectives: The Emergence of Ethnic Crime Writing." *Contemporary American Crime Fiction*. New York: Palgrave, 2001. 175–89.

"Black History Month: Walter Mosley." *Gale Cengage Learning*. 2009. http://www.gale.cengage.com/free_resources/bhm/bio/mosley_w.htm (accessed November 1, 2010).

Brady, Owen E., and Derek C. Maus. *Finding a Way Home: A Critical Assessment of Walter Mosley's Fiction*. Jackson: University Press of Mississippi, 2008.

Bunyan, Scott. "No Order from Chaos: The Absence of Chandler's Extra-Legal Space in the Detective Fiction of Chester Himes and Walter Mosley." *Studies in the Novel* 35.3 (2003): 339–65.

Cobb, John L. "Walter Mosley." *American Mystery and Detective Writers (Dictionary of Literary Biography* 306). Ed. George Parker Anderson. Detroit, MI: Thomson Gale, 2005. 285–96.

Crooks, Robert. "From the Far Side of the Urban Frontier: The Detective Fiction of Chester Himes and Walter Mosley." *Race-ing Representation: Voice, History, and Sexuality*. Ed. Kostas Myrsiades and Linda S. Myrsiades. Lanham, MD: Rowman & Littlefield, 1998. 175–99. Also available *College Literature* 22.3 (1995): 68–90.

"'Devil in a Blue Dress' Study Guide" *Gradesaver.com*. n.d. http://www.gradesaver.com/devil-in-a-blue-dress/study-guide/. (accessed November 1, 2010)

"The Easy Rawlings [*sic*] Novels." *Aalbc.com*. n.d. http://aalbc.com/authors/easy.htm—Brief summary of each novel (accessed November 1, 2010).

English, Daylanne K. "The Modern in the Postmodern: Walter Mosley, Barbara Neely, and the Politics of Contemporary African-American Detective Fiction." *American Literary History* 18.4 (2006): 772–96.

Ford, Elisabeth V. "Miscounts, Loopholes, and Flashbacks: Strategic Evasion in Walter Mosley's Detective Fiction." *Callaloo: A Journal of African Diaspora Arts and Letters* 28.4 (2005): 1074–90.

Frieburger, William. "James Ellroy, Walter Mosley, and the Politics of the Los Angeles Crime Novel." *Clues: A Journal of Detection* 17.2 (1996): 87–104.

Geherin, David. "Walter Mosley: South Central Los Angeles." *Scene of the Crime: The Importance of Place in Crime and Mystery Fiction*. Jefferson, NC: McFarland, 2008. 49–62.

Goeller, Alison D. "The Mystery of Identity: The Private Eye (I) in the Detective Fiction of Walter Mosley and Tony Hillerman." *Sleuthing Ethnicity: The Detective in Multiethnic Crime Fiction*. Ed. Dorothea Fischer-Hornung and Monika Mueller. Madison, NJ: 2003. 175–86.

Goodman, Robin Truth. "Terrorist Hunter: Walter Mosley, the Urban Plot, and the Terror War." *Cultural Critique* 66.(2007): 21–57.

Gray, W. Russel. "Hard-Boiled Black Easy: Genre Conventions in A Red Death." *African American Review* 38.3 (2004): 489–98.

Kennedy, Liam. "Black Noir: Race and Urban Space in Walter Mosley's Detective Fiction." *Diversity and Detective Fiction*. Ed. Kathleen Gregory Klein. Bowling Green, OH: Popular Press, 1999. 224–39.

King, Nicole. "'You Think Like You White': Questioning Race and Racial Community through the Lens of Middle-Class Desire(s)." *Novel: A Forum on Fiction* 35.2–3 (2002): 211–30.

Lock, Helen. "Invisible Detection: The Case of Walter Mosley." *MELUS: The Journal of the Society for the Study of the Multi-Ethnic Literature of the United States* 26.1 (2001): 77–89.

Lomax, Sara M. "Double Agent Easy Rawlins." *American Visions* 7.2 (April-May 1992): 32–34.

Mason, Theodore O., Jr. "Walter Mosley's Easy Rawlins: The Detective and Afro-American Fiction." *The Kenyon Review* 14.4 (1992): 173–83.

Mills, Alice. "Warring Ideals in Dark Bodies: Cultural Allegiances in the Work of Walter Mosley." *PALARA: Publication of the Afro-Latin/American Research Association* 4 (2000): 23–39.

Muller, Gilbert H. "Double Agent: The Los Angeles Crime Cycle of Walter Mosley." *Los Angeles in Fiction: A Collection of Essays: From James M. Cain to Walter Mosley*. Ed. David M. Fine. Albuquerque: University of New Mexico Press, 1995. 287–301.

Pepper, Andrew. "Bridges and Boundaries: Race, Ethnicity, and the Contemporary American Crime Novel." *Diversity and Detective Fiction*. Ed. Kathleen Gregory Klein. Bowling Green, OH: Popular Press, 1999. 240–59.

Wesley, Marilyn C. "Power and Knowledge in Walter Mosley's Devil in a Blue Dress." *African American Review* 35.1 (2001): 103–16.

Wilson, Charles E., Jr. *Walter Mosley: A Critical Companion*. Westport, CT: Greenwood, 2003.

Young, Mary. "Walter Mosley, Detective Fiction, and Black Culture." *Journal of Popular Culture* 32.1 (1998): 141–50.

Web Sites

Official Web site: http://www.waltermosley.com/.

"Mysteries of Walter Mosley." (fansite). No producer. n.d. http://www.math.buffalo.edu/~sww/mosley/mosley_walter_primer.html—Brief synopsis of major mysteries along with an overview of work as a whole (accessed November 1, 2010).

Muller, Marcia, 1944–

My fingertips touched the switch but before I could flip it, a dark figure appeared only a few feet away and then barreled into me, knocked me against the wall. My head bounced off the Sheetrock hard enough to blur my vision. In the next second I reeled backward through the door, spun around, and was down on my knees on the hard iron catwalk.

—*Locked In,* 2009

Biographical Sketch

Muller was born in Detroit, Michigan, the daughter of Henry J. and Kathryn Muller. She received B.A. and M.A. degrees from the University of Michigan, where a creative writing instructor told her she couldn't be a writer because she had nothing to say. After graduating, she worked as a freelance writer for magazines and held other jobs. Despite the instructor's verdict, she starting writing crime novels, but none was accepted for publication for several years. Her first publisher dropped its crime fiction line, and it was four years before another publisher accepted her work. Once she was over that hump, she went on to write more than thirty novels in the Sharon McCone series, as well as books in three other series. She has been married twice, the second time to Bill Pronzini, who is also a crime novelist. The couple shares the honor of both being named Grand Master. They live in Sonoma County, California.

Muller was the first author to make a success of a series featuring a hard-boiled female private detective, and she paved the way for authors such as Sue Grafton and Sara Paretsky. Muller is recognized for the realistic way in which she portrays her protagonist and for her vivid depiction of San Francisco. Over the course of the series, McCone learns more about her past as her life changes and her detective agency grows. In *Locked In,* one of the most recent entries in the series, McCone is shot in the head and paralyzed and can communicate only by blinking. Others carry out the burden of the action: it is an unusual approach for a crime novel to take. Muller's books have received critical praise, and she has received many awards from her peers and fans.

Categories: Hard-Boiled, Private Detective

Awards

Anthony Award for Best Novel (*Wolf in the Shadows,* 1994)
Anthony Award for Best Short Story Collection (*The McCone Files,* 1996)
Anthony Award for Lifetime Achievement (2005)
Edgar Grand Master Award for Lifetime Achievement (2005)
Shamus Award for Best PI Short Story ("Final Resting Place," *Justice for Hire,* ed. Bill Pronzini, 1991)
Shamus Eye Award for Lifetime Achievement (1993)
Shamus Award for Best Novel (*Locked In,* 2010)

Major Works

Sharon McCone series: *Edwin of the Iron Shoes* (1977), *Ask the Cards a Question* (1982), *The Cheshire Cat's Eye* (1983), *Games to Keep the Dark Away* (1984), *Leave a Message for Willie* (1984), *Double* (with Bill Pronzini, 1984), *There's Nothing to Be Afraid Of* (1985), *Eye of the Storm* (1988), *The Shape of Dread* (1989), *There's Something in a Sunday* (1989), *Trophies and Dead Things* (1990), *Where Echoes Live* (1991), *Pennies on a Dead Woman's Eyes* (1992), *Wolf in the Shadows* (1993), *Till the Butchers Cut Him Down* (1994), *A Wild and Lonely Place* (1995), *The McCone Files: The Complete Sharon McCone Stories* (1995), *The Broken Promise Land* (1996), *Both Ends of the Night* (1997), *While Other People Sleep* (1998), *Duo* (short stories with Bill Pronzini, 1998), *A Walk Through the Fire* (1999), *Listen to the Silence* (2000), *McCone and Friends* (short stories, 2000), *Season of Sharing* (with Bill Pronzini, 2001), *Dead Midnight* (2002), *The Dangerous Hour* (2004), *Vanishing Point* (2006), *The Ever-Running Man* (2007), *Burn Out* (2008), *Locked In* (2009), *Coming Back* (2010)

Elena Oliverez series: *The Tree of Death* (1983), *The Legend of the Slain Soldiers* (1985), *Beyond the Grave* (with Bill Pronzini, 1986)

Joanna Stark series: *The Cavalier in White* (1986), *There Hangs the Knife* (1988), *Dark Star* (1989)

Soledad County series: *Point Deception* (2001), *Cyanide Wells* (2003), *Cape Perdido* (2005)

Research Sources

Encyclopedias and Handbooks: BYA, CA (81–84, 242), CANR (41, 62, 97, 182), GWM, EMM, MCF, OCC, STJ, WWW

Bibliographies: FF, OM

Biographies and Interviews

Bibel, Barbara. "The Booklist Interview: Marcia Muller." *Booklist* 96.17 (May 1, 2000): 1596–97.

Clark, C. Hope. "Marcia Muller: Master Mystery Writer." *WOW! Women on Writing.* 2009. http://wow-womenonwriting.com/35-FE5-MarciaMuller.html (accessed November 1, 2010).

Grape, Jan. "Marcia Muller." *Speaking of Murder: Interviews with the Masters of Mystery and Suspense.* Ed. Ed Gorman and Martin H. Greenberg. New York: Berkley Prime Crime, 1998. 103–12.

Grape, Jan. "A Visit with Marcia Muller." *Deadly Women: The Woman Mystery Reader's Indispensable Companion.* Ed. Jan Grape et al. New York: Carroll & Graf, 1998. 307–12.

"Marcia Muller." *BookBrowse.com.* August 4, 2001. http://www.book browse.com/biographies/index.cfm/author_number/669/Marcia-Muller (accessed November 1, 2010).

"Marcia Muller." *Bookreporter.com.* July 2004. http://www.bookreporter. com/authors/au-muller-marcia.asp (accessed November 1, 2010).

"Marcia Muller: 2005 National Book Festival." (videocast) *Library of Congress.* September 24, 2005. http://www.loc.gov/today/cyberlc/feature_wdesc.php?rec=3739 (accessed November 1, 2010).

Koch, Pat. "PW Talks with Marcia Muller." *Publishers Weekly* 248.26 (June 25, 2001): 54.

Peters, Tim. "Muller and McCone: Parboiled Tough." *Publishers Weekly* 256.35 (August 31, 2009): 29.

Shechter, Andi. "Q&A: Marcia Muller & Bill Pronzini." *Library Journal.* 131.12 (July 15, 2006): 54. http://www.libraryjournal.com/article/CA6349034.html (accessed November 1, 2010).

Sims, Michael. "Marcia Muller Returns with Her 21st Sharon McCone Adventure." *BookPage.* 2000. http://www.bookpage.com/0008bp/marcia_muller.html (accessed November 1, 2010).

Criticism and Reader's Guides

Bairner, Alan. "Sharon McCone's San Francisco: The Role of the City in the Work of Marcia Muller." *Irish Journal of American Studies* 6 (1997): 117–38

Howe, Alexander N., and Christine A. Jackson, eds. *Marcia Muller and the Female Private Eye: Essays on the Novels that Defined a Subgenre.* Jefferson, NC: McFarland, 2008.

Isaac, Frederick. "Situation, Motivation, Resolution: An Afternoon with Marcia Muller." *Clues: A Journal of Detection* 5.2 (1984): 20–34.

Martin, Rebecca E. "Marcia Muller." *American Hard-Boiled Crime Writers* (*Dictionary of Literary Biography* 226). Ed. George Parker Anderson and Julie B. Anderson. Detroit, MI: Gale, 2000. 267–82.

Muller, Marcia. "A Novelist's Life Is Altered by Her Alter Ego." *Writers on Writing: More Collected Essays from the New York Times, II.* Ed. Jane Smiley. New York: Holt, 2003. 175–79.

Muller, Marcia. "Partners in Crime: Developing a Series Character." *They Wrote the Book: Thirteen Women Mystery Writers Tell All.* Ed. Helen Windrath. Duluth, MN: Spinsters Ink, 2000. 49–58.

Muller, Marcia. "The Real McCone." *Armchair Detective: A Quarterly Journal Devoted to the Appreciation of Mystery, Detective, and Suspense Fiction* 23.3 (1990): 260–69.

Wilson, Ann. "The Female Dick and the Crisis of Heterosexuality." *Feminism in Women's Detective Fiction.* Ed. Glenwood Irons. Toronto: University of Toronto Press, 1995. 148–56.

Web Site

Official Web site: http://marciamuller.com/ (accessed November 1, 2010).

Paretsky, Sara, 1947–

*I pointed the light at her chest, as if I might be able to detect her lungs,
and recoiled in horror. The front of her dress was black with blood. It had
oozed through the thin fabric, sticking it to her body like a large bandage.
Dirt and blood streaked her arms; her left humerus poked through the skin
like a knitting needle out of a skein of wool.*

—*Hard Time*, 1999

Biographical Sketch

Sara Paretsky was born in Ames, Iowa, the daughter of a scientist and a
librarian. She attended the University of Kansas, where she received a B.A.
She later received an M.B.A. and a Ph.D. in history from the University
of Chicago. She married Courtenay Wright, a professor, in 1976 and has
three children. She worked as a writer, publications manager, advertising
manager, and manager of direct marketing for various business organizations. In 1986, she became a full-time writer. She has a passion for social
justice and is involved in many groups that address various social problems.
This passion is reflected in her novels. She also wanted to create a strong
female character who would counteract some of the gender stereotypes in
the crime fiction genre at the time. In 1986, she founded Sisters in Crime,
an organization that supports women crime authors (http://www.sistersin-
crime.org/).

Paretsky's series character, V. I. Warshawski, is a half-Polish, half-Italian,
tough, street-wise private detective. Paretsky has been praised for her characterizations, and her novels address some of the social issues that are dear to
her heart through the fictional plots. They are set in her hometown of Chicago and give a gritty portrayal of the city. She has been widely recognized by
her peers and is popular with readers.

Categories: Hard-Boiled, Private Detective

Awards

Gold Dagger Award for Best Novel (*Blacklist*, 2004)
Silver Dagger Award for Runner-up for Best Novel (*Toxic Shock*, 1988)
Diamond Dagger Award for Lifetime Achievement (2002)
Shamus Award for Lifetime Achievement (2005)

Major Works

V. I. Warshawski series: *Indemnity Only* (1982), *Deadlock* (1984), *Killing Orders* (1985), *Bitter Medicine* (1987), *Blood Shot* (U.K. title *Toxic Shock*, 1988), *Burn Marks* (1990), *Guardian Angel* (1992), *Tunnel Vision* (1994), *Windy City Blues* (short stories, 1995), *Hard Time* (1999), *Total Recall* (2001), *Blacklist* (2003), *Fire Sale* (2005), *Hardball* (2009), *Body Work* (2010)
Nonfiction: *Writing in an Age of Silence* (2007)

Research Sources

Encyclopedias and Handbooks: 100, BYA, CA (129), CANR (59, 95, 184), CLC (135), EMM, GWM, MCF, OCC, STJ, WWW

Bibliographies: FF, OM

Biographies and Interviews

Abbe, Elfrieda. "Risky Business: Sara Paretsky Pushes the Boundaries of Her Detective Series." *The Writer*. 116.10 (October 2003): 22 +. http://www.writermag.com/wrt/default.aspx?c=a&id=1165 (accessed November 1, 2010).

Cornwell, Bob. "'Anger Is a Very Bad Place to Start' Says Sara Paretsky: An Interview." *Tangled Web UK Crimescene*. n.d. http://www.twbooks.co.uk/crimescene/Sara-Paretsky-An-interview-by-Bob-Cornwell.htm (accessed November 1, 2010).

Ensor, Sarah. "Interview: Sara Paretsky." *Socialist Review*. April 2008. http://www.socialistreview.org.uk/article.php?articlenumber=10351 (accessed November 1, 2010).

Goldenberg, Suzanne. "Interview." *Guardian.co.uk*. March 22, 2008. http://www.guardian.co.uk/lifeandstyle/2008/mar/22/familyandrelationships.crimebooks (accessed November 1, 2010).

Kaminsky, Stuart, and Laurie Roberts. "Sara Paretsky." *Behind the Mystery: Top Mystery Writers Interviewed*. Cohasset, Mass.: Hot House, 2005. 188–99.

Paretsky, Sara, and Monica Hileman. "Women, Mystery, and Sleuthing in the '80s." *Sojourner: The Women's Forum* 14.7 (March 1989): 16–17.

Peters, Barbara. "Sara Paretsky." (videocast—6 parts) *Poisoned Pen Bookstore*. August 8, 2007. http://www.poisonedpen.com/interviews/sarah-paretsky; Also at http://www.youtube.com/watch?v=jHSeGLKGKnM (accessed November 1, 2010).

Richards, Linda. "January Interview: Sara Paretsky." *January Magazine*. November 2001. http://januarymagazine.com/profiles/paretsky.html (accessed November 1, 2010).

Rozan, S. J. "Sara Paretsky: A Gun of One's Own." *Publishers Weekly* 246.43 (October 25, 1999): 44.

"Sara Paretsky." *Shots Magazine.* March 2006. http://www.shotsmag.co.uk/author_profiles/s_paretsky/s_paretsky.html (accessed November 1, 2010).

"Sara Paretsky." (audiocast) *WETA Book Studio.* n.d. http://www.thebookstudio.com/authors/sara-paretsky (accessed November 1, 2010).

"Sara Paretsky: Collaring Whitecollar Crime." *Crescent City Blues* 2.6 (1999). http://www.crescentblues.com/2_6issue/paretsky.shtml (accessed November 1, 2010).

"Sara Paretsky: 'Fire Sale.'" (videocast) *Library of Congress.* February 27, 2007. http://www.loc.gov/today/cyberlc/feature_wdesc.php?rec=4033. Also at http://www.youtube.com/watch?v=ikBfYY82Dp0 (accessed November 1, 2010).

"Sara Paretsky: Heartache in the Heartland." *Independent.co.uk.* March 28, 2008. http://www.independent.co.uk/arts-entertainment/books/features/sara-paretsky-heartache-in-the-heartland-801488.html (accessed November 1, 2010).

Swain, Don. "Interview with Sara Paretsky." (audiocast) *Wired for Books.* February 6, 1992. http://wiredforbooks.org/saraparetsky/index.htm (accessed November 1, 2010).

Criticism and Reader's Guides

Bakerman, Jane S. "Living 'Openly and with Dignity': Sara Paretsky's New-Boiled Feminist Fiction." *Midamerica: The Yearbook of the Society for the Study of Midwestern Literature* 12 (1985): 120–35.

Biamonte, Gloria A. "Funny, Isn't It?: Testing the Boundaries of Gender and Genre in Women's Detective Fiction." *Look Who's Laughing: Gender and Comedy.* Ed. Jane Finney. Langhorne, PA: Gordon and Breach, 1994. 231–54.

Bickford, Donna M. "Homeless Women and Social Justice in Sara Paretsky's Tunnel Vision." *Clues: A Journal of Detection* 25.2 (2007): 45–52.

Dayton, Tim. "New Maps of Chicago: Sara Paretsky's 'Blood Shot.'" *Clues: A Journal of Detection* 25.2 (2007): 65–77.

Décuré, Nicole. "V. I. Warshawski, a 'Lady with Guts': Feminist Crime Fiction by Sara Paretsky." *Women's Studies International Forum* 12.2 (1989): 227–38.

Dempsey, Peter. "Sara Paretsky." *American Mystery and Detective Writers* (*Dictionary of Literary Biography* 306). Ed. George Parker Anderson. Detroit, MI: Thomson Gale, 2005. 306–20.

Dolan, Jill. "Sara Paretsky." *100 Masters of Mystery and Detection, vol. 2.* Ed. Fiona Kelleghan. Pasadena, CA: Salem Press, 2001. 487–93.

Edgington, K. "Defining the Enemy: Housewives and Detectives." *Clues: A Journal of Detection* 25.2 (2007): 55–63.

Ford, Susan Allen. "Detecting (and Teaching) the Gothic." *Studies in Popular Culture* 24.1 (2001): 47–57.

Ford, Susan Allen. "Ruined Landscapes, Flooding Tunnels, Dark Paths: Sara Paretsky's Gothic Vision." *Clues: A Journal of Detection* 25.2 (2007): 7–18.

Geherin, David. "Sara Paretsky: Chicago." In *Scene of the Crime.* Jefferson, NC: McFarland, 2008. 81–92.

Gladsky, Thomas S. "Consent, Descent, and Transethnicity in Sara Paretsky's Fiction." *Clues: A Journal of Detection* 16.2 (1995): 1–15.

Goldstein, Philip. "The Politics of Sara Paretsky's Detective Fiction." *Reader: Essays in Reader-Oriented Theory, Criticism, and Pedagogy* 55 (2006): 71–84.

Irons, Glenwood H. "Gender and Genre: The Woman Detective and the Diffusion of Generic Voices." *Feminism in Women's Detective Fiction.* Toronto: University of Toronto Press, 1995. viii–xxii.

Irons, Glenwood H. "New Women Detectives: G Is for Gender-Bending." *Gender, Language, and Myth: Essays and Popular Narrative.* Toronto: University of Toronto Press, 1992. 127–41.

Johnson, Patricia E. "Sex and Betrayal in the Detective Fiction of Sue Grafton and Sara Paretsky." *Journal of Popular Culture* 27.4 (1994): 97–106.

Jones, Louise Conley. "Feminism and the P. I. Code: Or, 'Is a Hard-Boiled Warshawski Unsuitable to Be Called a Feminist?'" *Clues: A Journal of Detection* 16.1 (1995): 77–87.

Kaufman, Natalie Hevener, and Carrollee Kaufman Hevener. "Mythical Musical Connections: The Mother-Daughter Bond in the Work of Sara Paretsky." *Clues: A Journal of Detection* 25.2 (2007): 19–28.

Kinsman, Margaret. "A Band of Sisters." *The Art of Detective Fiction.* Basingstoke, England; New York: Macmillan; St. Martin's, with Institute of English Studies, School of Advanced Study, University of London, 2000. 153–69.

Kinsman, Margaret. "A Question of Visibility: Paretsky and Chicago." *Women Times Three.* Ed. Kathleen Gregory Klein. OH: Popular Press, 1995. 15–27.

Kinsman, Margaret. "'Different and Yet the Same': Women's Worlds/Women's Lives and the Classroom." *Diversity and Detective Fiction.* Ed. Kathleen Gregory Klein. Bowling Green, OH: Popular Press, 1999. 5–21.

Kinsman, Margaret. "Sara Paretsky." *Mystery and Suspense Writers: The Literature of Crime, Detection, and Espionage.* Ed. Robin W. Winks and Maureen Corrigan. New York: Scribner's, 1998. 699–713.

Littler, Alison. "Marele Day's 'Cold Hard Bitch': The Masculinist Imperatives of the Private-Eye Genre." *Journal of Narrative Technique* 21.1 (1991): 121–35.

Pope, Rebecca A. "'Friends Is a Weak Word for It': Female Friendship and the Spectre of Lesbianism in Sara Paretsky." *Feminism in Women's Detective Fiction.* Ed. Glenwood H. Irons. Toronto: University of Toronto Press, 1995. 157–70.

Reddy, Maureen T. "The Feminist Counter-Tradition in Crime: Cross, Grafton, Paretsky, and Wilson." *The Cunning Craft: Original Essays on Detective Fiction and Contemporary Literary Theory*. Ed. Ronald G. Walker and June M. Frazer. Macomb: Western Illinois University Press, 1990. 174–87.

Reynolds, Moira Davison. "Sara Paretsky." *Women Authors of Detective Series: Twenty-One American and British Writers, 1900–2000*. Jefferson, NC: McFarland, 2001. 139–44.

Schaffer, Rachel. "V. I. Talks Back: Sara Paretsky's Unlikable Characters as Foes and Foils." *Clues: A Journal of Detection* 25.2 (2007): 31–42.

Svoboda, Frederic. "Hard-Boiled Feminist Detectives and Their Families: Reimaging a Form." *Gender in Popular Culture: Images of Men and Women in Literature, Visual Media, and Material Culture*. Ed. Peter C. Rollins and Susan W. Rollins. Cleveland, OH: Ridgemont, 1995. 247–72.

Walton, Priscilla L. "Paretsky's V.I. as P.I.: Revising the Script and Recasting the Dick." *Lit: Literature Interpretation Theory* 4.3 (1993): 203–13.

Weatherston, Rosemary. "Reading Students Reading Detectives." *Murder 101: Essays on the Teaching of Detective Fiction*. Ed. Edward J. Reilly. Jefferson, NC: McFarland, 2009. 206–16.

Wilson, Ann. "The Female Dick and the Crisis of Heterosexuality." *Feminism in Women's Detective Fiction*. Ed. Glenwood H. Irons. Toronto: University of Toronto Press, 1995. 148–56.

Web Site

Official Web site—http://www.saraparetsky.com/ (accessed November 1, 2010).

Parker, Robert B., 1932–2010

"Look, Dr. Forbes, I went to college once, I don't wear my hat indoors. And if a clue comes along and bites me on the ankle, I grab it. I am not, however, an Oxford don. I am a private detective. Is there something you'd like me to detect, or are you just polishing up your elocution for next year's commencement?"

—The Godwulf Manuscript, 1974

Biographical Sketch

Born in Springfield, Massachusetts, Parker attended Colby College, where he met his future wife, Joan Hall. After receiving a B.A., in 1954, he served in the U.S. Army in Korea. He received an M.A. in English from Boston University and later achieved a Ph.D. in American and English literature from that same institution in 1971. Prior to that, he worked as a technical and business writer before becoming an English educator at various institutions of higher education in Massachusetts. He was a professor at Northeastern University, when he submitted his first manuscript, *The Godwulf Manuscript,* for publication. It was quickly accepted, and he was launched on a career that saw the publication of more than sixty books. He and his wife had two sons and an enduring marriage—he dedicated most of his books to her.

Parker did his dissertation on Chandler and Hammett, and his hero, Spenser, is cast in that same mold, brought up to date for the late twentieth century. His books are praised for their sharp dialog and vivid characterizations, as well as their strong depiction of the Boston area. He was also the author of a western series about itinerant lawmen. Before his death, he received three major lifetime achievement awards for his crime fiction.

Categories: Hard-Boiled, Private Detective

Awards

Anthony Award for Lifetime Achievement (2006)
Edgar Award for Best Novel *(Promised Land,* 1977)
Edgar Grand Master Award for Lifetime Achievement (2002)
Shamus Eye Award for Lifetime Achievement (1995)

Major Works

Spenser series: *The Godwulf Manuscript* (1974), *God Save the Child* (1974), *Mortal Stakes* (1975), *Promised Land* (1976), *The Judas Goat* (1978), *Looking for Rachel Wallace* (1980), *Early Autumn* (1981), *A Savage Place* (1981), *Ceremony* (1982), *The Widening Gyre* (1983), *Valediction* (1984), *A Catskill Eagle* (1985), *Taming a Sea-Horse* (1986), *Pale Kings and Princes* (1987), *Crimson Joy* (1988), *Playmates* (1989), *Stardust* (1990), *Pastime* (1991), *Double Deuce* (1992), *Paper Doll* (1993), *Walking Shadow* (1994), *Thin Air* (1995), *Chance* (1996), *Small Vices* (1997), *Sudden Mischief* (1998), *Hush Money* (1999), *Potshot* (2001), *Hugger Mugger* (2001), *Widow's Walk* (2002), *Back Story* (2003), *Bad Business* (2004), *Cold Service* (2005), *School Days* (2005), *Hundred-Dollar Baby* (2006), *Now and Then* (2007), *Rough Weather* (2008), *The Professional* (2009), *Painted Ladies* (2010)
Jesse Stone series: *Night Passage* (1997), *Trouble in Paradise* (1998), *Death in Paradise* (2001), *Stone Cold* (2003), *Sea Change* (2006), *High Profile* (2007), *Stranger in Paradise* (2008), *Night and Day* (2009), *Split Image* (2010)
Sunny Randall series: *Family Honor* (1999), *Perish Twice* (2000), *Shrink Rap* (2002), *Melancholy Baby* (2004), *Blue Screen* (2006), *Spare Change* (2007)

Nonseries novels: *Wilderness* (1979), *Poodle Springs* (with Raymond Chandler, 1989), *Perchance to Dream* (a sequel to Chandler's *The Big Sleep*, 1991), *All Our Yesterdays* (1994)

Nonfiction: *Order and Diversity: The Craft of Prose* (with Peter L. Sandberg, 1973), *The Private Eye in Hammett and Chandler* (1984), *Parker on Writing* (1985)

Research Sources

Encyclopedias and Handbooks: 100, BEA, BEB, CA (49–52), CANR (1, 26, 52, 89, 128, 165), CLC (27), EMM, MCF, OCC, STJ, WWW

Bibliographies: FF, OM

Biographies and Interviews

Berlin, Eric. "Dumpster Bust Interviews Robert B. Parker." *BlogCritics.* March 14, 2005. http://blogcritics.org/books/article/dumpster-bust-interviews-robert-b-parker/ (accessed October 13, 2010).

Carr, John C. "Robert B. Parker." *The Craft of Crime: Conversations with Crime Writers.* Boston: Houghton Mifflin, 1983. 143–75.

Kaminsky, Stuart, and Laurie Roberts. "Robert B. Parker." *Behind the Mystery: Top Mystery Writers Interviewed.* Cohasset, MA: Hot House, 2005. 80–91.

Kurata, Marilyn J. "Robert B. Parker: An Interview." *Clues: A Journal of Detection* 12.1 (1991): 1–31.

Leith, Sam. "Robert B. Parker: Hard-Boiled, Old School and Y'know, a Bit Sloppy." *Telegraph.co.uk.* February 23, 2008. http://www.telegraph.co.uk/culture/books/3671370/Robert-B-Parker-Hard-boiled-old-school-and-yknow-a-bit-sloppy.html (accessed November 1, 2010).

Liukkonen, Petri. "Robert B(rown) Parker (1932–2010)." *Books and Writers.* 2010. http://www.kirjasto.sci.fi/parker.htm (accessed November 1, 2010).

Neary, Lynn. "Parker Explores the Shadows of Boston's Back Bay." (audiocast) *Morning Edition, NPR.* July 11, 2008. http://www.npr.org/templates/story/story.php?storyId=92374946 (accessed November 1, 2010).

Older, J. "Private I" [Interview with R. B. Parker]. *Yankee* 67.8 (October 2003): 72–75.

Parker, R. B. "How I Write." *The Writer* 116.1 (January 2003): 66. http://www.writermag.com/Articles/2002/12/Robert%20B%20Parker.aspx (accessed November 1, 2010).

Ponder, Anne. "A Dialogue with Robert B. Parker." *Armchair Detective: A Quarterly Journal Devoted to the Appreciation of Mystery, Detective, and Suspense Fiction* 17.4 (1984): 340–48.

"Robert B. Parker." *Bookreporter.com*. April 4, 2000. http://www.bookre porter.com/authors/au-parker-robert.asp (accessed November 1, 2010).

"Robert B. Parker." (obituary) *The Telegraph*. January 20, 2010. http:// www.telegraph.co.uk/news/obituaries/culture-obituaries/books-obituaries/7038200/Robert-B-Parker.html (accessed November 1, 2010).

"Robert B. Parker." *ThrillingDetective.com*. 2010. http://www.thrillingdetec tive.com/trivia/parker.html (accessed November 1, 2010).

"Robert B. Parker: An Interview." *New Black Mask* 1 (1985): 1–10.

"Robert B. Parker: Bookfest 04." (videocast) *Library of Congress*. October 9, 2004. http://www.loc.gov/today/cyberlc/feature_wdesc.php?rec=3621 (accessed November 1, 2010).

Silet, Charles L. P. "Robert B. Parker." In *Speaking of Murder, vol. 2: In-terviews with the Masters of Mystery and Suspense*. Ed. Ed Gorman and Martin H. Greenberg. New York: Berkley Prime Crime, 1999. 211–24.

Silet, Charles L. P. "Robert B. Parker Author Interview on Writing Myster-ies." *MysteryNet.com*. n.d. http://www.mysterynet.com/books/testimony/ fivepages/ (accessed November 1, 2010).

Swaim, Don. "Audio Interviews with Robert B. Parker." (audiocasts) *Wired for Books*. May 11, 1984; June 11, 1986. http://wiredforbooks.org/robert parker/ (accessed November 1, 2010).

Weber, Bruce. "Robert B. Parker, the Prolific Writer Who Created Spenser, Is Dead at 77." *New York Times*. January 20, 2010. http://www.nytimes. com/2010/01/20/books/20parker.html (accessed November 1, 2010).

Zaleski, Jeff. "*PW* Talks with Robert B. Parker." *Publisher's Weekly* 248.41 (October 8,2001): 46–47.

Criticism and Reader's Guides

Amis, Martin. "Chandler Prolonged." *The War against Cliché*. New York: Hyperion, 2001. 215–18.

Carter, Steven R. "Spenserian Ethics: The Unconventional Morality of Rob-ert B. Parker's Traditional American Hero." *Clues: A Journal of Detec-tion* 1.2 (1980): 109–18.

Casella, Donna R. "The Trouble with Susan: Women in Robert B. Parker's Spenser Novels." *Clues: A Journal of Detection* 10.2 (1989): 93–105.

Corrigan, Maureen. "Robert B. Parker." *Mystery and Suspense Writers: The Literature of Crime, Detection, and Espionage, II*. Ed. Robin W. Winks and Maureen Corrigan. New York: Scribner's, 1998. 715–32.

Eisman, Gregory D. "The Catskill Eagle Crashed: The Moral Demise of Spenser in Robert B. Parker's *A Catskill Eagle*." *Clues: A Journal of De-tection* 11.1 (1990): 107–17.

Fackler, Herbert V. "Dialectic in the Corpus of Robert B. Parker's Spenser Novels." *Clues: A Journal of Detection* 16.1 (1995): 13–24.

Fackler, Herbert V. "Spenser's New England Conscience." *Colby Quarterly* 34.3 (1998): 253–60.

Freier, Mary P. "Information Ethics in the Detective Novel." *Clues: A Journal of Detection* 24.1 (2005): 18–26.

Geherin, David. "Robert B. Parker." *Sons of Sam Spade: The Private-Eye Novel in the 70s.* New York: Ungar, 1982. 5–82.

Geherin, David. "Spenser." *The American Private Eye: The Image in Fiction.* New York: Ungar, 1985. 164–66.

Gray, W. Russel. "Reflections in a Private Eye: Robert B. Parker's Spenser." *Clues: A Journal of Detection* 5.1 (1984): 1–13.

Greiner, Donald J. "Robert B. Parker and the Jock of the Mean Streets." *Critique: Studies in Contemporary Fiction* 26.1 (1984): 36–44.

Harper, Donna Waller. "Robert B. Parker." *American Mystery and Detective Writers* (*Dictionary of Literary Biography* 306). Ed. George Parker Anderson. Detroit, MI: Thomson Gale, 2005. 321–32.

Hoffman, Carl. "Spenser: The Illusion of Knighthood." *Armchair Detective: A Quarterly Journal Devoted to the Appreciation of Mystery, Detective, and Suspense Fiction* 16.2 (1983): 131–43.

Lorenz, Janet E. "Robert B. Parker." *100 Masters of Mystery and Detection, vol. 2.* Ed. Fiona Kelleghan. Pasadena, CA: Salem Press, 2001. 494–501.

Parker, Robert B. "Spenser." *The Lineup: The World's Greatest Crime Writers Tell the Inside Story of Their Greatest Detectives.* Ed. Otto Penzler. New York: Little, Brown, 2009. 291–332.

Parker, Robert B., and Anne Ponder. "What I Know about Writing Spenser Novels." *Colloquium on Crime: Eleven Renowned Mystery Writers Discuss Their Work.* Ed. Robin W. Winks. New York: Scribner's, 1996. 189–203.

Presley, John W. "Theory into Practice: Robert Parker's Re-Interpretation of the American Tradition." *Journal of American Culture* 12.3 (1989): 27–30.

Robinson, Doug. *No Less a Man: Masculist Art in a Feminist Age.* Bowling Green, OH: Popular Press, 1994.

Root, Christina. "Silence of the Other: Women in Robert Parker's Spenser Series." *Clues: A Journal of Detection* 19.1 (1998): 25–38.

Rose, Lloyd. "A Literary Hybrid." *Atlantic* 264.4 (October, 1989): 113+.

Saylor, V. Louise. "The Private Eye and His Victuals." *Clues: A Journal of Detection* 5.2 (1984): 111–18.

Schaefer, Eric, and Eithne Johnson. "Quarantine! A Case Study of Boston's Combat Zone." *Hop on Pop: The Politics and Pleasures of Popular Culture.* Ed. Henry Jenkins, et al. Durham, NC: Duke University Press, 2002. 430–53.

So, Gerald. "Spencer and Hawk: A Study of Good and Evil in the Fiction of Robert B. Parker." *ThrillingDetective.com.* October 2002. http://www.thrillingdetective.com/non_fiction/e001.html. (accessed November 1, 2010)

"Spencer." *ThrillingDetective.com*. 2010. http://www.thrillingdetective.com/ spenser.html (accessed November 1, 2010).

Svoboda, Frederic. "Hard-Boiled Feminist Detectives and Their Families: Re-imaging a Form." *Gender in Popular Culture: Images of Men and Women in Literature, Visual Media, and Material Culture*. Ed. Peter C. Rollins and Susan W. Rollins. Cleveland, OH: Ridgemont, 1995. 247–72.

Tallett, Dennis. *The Spenser Companion: The Godwulf Manuscript to Hugger Mugger, a Reader's Guide*. California: Companion Books, 2001.

Taylor, Rhonda Harris. "'It's about Who Controls the Information': Mystery Antagonists and Information Literacy." *Clues: A Journal of Detection* 24.1 (2005): 7–17.

Zalewski, James W., and Lawrence B. Rosenfield. "Rules for the Game of Life: The Mysteries of Robert B. Parker and Dick Francis." *Clues: A Journal of Detection* 5.2 (1984): 72–81.

Web Sites

Official Web site: http://www.robertbparker.net/ (accessed November 1, 2010).

Robert B. Parker blog: http://robertbparker.typepad.com/robertbparker/— last updated in May 2009 (accessed November 1, 2010).

If You Like Robert B. Parker

Parker is best known for his series of novels about Spenser, a Boston P.I. A notable feature of the books is his relationship with his girlfriend, Susan Silverman, and his friend Hawk. Although the books are classified as hard-boiled, Spenser is more introspective than many private eyes in the genre.

You Might Like

Philip R. Craig

The Martha's Vineyard series features J. W. Jackson, a retired policeman who does odd jobs and security work and occasionally is hired as a private inves-tigator. His relationship with his girlfriend (later wife), Zee Madieras, is an important part of the stories, as is his love of fishing and eating. Titles include *A Beautiful Place to Die* and *The Woman Who Walked into the Sea*; there are 17 more.

Harlen Coben

Coben's Myron Bolitar books all have sports themes that grow out of Boli-tar's work as an agent for professional athletes. Myron, his friend Win, and his assistant, Esperanza, solve a variety of mysterious happenings during the course of nine books. The amoral Win is somewhat reminiscent of Hawk. The series begins with *Deal Breaker*.

Jeremiah Healy

The John Francis Cuddy books share the Boston ambience of the Spenser books. Private investigator Cuddy's wife is dead, but he often visits her graveside to chat. The Cuddy books are gritty and hard-boiled, and the series starts with *Blunt Darts*.

Bill Pronzini

Pronzini's series is known as the "Nameless" detective series; we never find out the name of the chief protagonist. "Nameless" runs a detective agency with the aid of a young black woman and an ex-cop. Set in San Francisco, the novels have a noirish feel but are not as violent as some others in the genre. Start with *The Snatch,* followed by *The Vanished* and more than thirty other titles.

William G. Tapply

Another series set in Boston, the Brady Coyne books depict a lawyer-sleuth whose cases often arise from bad things that have happened to friends and loved ones. This series features strong plotting and an appealing protagonist. Titles in this long-running series include *Death at Charity's Point* and *The Dutch Blue Error.*

Patterson, James, 1947–

God, the woods were almost pitch-black back in here. A quarter moon drooping over the thick forest canopy did little to light the ground below. Trees were shadows. Thorns and brambles were invisible in the underbrush; they pierced and raked her legs bloody as she pushed through. What little she'd been wearing to begin with—just an expensive black lace teddy—now hung in shreds off her shoulders.

—*I, Alex Cross,* 2009

Biographical Sketch

Born in Newbaugh, New York, Patterson attended Manhattan College, where he graduated summa cum laude, and Vanderbilt University, from which he received an M.A. in 1970. He started working for J. Walter Thompson advertising agency as a junior copywriter and eventually rose to be CEO and then chairman of the company. He is very active in the support of literacy and sponsors the Pageturner Awards, has a Web site that aims to hook young people up with good books, and donates thousands of books to troops overseas. In 2007, he received the ThrillerMaster Award from the International Thriller Writers. He is married and has two children.

Patterson's books have been wildly popular with the reading public, having sold an estimated one hundred and seventy million copies worldwide (official website). His most notable series is the Alex Cross novels. In recent years, most of the books appearing under his name have been coauthored with others. In addition to his adult books, Patterson is also the author of the Maximum Ride series for young adults, which is also very popular and which has spun off a graphic novel adaptation series.

Categories: Police Procedural, Thriller

Awards

Edgar Award for Best First Novel by American Author (*The Thomas Berryman Number,* 1977)

Major Works (only solo-authored works are listed)

Alex Cross series: *Along Came a Spider* (1993), *Kiss the Girls* (1995), *Jack and Jill* (1996), *Cat and Mouse* (1997), *Pop Goes the Weasel* (1999), *Roses are Red* (2000), *Violets Are Blue* (2001), *Four Blind Mice* (2002), *The Big Bad Wolf* (2003), *London Bridges* (2004), *Mary, Mary* (2005), *Cross* (2006), *Double Cross* (2007), *Cross Country* (2008), *I, Alex Cross* (2009), *Cross Fire* (2010)

Nonseries novels: *The Thomas Berryman Number* (1976), *Season of the Machete* (1977), *The Jericho Commandment* (reprinted as *See How They Run,* 1979), *Virgin* (reprinted as *Cradle and All*, 1980), *Black Market* (reprinted as *Black Friday,* 1986), *The Midnight Club* (1989), *Hide and Seek* (1996), *When the Wind Blows* (1998), *The Lake House* (2003)

Research Sources

Encyclopedias and Handbooks: 100, CA (133), CANR (71, 113, 168), MCF

Bibliographies: FF, OM

Biographies and Interviews

Brookman, R. "Have You Read a Patterson Lately?" *Book* (Summit, NJ) 27 (March–April 2003): 44–48.

"First Book Interview with James Patterson." *First Book.* May 20, 2006. http://www.youtube.com/watch?v=urzcoUcE-gU (accessed November 1, 2010).

Frumkes, Lewis Burke. "A Conversation with James Patterson." *Writer* 113.11 (2000): 13.

Gross, Andrew. "The Patterson School of Writing." *Publishers Weekly* 254.18 (April 30, 2007): 168.

Grossman, Lev. "James Patterson: The Man Who Can't Miss." *Time* 167.12 (2006): 106–15. http://www.time.com/time/magazine/article/0,9171,1172251,00.html (accessed November 1, 2010).

Harmon, Melissa Burdick. "Tangents." *Biography* 2.5 (1998): 28+.

Hayward, Lisa. "Legends and Legacies: James Patterson." *WPBF.* November 5, 2007. http://www.youtube.com/watch?v=FHA1XibOHB4 (accessed November 1, 2010).

"James Patterson: 2009 National Book Festival." (audiocast and videocast) *Library of Congress.* September 26, 2009. http://www.loc.gov/today/cyberlc/feature_wdesc.php?rec=4720 (accessed November 1, 2010).

"James Patterson." *Bookreporter.com.* December 21, 2001. http://www.bookre porter.com/authors/au-patterson-james.asp (accessed November 1, 2010).

"James Patterson." *Jrank.org.* n.d. http://biography.jrank.org/pages/1884/Patterson-James-1947.html (accessed November 1, 2010).

"James Patterson Interviewed for the London Book Fair." *London Book Fair.* June 17, 2009. http://www.youtube.com/watch?v=KXTo1sNvlJ4 (part 1); http://www.youtube.com/watch?v=dxAbV9nsGZ0 (part 2) (accessed November 1, 2010).

Kellner, Tomas. "Stranger Than Fiction." *Forbes* 170.9 (2002): 110–14.

Leddy, Chuck. "Authors Face Pressure to Commit to One-Book-a-Year Schedule." *Writer* 122.1 (2009): 8–9.

Mahler, Jonathan. "James Patterson, Inc." *New York Times.* January 20, 2010. http://www.nytimes.com/2010/01/24/magazine/24patterson-t.html (accessed November 1, 2010).

"Man with a Mission." *Booklist* 102.18 (2006): 54.

McMains, A. "James Patterson: On the Spot." *Adweek* 45.45 (November 29, 2004): 20.

"Profile: James Patterson." *Sunday Times.* February 10, 2008. http://entertainment.timesonline.co.uk/tol/arts_and_entertainment/books/article3341748.ece (accessed November 1, 2010).

Rich, Motoko. "An Author Looks beyond Age Limits." *New York Times* (February 20, 2008): 1. http://www.nytimes.com/2008/02/20/books/20patt.html (accessed October 31, 2010).

Speidel, Maria. "A Killer at Thrillers." *People* 43.11 (1995): 83.

Thornton, Matthew. "Patterson Aplenty." *Publishers Weekly* 255.18 (May 5, 2008): 27. http://www.publishersweekly.com/article/391991-Patterson_Aplenty.php (accessed November 1, 2010).

Wood, Gaby. "The World's No. 1 Bestseller." *Guardian.co.uk: The Observer.* April 5, 2009. http://www.guardian.co.uk/books/2009/apr/05/james-patterson-author-bestseller (accessed November 1, 2010).

Zaleski, Jeff. "The James Patterson Business." *Publishers Weekly* 249.44 (November 4, 2002): 43–55.

Criticism and Reader's Guides

Gregoriou, Christiana. "Criminally Minded: The Stylistics of Justification in Contemporary American Crime Fiction." *Style* 37.2 (2003): 144–59.

Gregoriou, Christiana. "Demystifying the Criminal Mind: Linguistic, Social and Generic Deviance in Contemporary American Crime Fiction." *Working with English: Medieval and Modern Language, Literature and Drama* 1 (2003): 1–15.

Kotker, Joan G. *James Patterson: A Critical Companion.* Westport, CT: Greenwood, 2004.

Taylor, Rhonda Harris. "'It's about Who Controls the Information': Mystery Antagonists and Information Literacy." *Clues: A Journal of Detection* 24.1 (2005): 7–17.

Web Site

Official Web site: http://www.jamespatterson.com/ (accessed November 1, 2010).

Perry, Anne (Juliet Hulme), 1938–

"Bruises." Cutler answered gravely.

Pitt frowned. "I saw none."

"On the heels. Quite hard. If you came upon a man in his bath, it would be far easier to drown him by grasping hold of his heels and pulling them upward, thereby forcing his head under the water, than it would be to try forcing his shoulders down, leaving his arms free to struggle with you."

—Bluegate Fields, 1984

Biographical Sketch

Juliet Marion Hulme was born in Blackheath, England. She suffered from a number of illnesses as a child and was eventually sent to the Bahamas to live with a foster family in order to restore her health. The family moved to an island off New Zealand, and she received a spotty education, mostly at home. Many years later, she acknowledged that, while a teen, she was tried and convicted in New Zealand of helping a friend murder the friend's mother. This revelation came about as a result of the release of the film *Heavenly Creatures,* which was based on a newspaper account of the crime. As an adult, she lived in England and California and had a number of different jobs, including flight attendant, salesclerk, insurance underwriter, and limousine dispatcher. She finally returned to England when her stepfather became ill. She was writing all this time, but it took a number of years before anything was accepted for publication and she was finally able to become a full-time writer. She now lives in Scotland.

Perry's books have been praised for their strong plotting and characterizations, as well as for their attention to social problems and injustices of Victorian times. The Reavley series, set during World War I, carries the mystery through all five books as the Reavley siblings attempt to find the person responsible for the murder of their parents. The horrors of trench warfare and the overall hardships of the war are strong elements of the novels. Perry's novels have found a large and loyal following and are critically well regarded.

Categories: Historical, Police Procedural

Awards

Agatha Malice Domestic Lifetime Achievement Award (2009)
Edgar Award for Best Short Story ("Heroes," *Murder and Obsession,* ed. Otto Penzler, 2000)

Major Works

Thomas and Charlotte Pitt series: *The Cater Street Hangman* (1979), *Callander Square* (1980), *Paragon Walk* (1981), *Resurrection Row* (1981), *Rutland Place* (1983), *Bluegate Fields* (1984), *Death in the Devil's Acre* (1985), *Cardington Crescent* (1987), *Silence in Hanover Close* (1988), *Bethlehem Road* (1990), *Highgate Rise* (1991), *Belgrave Square* (1992), *Farriers' Lane* (1993), *The Hyde Park Headsman* (1994), *Traitors Gate* (1995), *Pentecost Alley* (1996), *Ashworth Hall* (1997), *Brunswick Gardens* (1998), *Bedford Square* (1999), *Half Moon Street* (2000), *The Whitechapel Conspiracy* (2001), *Southampton Row* (2002), *Seven Dials* (2003), *Long Spoon Lane* (2005), *Africa Passage* (2007), *Buckingham Palace Gardens* (2008), *Betrayal at Lisson Grove* (2011)
William Monk series: *The Face of a Stranger* (1990), *A Dangerous Mourning* (1991), *Defend and Betray* (1992), *A Sudden, Fearful Death* (1993), *The Sins of the Wolf* (1994), *Cain His Brother* (1995), *Weighed in the Balance* (1996), *The Silent Cry* (1997), *A Breach of Promise* (1998), *The Twisted Root* (1999), *Slaves of Obsession* (2000), *Funeral in Blue* (2002), *Death of a Stranger* (2002), *The Shifting Tide* (2004), *Dark Assassin* (2006), *Execution Dock* (2009)
World War One Reavley Family series: *No Graves as Yet: 1914* (2003), *Shoulder the Sky: 1915* (2004), *Angels in the Gloom: 1916* (2005), *At Some Disputed Barricade: 1917* (2007), *We Shall Not Sleep* (2007)
Historical Christmas series: *A Christmas Journey* (2003), *A Christmas Visitor* (2004), *A Christmas Guest* (2005), *A Christmas Secret* (2006),

A Christmas Beginning (2007), *A Christmas Grace* (2008), *A Christmas Promise* (2009)

Nonseries novels: *The Fashionable Funeral* (1992), *A Dish Taken Cold* (1999), *The Sheen on the Silk* (2010)

Nonfiction: *Letters from the Highlands* (2004)

Research Sources

Encyclopedias and Handbooks: 100, BYA, CA (101), CANR (22, 50, 84, 150, 177), CLC (126), GWM, MCF, STJ, WWW

Bibliographies: FF, OM

Biographies and Interviews

"Anne Perry: Victorian Muse." *Crescent Blues* 2.2 (1999). http://www.crescentblues.com/2_2issue/perry.shtml (accessed November 1, 2010).

Brainard, Dulcy. "Anne Perry: 'A Structure in Which to Grow.'" *Publishers Weekly* 242.13 (March 27, 1995): 64.

Clark, Diana Cooper. "Interview with Anne Perry." *Clues* 3.2: 52–65. Also published in her *Dreams of Darkness: Interviews with Detective Novelists.* Bowling Green, OH: Popular Press, 1983. 205–23.

Douglas, Carole Nelson. "At Home Online: Anne Perry Interviewed." *Mystery Readers International.* n.d. http://www.mysteryreaders.org/athomeperry.html (accessed November 1, 2010).

Goldman, David. "Shocking, Lurid, and True!" *Biography* 1.7 (July 1997): 10.

"Ian Rankin Talks to Anne Perry (Juliet Hulme)." (videocast) *YouTube.com.* August 18, 2007. http://www.youtube.com/watch?v=b_oYT9mvChw (accessed November 1, 2010).

Menconi, Ralph, and Jeff Zaleski. "Murder on the Eve of War." *Publishers Weekly* 250.26 (June 30, 2003): 60.

Muller, Adrian. "Anne Perry." *Speaking of Murder: Interviews with the Masters of Mystery and Suspense.* Ed. Ed Gorman and Martin H. Greenberg. New York: Berkley Prime Crime, 1998. 223–34.

Neustatter, Angela. "I Was Guilty. I Did My Time." *Guardian.co.uk.* November 12, 2003. http://www.guardian.co.uk/books/2003/nov/12/crimebooks.features11 (accessed November 1, 2010).

Peters, Barbara. "Ann Perry." (videocast—6 parts) *Poisoned Pen Bookstore.* n.d. http://www.poisonedpen.com/interviews/ann-perry; also available at http://www.youtube.com/watch?v=tn31QPcShDI (accessed November 1, 2010).

Richards, Linda. "The Mysteries of Anne Perry." *January Magazine.* November 1998. http://januarymagazine.com/profiles/perry.html (accessed November 1, 2010).

Stedman, Jane W. "Anne Perry Biography—Anne Perry Comments." *Jrank. org.* n.d. http://biography.jrank.org/pages/4653/Perry-Anne.html (accessed November 1, 2010).

Weinberg, A. "Secrets and Lies." *Book* 26 (January-February 2003): 22.

Wickens, Barbara. "Haunted by Homocide." *Maclean's* 108.13 (1995): 61.

Criticism and Reader's Guides

Alter, Iska S. "Class, Gender, and the Possibilities of Detection in Anne Perry's Victorian Reconstructions." *Theory and Practice of Classic Detective Fiction.* Ed. Jerome Delamater and Ruth Prigozy. Westport, CT: Greenwood, 1997. 159–68.

Clowers, Myles L. "She Snoops to Conquer: The Historical Detective Novels of Anne Perry." *Clues: A Journal of Detection* 16.1 (1995): 25–34.

DuBose, Martha Hailey. "Anne Perry: Past Imperfect." *Women of Mystery: The Lives and Works of Notable Women Crime Novelists.* New York: St. Martin's Minotaur, 2000. 425–32.

Foxwell, Elizabeth. "Anne Perry's Hester Latterly." *Clues: A Journal of Detection* 22.2 (2001): 63–72.

Hadley, Mary. "Social Injustices in Anne Perry's Victorian England." *Clues: A Journal of Detection* 20.2 (1999): 1–12.

Leaker, Cathy, and Julie Anne Taddeo. "Defend and Preserve: Imminent Nostalgia in the Victorian Mysteries of Anne Perry." *Clues: A Journal of Detection* 17.1 (1996): 77–106.

Perry, Anne. "Charlotte and Thomas Pitt." *The Lineup: The World's Greatest Crime Writers Tell the Inside Story of Their Greatest Detectives.* Ed. Otto Penzler. New York: Little, Brown, 2009. 333–48.

Perry, Anne. "Drawing Sympathetic Characters." *Writer* 120.7 (2007): 24–25.

Perry, Anne. "Set Your Characters in Their Time & Place." *Writer* 121.7 (2008): 30–33.

Perry, Anne. "Writing the Historical Mystery." *Writer* 112.12 (1999): 10.

Rye, Marilyn. "Anne Perry." *British Mystery and Thriller Writers since 1960 (Dictionary of Literary Biography 276).* Ed. Gina Macdonald. Detroit, MI: Gale, 2003. 269–83.

Town, Caren J. "'Naked into the World's Gaze': The Dark Secret in Anne Perry's Novels." *Studies in Popular Culture* 27.1 (2004): 45–60.

Web Site

Official web site: http://www.anneperry.net/ (accessed November 1, 2010).

If You Like Anne Perry

Anne Perry's books are atmospheric historical mysteries set in Victorian London. The novels depict a range of social classes and present a vivid picture of the times.

Then You Might Like

Bruce Alexander

Alexander wrote a series of crime novels set in eighteenth-century London. A real person, Sir John Fielding, the blind magistrate and half-brother to novelist Henry Fielding, is the detective in these stories, which are told through the eyes of Fielding's assistant, Jeremy Proctor. There are eleven books in the Fielding series, including *Blind Justice* and *Murder in Grub Street.*

Caleb Carr

Carr has not published many books, but his best-known work, *The Alienist,* was extremely popular. Set in New York City during the closing years of the nineteenth century, the book recounts the struggle to find a serial killer by alienist (psychologist) Dr. Laszlo Kreizler and friends. Police Commissioner Theodore Roosevelt lends his support. *The Angel of Darkness* is the sequel.

Barbara Hambly

The Benjamin January series of crime novels, beginning with *A Free Man of Color,* has as its protagonist a free African American living in New Orleans during the 1830s. January trained as a physician in Paris but has returned to his family in New Orleans, where life is very different for blacks and whites. Gritty and atmospheric, this series portrays a time, place, and way of life that are fascinating for historical mystery fans.

Cynthia Peale

The three titles in the Beacon Hill mystery series are set in nineteenth-century Boston, very much the same times as Perry's novels. Addington Ames, his sister Caroline, and their boarder Dr. John MacKenzie solve the mysteries, while a romance develops between Caroline and Dr. MacKenzie. The first title is *The Death of Colonel Mann.*

Deanna Raybourn

Raybourn's romantic Victorian mystery series features Lady Julia Grey, widowed in the first book of the series. Her on-again, off-again relationship with private detective Nicholas Brisbane, along with her independent nature and insatiable curiosity, lead Lady Julia into wittily described escapades. The series starts with *Silent in the Grave,* followed by *Silent in the Sanctuary* and additional titles.

Victoria Thompson

Thompson's Gaslight Mystery series is set in New York in the early years of the twentieth century. Midwife Sarah Brandt solves crimes in collaboration with her friend Detective Malloy. Like Charlotte Pitt in one of Perry's series, Sarah comes from a prominent family and has defied convention in her choice to be a midwife. Start with *Murder on Astor Place.*

Peters, Elizabeth (aka Barbara Mertz, Barbara Michaels), 1927–

My eldest brother James went so far as to threaten legal proceedings, on the basis of unsound mind and undue influence. This ill-considered burst of temper, which was characteristic of James, was easily stopped by Mr. Fletcher, Papa's excellent solicitor. Other attempts ensued. I was visited by a stream of attentive nieces and nephews assuring me of their devotion—which had been demonstrated, over the past years, by their absence.

—*Crocodile on the Sandbank,* 1975

Biographical Sketch

Barbara Gross was born in Canton, Illinois, but the family moved to Chicago when she was in elementary school. She attended the University of Chicago, where she received a Bachelor of Philosophy, and later studied at the Oriental Institute, receiving an M.A. and a Ph.D. in Egyptology. She never worked in her chosen field, instead marrying Richard Mertz, a professor of history, in 1950. They had two children before divorcing in 1968. Her first two published books (under the name Barbara Mertz) were nonfiction historical studies of Egypt, and both have been republished in revised editions. Mertz wrote a number of crime and suspense novels before having one accepted for publication. Her first novels were published under the name Barbara Michaels and were romantic suspense tales with supernatural elements. She writes humorous mysteries under the name of Elizabeth Peters and is best known for her Amelia Peabody novels, the first of which was published in 1975. She now lives in Maryland.

All of Mertz's novels feature strong, capable female characters. She has been praised for her settings (many of her books are set in Egypt), her plotting, and her humorous approach to the conventions of the crime novel. In the Amelia Peabody series, the characters progress through their lives, and followers of the series are fascinated by the developing relationships among them. Mertz has received three lifetime achievement awards, including the Grand Master Award.

Categories: Amateur Detective, Historical, Romantic Suspense

Awards

Agatha Award for Best Novel (*Naked Once More,* 1989)
Agatha Malice Domestic Award for Lifetime Achievement (2003)

Anthony Award for Lifetime Achievement (1986)
Grand Master Award for Lifetime Achievement (1998)

Major Works

Amelia Peabody series: *Crocodile on the Sandbank* (1975), *The Curse of the Pharaohs* (1981), *The Mummy Case* (1985), *Lion in the Valley* (1986), *Deeds of the Disturber* (1988), *The Last Camel Died at Noon* (1991), *The Snake, the Crocodile, and the Dog* (1992), *The Hippopotamus Pool* (1996), *Seeing a Large Cat* (1997), *The Ape Who Guards the Balance* (1998), *The Falcon at the Portal* (1999), *He Shall Thunder in the Sky* (2000), *Lord of the Silent* (2001), *The Golden One* (2002), *Children of the Storm* (2003), *Guardian of the Horizon* (2004), *The Serpent on the Crown* (2005), *Tomb of the Golden Bird* (2006), *A River in the Sky* (2010)

Jacqueline Kirby series: *The Seventh Sinner* (1972), *The Murders of Richard III* (1974), *Die for Love* (1984), *Naked Once More* (1989)

Vicky Bliss series: *Borrower of the Night* (1973), *Street of the Five Moons* (1978), *Silhouette in Scarlet* (1983), *Trojan Gold* (1987), *Night Train to Memphis* (1994), *The Laughter of Dead Kings* (2008)

Nonseries novels: *The Jackal's Head* (1968), *The Camelot Caper* (1969), *The Dead Sea Cipher* (1970), *The Night of 400 Rabbits* (1971), *Legend in Green Velvet* (1976), *Devil-May-Care* (1977), *Summer of the Dragon* (1979), *The Love Talker* (1980), *The Copenhagen Connection* (1982)

Novels as Barbara Michaels: *The Master of Blacktower* (1966), *Sons of the Wolf* (1967, reprinted as *Mystery on the Moors*), *Ammie, Come Home* (1968), *Prince of Darkness* (1968), *Dark on the Other Side* (1970), *The Crying Child* (1971), *Greygallows* (1972), *Witch* (1973), *House of Many Shadows* (1974), *The Sea King's Daughter* (1975), *Patriot's Dream* (1976), *Wings of the Falcon* (1977), *Wait for What Will Come* (1978), *The Walker in the Shadows* (1979), *The Wizard's Daughter* (1980), *Someone in the House* (1981), *Black Rainbow* (1982), *Here I Stay* (1983), *Dark Duet* (1983), *The Grey Beginning* (1984), *Be Buried in the Rain* (1985), *Shattered Silk* (1986), *Search the Shadows* (1987), *Smoke and Mirrors* (1989), *Into the Darkness* (1990), *Vanish with the Rose* (1992), *Houses of Stone* (1993), *Stitches in Time* (1995), *The Dancing Floor* (1997), *Other Worlds: The Bell Witch and the Stratford Haunting* (1999)

Nonfiction: *Amelia Peabody's Egypt: A Compendium to Her Journals* (with Kristen Whitbread, 2003)

Research Sources

Encyclopedias and Handbooks: 100, BYA, CA (21–24R), CANR (11, 36, 63, 82, 135, 175), EMM, GWM, MCF, STJ, WWW

Bibliographies: FF, OM

Biographies and Interviews

"Elizabeth Peters Discusses Amelia Peabody's Egypt." (videocast) *Library of Congress.* November 4, 2003. http://www.loc.gov/locvideo/peters// (accessed November 1, 2010).

James, Dean. "Elizabeth Peters." *Speaking of Murder: Interviews with the Masters of Mystery and Suspense.* Ed. Ed Gorman and Martin H. Greenberg. New York: Berkley Prime Crime, 1998. 163–70.

James, Dean. "Interview with Elizabeth Peters." *Deadly Women: The Woman Mystery Reader's Indispensable Companion.* Ed. Jan Grape et al. New York: Carroll & Graf, 1998. 80–85.

Mussell, Kay. "Paradoxa Interview with Barbara G. Mertz." *Paradoxa: Studies in World Literary Genres* 3.1–2 (1997): 180–83.

"Powell's Q&A with Elizabeth Peters." *Powells Bookstore.* n.d. http://www.powells.com/ink/elizabethpeters.html (accessed November 1, 2010).

Rehm, Diane. "Elizabeth Peters: Lord of the Silent" (audiocast) *Diane Rehm Show.* May 29, 2001. http://wamu.org/programs/dr/01/05/29.php (accessed November 1, 2010).

Rose, Mark. "Queen of the Novel." *Archaeology* 58.2 (2005): 46–51.

Slung, Michele. "Sleuthing the Sahara." *Victoria* 16.7 (2002): 102.

Smith, L. "The Jewel of the Nile." *Book* (Summit, NJ) 27 (March-April 2003): 30–2.

Swanson, Jean. "*PW* Talks with Elizabeth Peters." *Publisher's Weekly* 248.17 (November 1, 2001): 53.

Ward, Jean Marie. "Elizabeth Peters: Adventuring with Amelia." *Crescent Blues* 2.3 (1999). http://www.crescentblues.com/2_3issue/peters.shtml (accessed November 1, 2010).

Williams, Wilda. "The Three Faces of Mertz/Peters/Michaels." *Library Journal* 117.12 (1992): 128.

Zaleski, Jeff. "*PW* Talks with Elizabeth Peters." *Publishers Weekly* 248.17 (2001): 53.

Criticism and Reader's Guides

Elkins, Aaron. "A Thousand Miles up the Nile with Amelia Peabody." *Mystery Scene* 71 (2001): 22–24.

Freier, Mary P. "Information Ethics in the Detective Novel." *Clues: A Journal of Detection* 24.1 (2005): 18–26.

Hauser, Amy. "Digging beneath the Surface: Victorian Archaeologist Amelia Peabody." *Clues: A Journal of Detection* 22.2 (2001): 125–40.

Larew, Marilynn M. "Elizabeth Peters." *100 Masters of Mystery and Detection, vol. 2.* Ed. Fiona Kelleghan. Pasadena, CA: Salem Press, 2001. 502–10.

Mertz, Barbara. "Summer Lite." *The Writing Life: Writers on How They Think and Work.* Ed. Marie Arana. New York: PublicAffairs, 2003. 271–75.

Peters, Elizabeth. "Series Characters: Love 'em or Leave 'em." *Writer* 107.4 (April 1994): 5+.

Peterson, Barbara. "The Gifts of Mystery—Author Elizabeth Peters." *EzineArticles.com.* n.d. http://ezinearticles.com/?The-Gifts-of-Mystery--Author-Elizabeth-Peters&id=1886762 (accessed November 1, 2010).

Tavernier-Courbin, Jacqueline. "Sleuthing and Excavating in Egypt: Elizabeth Peters's Humor." *Thalia: Studies in Literary Humor* 20.1–2 (2000): 24–54.

Web Sites

Official Web site: http://www.mpmbooks.com/ (accessed November 1, 2010).

Official Web site for Amelia Peabody series: http://www.ameliapeabody.com (accessed November 1, 2010).

Pickard, Nancy, 1945–

You know how the sound of thunder may first reach your ears form a long way off? So far away that it registers only as a rumble in your subconscious? There, for a moment, you felt something, an unease, but what was it? A truck going by on the highway, an airplane overhead? You shake your head, you go back to whatever you were doing.

—*Bum Steer,* 1990

Biographical Sketch

Picard was born in Kansas City, Missouri, and graduated from the Missouri School of Journalism with a B.A. in 1967. She married Guy Picard in 1976, and they had one son, but the couple later divorced. She has worked as a newspaper reporter and editor and as a business supervisor. She became a freelance writer in 1973, then turned to writing fiction in 1981. She has won a number of awards for both her novels and her short stories.

Picard's stories have both humor and serious themes but have become darker over the years. Her most recent novels are stand-alones set in Kansas. *The Virgin of Small Plains* has been her biggest critical success thus far and is popular with book clubs; it has also been chosen as a statewide reading novel for Kansas Reads.

Categories: Amateur Detective, Cozy

Awards

Agatha Award for Best Novel (*Bum Steer,* 1990; *I.O.U.,* 1991; *The Virgin of Small Plains,* 2006)

Agatha Award for Best Short Story ("Out of Africa," *Mom, Apple Pie & Murder,* ed. Nancy Pickard, 1999)

Anthony Award for Best Paperback Original (*Say No to Murder,* 1986)

Anthony Award for Best Short Story ("Afraid All the Time," *Sisters in Crime,* 1990)

Barry Award for Best Short Story ("There Is No Crime on Easter Island," *Ellery Queen Mystery Magazine,* September-October 2005, 2006)

Macavity Award for Best Novel (*Marriage Is Murder,* 1988; *I.O.U.,* 1992; *The Virgin of Small Plains,* 2007)

Macavity Award for Best Short Story ("Afraid All the Time," *Sisters in Crime,* 1990; "There Is No Crime on Easter Island," *Ellery Queen Mystery Magazine,* September-October 2005, 2006)

Shamus Award for Best Short Story ("Dust Devil," *The Armchair Detective,* Winter 1991, 1992)

Major Works

Jenny Cain series: *Generous Death* (1984), *Say No to Murder* (1985), *No Body* (1986), *Marriage is Murder* (1987), *Dead Crazy* (1989), *Bum Steer* (1990), *I.O.U.* (1991), *But I Wouldn't Want to Die There* (1993), *Confession* (1994), *Twilight* (1995)

Marie Lightfoot series: *The Whole Truth* (2000), *Ring of Truth* (2001), *The Truth Hurts* (2002)

Eugenia Potter series: *The Twenty-Seven Ingredient Chili Con Carne Murders* (1993), *The Blue Corn Murders* (1998), *The Secret Ingredient Murders* (2001)

Nonseries novels: *Storm Warnings* (1999), *The Virgin of Small Plains* (2006), *The Scent of Rain and Lightening* (2010)

Nonfiction: *Seven Steps on the Writer's Path: The Journey from Frustration to Fulfillment* (with Lynn Lott, 2003)

Research Sources

Encyclopedias and Handbooks: BYA, CA (153), CANR (73, 145, 178), GWM, MCF, STJ, WWW

Bibliographies: FF, OM

Biographies and Interviews

Hall, Melissa Mia. "Small Miracles." *Publishers Weekly* 253.13 (March 27, 2006): 61.

Marks, Jeffrey. "Interview with Nancy Pickard." *Deadly Women: The Woman Mystery Reader's Indispensable Companion.* Ed. Jan Grape et al. New York: Carroll & Graf, 1998. 243–46.

Peters, Barbara. "Nancy Pickard Interview." *Poisoned Pen Bookstore.* n.d. http://www.poisonedpen.com/interviews/nancy-pickard; also available at http://www.youtube.com/watch?v=8yc5GxvzG7Q&feature=PlayList& p=32D32DA0C805D488&index=0 (accessed November 1, 2010).

Randisi, Robert J. "Nancy Pickard." *Speaking of Murder, vol. 2: Interviews with the Masters of Mystery and Suspense.* Ed. Ed Gorman and Martin H. Greenberg. New York: Berkley Prime Crime, 1999. 225–32.

Shindler, Dorman T. "The Third Stage of Evolution." *Publishers Weekly* 249.31 (August 5, 2002): 48.

Criticism and Reader's Guides

"Nancy Pickard." *Kansas Literature.* n.d. http://www.washburn.edu/reference/ cks/mapping/pickard/ (accessed November 1, 2010).

"2009 Kansas Reads: The Virgin of Small Plains." *Kansas Center for the Book.* 2008. http://www.kcfb.info/plains.htm–Includes discussion questions, classroom resources and other materials (accessed November 1, 2010).

"The Virgin of Small Plains." (reading guide) *BKMT Reading Guides.* n.d. http://www.bookmovement.com/app/readingguide/view.php?reading GuideID=1660 (accessed November 1, 2010).

"The Virgin of Small Plains." (reading guide) *LitLovers.com.* 2006. http:// www.litlovers.com/guide_virgin_of_small%20_plains.html (accessed November 1, 2010).

"The Virgin of Small Plains." (reading guide) *Random House.* 2007. http:// www.randomhouse.com/rhpg/rc/library/display.pperl?isbn=9780345471 000&view=qa (accessed November 1, 2010).

Web Sites

Official Web site: http://www.nancypickard.com/ (accessed November 1, 2010).

Facebook: http://www.facebook.com/people/Nancy-Pickard/100000468620446 (accessed November 1, 2010).

Reichs, Kathy, 1950–

I wasn't thinking about the man who'd blown himself up. Earlier I had. Now I was putting him together. Two sections of skull lay in front of me, and a third jutted from a sand-filled stainless steel bowl, the glue still drying on its reassembled fragments. Enough bone to confirm identity. The coroner would be pleased.

—*Deja Dead,* 1997

Biographical Sketch

Kathy Reichs was born in Chicago and received a Ph.D. from Northwestern University. She is a forensic anthropologist and is a professor in the anthropology department at the University of North Carolina at Charlotte. Reichs consults on forensic anthropology for the State of North Carolina Office of the Medical Examiner and for the Laboratoire de Sciences Judiciaires et de Médecine Légale in Quebec. She has also worked with the FBI, other law enforcement organizations, and the U.N. in criminal and war-related investigations. She was awarded the Arthur Ellis Award for Best First Novel (*Deja Dead,* 1997) by the Crime Writers of Canada. The popular television series *Bones* is based on her books, and she is an executive producer. Currently, she divides her time between North Carolina and Quebec.

Her work to date largely consists of the Temperance Brennan novels, which have generally been favorably reviewed. Brennan works as a forensic anthropologist, and Reichs uses her considerable professional expertise to give the series a realistic foundation.

Categories: Forensic, Police Procedural

Major Works

Temperance Brennan series: *Deja Dead* (1997), *Death du Jour* (1999), *Deadly Decisions* (2000), *Fatal Voyage* (2001), *Grave Secrets* (2002), *Bare Bones* (2003), *Monday Mourning* (2004), *Cross Bones* (2005), *Bones: Buried Deep* (with Allan Collins, 2006), *Break No Bones* (2006), *Bones to Ashes* (2007), *Devil Bones* (2008), *206 Bones* (2009), *Spider Bones* (2010)
Nonseries novel: *I'd Kill for That* (2005)

Research Sources

Encyclopedias and Handbooks: CA (174), CANR (149), MCF

Bibliographies: FF, OM

Biographies and Interviews

Bertrand, Steve. "Meet the Writers: Kathy Reichs." *Barnes and Noble.* September 14, 2009. http://www.youtube.com/watch?v=WJ1rI5Xmwpo (accessed November 1, 2010).

Dunn, Adam, and Jeff Zaleski. "Writing Forensics." *Publishers Weekly* 250.18 (May 5, 2003): 194.

Foster, Jordan. "No Bones about It." *Publishers Weekly* 255.23 (September 6, 2008): 26.

"Kathy Reichs." *Bookreporter.com.* July 12, 2002. http://www.bookreporter.com/authors/au-reichs-kathy.asp (accessed November 1, 2010).

"Kathy Reichs." *Literati.net*. n.d. http://literati.net/Reichs/index.htm (accessed November 1, 2010).

Lindsey, Elizabeth "Best Selling Author Kathy Reichs—Author Biographies." *EzineArticles.com*. September 3, 2009. http://ezinearticles.com/?Best-Selling-Author-Kathy-Reichs-Author-Biographies&id=2861774 (accessed November 1, 2010).

Lineberry, Cate. "On the Case." *Smithsonian* 38.5 (2007): 84–85.

Peters, Barbara. "Kathy Reichs Interview." (videocast—6 parts) *Poisoned Pen Bookstore*. n.d. http://www.poisonedpen.com/interviews/kathy-reichs-interview; also available at http://www.youtube.com/watch?v=y71Q8ZeoIaI (accessed November 1, 2010).

Turbide, Diane. "Alas, Poor Victim: A Forensic Expert Spins a Gruesome Thriller." *Maclean's* 110 (1997): 72–3. http://www.thecanadianencyclopedia.com/index.cfm?PgNm=TCE&Params=M1ARTM0011394 (accessed November 1, 2010).

Wayman, E. R. "Forensic Anthropology." *Current Anthropology* 47.4 (2006): 567.

Web Site

Official Web site: http://kathyreichs.com (accessed November 1, 2010).

Rendell, Ruth (aka Barbara Vine), 1930–

Scorpio is metaphysics, putrefaction and death, regeneration, passion, lust and violence, insight and profundity; inheritance, loss, occultism, astrology, borrowing and lending, others' possessions. Scorpians are magicians, astrologers, alchemists, surgeons, bondsmen, and undertakers. The gem for Scorpio is the snakestone, the plant the cactus; eagles and wolves and scorpions are its creatures, its body part is the genitals, its weapon the Obligatory Pain, and its card in the Tarot is Death.

—The Lake of Darkness, 1980

Biographical Sketch

Ruth Grasemann was born in London, the daughter of two teachers, and attended Loughton Country High School in Essex. Her mother was Swedish and had difficulty pronouncing the name Ruth, so she called her Barbara. She worked as a reporter and journalist for small newspapers, at one of which she met her husband, Donald Rendell. They had one son. The couple divorced but remarried in 1977. She wrote several novels before having one accepted for publication. She was made a life peer in 1997 with the title Baroness Rendell of Babergh and takes her duties in the House of Lords seriously. She lives in London. Rendell's novels are noted for their depth and psychological insights. She frequently deals with social issues, and her Wexford series is considered to transcend the bounds of the police procedural genre. She has said that she considers the Barbara Vine books to be about ordinary people under extraordinary pressures, while the stand-alone Rendell books are stories of psychological suspense (Reynolds, *Women Authors of Detective Series*). She has been given lifetime achievement awards in both England and the United States, and her list of other awards is a lengthy one. She is highly regarded by many critics for suspenseful yet literate portrayals of the pressures of modern society.

Categories: Police Procedural, Psychological

Awards

Gold Dagger Award for Best Novel (*A Demon in My View,* 1976; *Live Flesh,* 1986; *A Fatal Inversion,* as Barbara Vine, 1987; *King Solomon's Carpet,* as Barbara Vine, 1991)

Silver Dagger Award for Runner-up for Best Novel (*The Tree of Hands,* 1984)

Diamond Dagger for Lifetime Achievement (1991)

Edgar Award for Best Novel (*A Dark-Adapted Eye,* as Barbara Vine, 1987)

Edgar Award for Best Short Story ("The Fallen Curtain," *Ellery Queen Mystery Magazine,* May 1974; "The New Girlfriend," *Ellery Queen Mystery Magazine,* August 1983)

Grand Master Award for Lifetime Achievement (1997)

Major Works

Inspector Wexford series: *From Doon with Death* (1964), *Wolf to the Slaughter* (1967), *A New Lease of Death* (1967; reprinted as *Sins of the Fathers*), *The Best Man to Die* (1969), *A Guilty Thing Surprised* (1970), *No More Dying Then* (1971), *Murder Being Once Done* (1972), *Some Lie and Some Die* (1973), *Shake Hands Forever* (1975), *A Sleeping Life* (1978), *Put On by Cunning* (1981, reprinted as *Death Notes*), *The Speaker of Mandarin* (1983), *An Unkindness of Ravens* (1985), *The Veiled One* (1988), *Kissing the Gunner's Daughter* (1992), *Simisola* (1995), *Road Rage* (1997), *Harm Done* (1999), *The Babes in the Wood* (2002), *End in Tears* (2006), *Not in the Flesh* (2007), *The Monster in the Box* (2009)

Nonseries novels: *To Fear a Painted Devil* (1965), *Vanity Dies Hard* (1966, reprinted as *In Sickness and in Health*), *The Secret House of Death* (1968), *One Across, Two Down* (1971), *The Face of Trespass* (1974), *A Demon in My View* (1977), *A Judgment in Stone* (1977), *Make Death Love Me* (1979), *The Lake of Darkness* (1980), *Master of the Moor* (1982), *The*

Killing Doll (1984), *The Tree of Hands* (1984), *Live Flesh* (1986), *Heart-stones* (1987), *Talking to Strangers* (1987, reprinted as *Talking to Strange Men*), *The Bridesmaid* (1989), *Going Wrong* (1990), *The Crocodile Bird* (1993), *Ginger and the Kingsmarkham Chalk Circle* (1966), *The Keys to the Street* (1996), *Whydunit (Perfectly Criminal 2)* (1997), *Thornapple* (1998), *A Sight for Sore Eyes* (1999), *Adam and Eve and Pinch Me* (2001), *The Rottweiler* (2004), *Thirteen Steps Down* (2004), *The Thief* (2006), *The Water's Lovely* (2007), *Portobello* (2010)

Short-story collections: *The Fallen Curtain and Other Stories* (1976), *Means of Evil and Other Stories* (1979), *The Fever Tree and Other Stories* (1982), *The New Girlfriend and Other Stories* (1985), *The Copper Peacock and Other Stories* (1991), *Blood Lines: Long and Short Stories* (1996), *Piranha to Scurfy and Other Stories* (2002)

Novels as Barbara Vine: *A Dark-Adapted Eye* (1985), *A Fatal Inversion* (1987), *The House of Stairs* (1989), *Gallowglass* (1990), *King Solomon's Carpet* (1992), *Anna's Book* (1993), *No Night Is Too Long* (1994), *The Brimstone Wedding* (1996), *The Chimney Sweeper's Boy* (1998), *Grasshopper* (2000), *The Blood Doctor* (2002), *The Minotaur* (2005), *The Birthday Present* (2009)

Research Sources

Encyclopedias and Handbooks: 100, BEA, BEB, BYA, CA (109), CANR (35, 52, 74, 127, 162, 190), CLC (28, 48, 50), EMM, GWM, OCC, MCF, WWW

"Ruth Rendell." *Encyclopedia of World Biography.* 2007. http://www. notablebiographies.com/newsmakers2/2007-Pu-Z/Rendell-Ruth.html (accessed November 1, 2010).

Bibliographies: FF

Biographies and Interviews

Anable, Stephen. "PW talks with Ruth Rendell." *Publishers Weekly* 249.4 (January 28, 2002): 275.

Carr, John C. "Ruth Rendell." *The Craft of Crime: Conversations with Crime Writers.* Boston: Houghton Mifflin, 1983. 227–57.

Cooper-Clark, Diana. "Interview with Ruth Rendell." *Armchair Detective: A Quarterly Journal Devoted to the Appreciation of Mystery, Detective, and Suspense Fiction* 14.2 (1981): 108–17.

Farndale, Nigel. "Ruth Rendell: A Tough Case to Crack." *Telegraph.co.uk.* August 10, 2008. http://www.telegraph.co.uk/culture/donotmigrate/3558328/ Ruth-Rendell-a-tough-case-to-crack.html (accessed November 1, 2010).

House, Christian. "Ruth Rendell: My Parliamentary Sex Scandal." *Independent.co.uk.* August 24, 2008. http://www.independent.co.uk/arts-entertain

ment/books/features/ruth-rendell-my-parliamentary-sex-scandal-904872. html (accessed November 1, 2010).

McDermid, Val. "Val McDermid on Ruth Rendell." *Twbooks.co.uk.* April 9, 2007. http://www.twbooks.co.uk/cwa/mcdermidonrendell.html (accessed November 1, 2010).

Macdonald, Marianne. "Her Dark Materials." *Telegraph.co.uk.* April 11, 2005. http://www.telegraph.co.uk/culture/donotmigrate/3640185/Her-dark-materials.html (accessed November 1, 2010).

Marsden, Michael, and Marilyn Motz. "Interview with Ruth Rendell." *Clues: A Journal of Detection* 10.2 (1989): 81–92.

"Ruth Rendell, Taking Readers '13 Steps Down.'" (audiocast) *All Things Considered, NPR.* October 9, 2005. http://www.npr.org/templates/story/ story.php?storyId=4948848 (accessed November 1, 2010).

Swaim, Don. "Ruth Rendell Interview." (audiocast) *Wired for Books.* November 10, 1990. http://wiredforbooks.org/ruthrendell/ (accessed November 1, 2010).

Walker, Fiona. "Tribute to Ruth Rendell." *Mystery Ink.* n.d. http://www. mysteryinkonline.com/2005/01/ruth_rendell_a_.html (accessed November 1, 2010).

Criticism and Reader's Guides

Bakerman, Jane S. "Ruth Rendell." *10 Women of Mystery.* Ed. Earl F. Bargainnier. Bowling Green, OH: Popular Press, 1981. 124–49.

Canfield-Reisman, Rosemary M. "Ruth Rendell." *100 Masters of Mystery and Detection, vol. 2.* Ed. Fiona Kelleghan. Pasadena, CA: Salem Press, 2001. 546–52.

Clark, Susan L. "A Fearful Symmetry." *Armchair Detective: A Quarterly Journal Devoted to the Appreciation of Mystery, Detective, and Suspense Fiction* 22.3 (1989): 228–35.

DuBose, Martha Hailey. "Ruth Rendell: Triple Threatening." *Women of Mystery: The Lives and Works of Notable Women Crime Novelists.* New York: St. Martin's Minotaur, 2000. 362–73.

Gabilondo, Patricia A. "Ruth (Barbara) Rendell." *British Mystery and Thriller Writers Since 1960 (Dictionary of Literary Biography 276).* Ed. Gina Macdonald. Detroit, MI: Gale, 2003. 315–17, 332.

Giffone, Tony. "Disoriented in the Orient: The Representation of the Chinese in Two Contemporary Mystery Novels." *Cultural Power/Cultural Literacy: Selected Papers from the Fourteenth Annual Florida State University Conference on Literature and Film.* Ed. Bonnie Braendlin. Tallahassee: Florida State University Press, 1991. 143–51.

Hendershot, Cyndy. "Gender and Subjectivity in Ruth Rendell's 'The New Girlfriend.'" *Clues: A Journal of Detection* 15.2 (1994): 75–83.

Kadonaga, Lisa. "Strange Countries and Secret Worlds in Ruth Rendell's Crime Novels." *Geographical Review* 88.3 (1998): 413–28.

Leavey, Barbara Fass. "A Folklore Plot in Ruth Rendell's Wexford Series." *Clues: A Journal of Detection* 20.2 (1999): 49–62.

Leitch, Thomas M. "Not Just Another Whodunit: Disavowal as Evolution in Detective Fiction." *Clues: A Journal of Detection* 20.1 (1999): 63–76.

Penuel, Suzanne. "Relocating the Heart of Darkness in Ruth Rendell." *Race and Religion in the Postcolonial British Detective Story: Ten Essays*. Ed. Julie H. Kim. Jefferson, NC: McFarland, 2005. 51–70.

Rahn, B. J. "Ruth Rendell." *Mystery and Suspense Writers: The Literature of Crime, Detection, and Espionage, II*. Ed. Robin W. Winks and Maureen Corrigan. New York: Scribner's, 1998. 773–90.

Reynolds, Moira Davison. "Ruth Rendell." *Women Authors of Detective Series: Twenty-One American and British Writers, 1900–2000*. Jefferson, NC: McFarland, 2001. 111–18.

Rowland, Susan. "The Horror of Modernity and the Utopian Sublime: Gothic Villainy in P. D. James and Ruth Rendell." *The Devil Himself: Villainy in Detective Fiction and Film*. Ed. Stacy Gillis and Philippa Gates. Westport, CT: Greenwood, 2002. 135–46.

Russett, Margaret. "Three Faces of Ruth Rendell: Feminism, Popular Fiction, and the Question of Genre." *Genre: Forms of Discourse and Culture* 35.1 (2002): 143–65.

Web Sites

"Demons in Her View: The Ruth Rendell Information Site: (fan site): http://www.gusworld.com.au/books/rendell/default.htm—Includes information about books written under the name of Ruth Rendell and links to other sources (accessed November 1, 2010).

"Fatal Inversions: The Barbara Vine Information Web" (fan site): http://www.gusworld.com.au/books/vine/default.htm—Includes information about books written under the name of Barbara Vine and links to other sources (accessed November 1, 2010).

Sayers, Dorothy L., 1893–1957

At Mr. Hankin's mildly sarcastic accents, the scene dislimned as by magic. The door-post drapers and Miss Parton's bosom-friend melted out into the passage,... Miss Rossiter, clutching Mr. Armstrong's carbons in her hand, was able to look businesslike, and did so. Mr. Ingleby alone, disdaining pretence, set down his cup with a slightly impudent smile and advanced to obey his chief's command.

—Murder Must Advertise, 1933

Biographical Sketch

Dorothy Leigh Sayers was born in Oxford, the only child of a clergyman. Her parents recognized Dorothy's intellectual skills and sent her to boarding school at Godolphin School in order to prepare her to attend a women's college at Oxford. She won a scholarship to Somerville College, Oxford, and passed examinations in 1915 that would have given her a first-class degree. However, she had to wait until 1920, when degrees were finally award to women. Since she had done postgraduate work, she received an M.A. at the same time. Sayers worked as a teacher for several years in England and France and as an editor for a publishing firm, then joined an advertising agency as a copywriter for seven years. After several love affairs and an illegitimate child, Sayers married Oswald Fleming in 1926. Sayers's son was adopted by Fleming but did not realize that Sayers was his real mother until he was an adult.

Sayers wrote crime novels to make money, and her real interests lay with more scholarly works. Her books about Lord Peter Wimsey and, later, Harriet Vane were very successful, but her more serious writing consumed much of her time and energy and consisted of plays, poetry, essays, and translations. Her translation of Dante's *Inferno* was admired, although it had to be finished by a friend after she died. Her crime novels continue to be popular with the reading public because of their high standard of literate writing, their interesting characters, and the developing relationship between Wimsey and Vane. Wimsey as a character has received a mixed critical reception over the years, and readers do not universally admire him. However, his character does develop over the course of the series, and he becomes much more human with time. Sayers combined the detective novel with the novel of manners and was, for the most part, very successful at it.

Categories: Amateur Detective, English Setting

Major Works

Lord Peter Wimsey series: *Whose Body?* (1923), *Clouds of Witness* (1925), *Unnatural Death* (1927), *The Unpleasantness at the Bellona Club* (1928), *The Documents in the Case* (with Robert Eustace, 1930), *Strong Poison* (1930), *The Five Red Herrings* (originally titled *Suspicious Characters* in U.S., 1931), *Have His Carcase* (1932), *Murder Must Advertise* (1933), *The Nine Tailors: Changes Rung on an Old Theme in Two Short Touches and Two Full Peals* (1934), *Gaudy Night* (1935), *Busman's Honeymoon: A Love Story with Detective Interruptions* (1937), *Thrones, Dominations* (with Jill Paton Walsh, 1998)

Short-story collections: *Lord Peter Views the Body* (1929), *Hangman's Holiday* (1933), *Six Against Scotland Yard* (with others, 1936), *In the Teeth of the Evidence, and Other Stories* (1939)

Other: *Papers Relating to the Family of Wimsey* (privately printed, 1936), *An Account of Lord Mortimer Wimsey, the Hermit of the Wash* (privately printed, 1937), *The Wimsey Papers* (published serially in *Spectator*, 1939–1940), *The Wimsey Family: A Fragmentary History Compiled from Correspondence with Dorothy L. Sayers* (compiled by C. W. Scott-Giles, 1977)

Nonfiction: *The Letters of Dorothy L. Sayers, 1899–1936: The Making of a Detective Novelist* (edited by Barbara Reynolds, 1996)

Research Sources

Encyclopedias and Handbooks: BEA, BEB, CA (119), CANR (60), EMM, OCC, STJ, TCLC (2, 15), WWW

Bibliographies: FF

Biographies and Interviews

Brabazon, James. *Dorothy L. Sayers: A Biography.* New York: Scribner, 1981.

Coomes, David. *Dorothy L. Sayers: A Careless Rage for Life.* Oxford: Lion, 1992.

Dale, Alzina Stone. *Maker and Craftsman: The Story of Dorothy L. Sayers.* Grand Rapids, MI: Eerdmans, 1978.

"Dorothy L. Sayers Biography." *Biographybase.com.* n.d. http://www.biogra-phybase.com/biography/Sayers_Dorothy_L.html (accessed November 1, 2010).

Hitchman, Janet. *Such a Strange Lady: A Biography of Dorothy L. Sayers.* New York: Harper and Row, 1975.

Hone, Ralph E. *Dorothy L. Sayers: A Literary Biography.* Kent, OH: Kent State University Press, 1979.

Kenney, Catherine. *The Remarkable Case of Dorothy L. Sayers.* Kent, OH: Kent State University Press, 1990.

Reynolds, Barbara. *Dorothy L. Sayers: Her Life and Soul.* New York: St. Martin's Press, 1993.

Sayers, Dorothy L., and Barbara Reynolds. *The Letters of Dorothy L. Sayers.* New York: St. Martin's Press, 1996–1998.

Yoder, Rodney. "Biography of Dorothy L. Sayers." Personal Web page. n.d. http://pbpl.physics.ucla.edu/~yoder/mystery/sayers-bio.html (accessed November 1, 2010).

Criticism and Reader's Guides

Dale, Alzina Stone. *Dorothy L. Sayers: The Centenary Celebration.* New York: Walker, 1993.

"Dorothy L. Sayers." *Guardian.co.uk.* July 22, 2008. http://www.guardian.co.uk/books/2008/jun/11/dorothylsayers (accessed November 1, 2010).

"Dorothy L. Sayers." *British Mystery Writers, 1920–1939 (Dictionary of Literary Biography* 77). Ed. Bernard Benstock and Thomas F. Staley. Detroit, MI: Gale, 1989. 254–72.

DuBose, Martha Hailey. "Dorothy L. Sayers: The Passionate Mind." *Women of Mystery: The Lives and Works of Notable Women Crime Novelists.* New York: St. Martin's Minotaur, 2000. 161–224.

Gillis, Stacy. "Consoling Fictions: Mourning, World War One, and Dorothy L. Sayers." *Modernism and Mourning.* Ed. Patricia Rae. Lewisburg, PA.: Bucknell University Press, 2007. 185–97.

Gorman, Anita G., and Leslie R. Mateer. "The Medium Is the Message: Busman's Honeymoon as Play, Novel, and Film." *Clues: A Journal of Detection* 23.4 (2005): 54–62.

Grost, Mike. "Dorothy L. Sayers." (fansite) *A Guide to Classic Mystery and Detection.* n.d. http://mikegrost.com/sayers.htm (accessed November 1, 2010).

Heilbrun, Carolyn G. "Sayers, Lord Peter, and Harriet Vane at Oxford." *Hamlet's Mother and Other Women.* New York: Columbia University Press, 1990. 252–59.

Klein, Kathleen Gregory. "Dorothy L. Sayers: From First to Last." *In the Beginning: First Novels in Mystery Series.* Bowling Green, OH: Popular Press, 1995. 5–18.

Klein, Kathleen Gregory. "Dorothy Leigh Sayers." *10 Women of Mystery.* Ed. Earl F. Bargainnier. Bowling Green, OH: Popular Press, 1981. 8–39.

LaGrand, Virginia, and Craig E. Mattson. "Peter Wimsey and Precious Ramotswe: Castaway Detectives and Companionate Marriage." *Christianity and Literature* 56.4 (2007): 633–64.

Lipscomb, Elizabeth Johnston. "Dorothy L. Sayers." *100 Masters of Mystery and Detection, vol. 2.* Ed. Fiona Kelleghan. Pasadena, CA: Salem Press, 2001. 569–78.

Mann, Jessica. "Dorothy L Sayers." *Deadlier Than the Male: Why Are Respectable English Women So Good at Murder?* New York: Macmillan, 1981. 154–88.

McClellan, Ann. "Alma Mater: Women, the Academy, and Mothering in Dorothy L. Sayers's *Gaudy Night.*" *Lit: Literature Interpretation Theory* 15.4 (2004): 321–46.

McGregor, Robert Kuhn, and Ethan Lewis. *Conundrum for the Long-Weekend: England, Dorothy L. Sayers, and Lord Peter Wimsey.* Kent, OH: Kent State University Press, 2000.

Merry, Bruce. "Dorothy L. Sayers: Mystery and Demystification." *Art in Crime Writing: Essays on Detective Fiction.* Ed. Bernard Benstock. New York: St. Martin's, 1983. 18–32.

Papinchak, Robert Allen. "Dorothy L. Sayers." *Mystery and Suspense Writers: The Literature of Crime, Detection, and Espionage, II.* Ed. Robin W. Winks and Maureen Corrigan. New York: Scribner's, 1998. 805–28.

Pitt, Valerie. "Dorothy Sayers: The Masks of Lord Peter." *Twentieth-Century Suspense: The Thriller Comes of Age*. Ed. Clive Bloom. New York: St. Martin's, 1990. 97–113.

Rawdon, Michael. "Dorothy L. Sayers: The Peter Wimsey Stories." Personal Web page. 2004. http://www.leftfield.org/~rawdon/books/mystery/sayers.html (accessed November 1, 2010).

Reynolds, Moira Davison. "Dorothy L. Sayers." *Women Authors of Detective Series: Twenty-One American and British Writers, 1900–2000*. Jefferson, NC: McFarland, 2001. 33–44.

Rowland, Susan. *From Agatha Christie to Ruth Rendell: British Women Writers in Detective and Crime Fiction*. New York: Palgrave, 2001.

Rzepka, Charles J. *Detective Fiction*. Cambridge, U.K.: Polity Press, 2005. 161–75.

Scutts, Joanna. "Second Glance: Dorothy L. Sayers and the Last Golden Age." *Open Letters Monthly: An Arts and Literature Review*. n.d. http://www.openlettersmonthly.com/second-glancedorothy-sayers/ (accessed November 1, 2010).

Trembley, Elizabeth A. "Collaring the Other Fellow's Property': Feminism Reads Dorothy L. Sayers." *Women Times Three: Writers, Detectives, Readers*. Ed. Kathleen Gregory Klein. Bowling Green, OH: Popular Press, 1995. 81–99.

Wald, Gayle F. "Strong Poison: Love and the Novelistic in Dorothy Sayers." *The Cunning Craft: Original Essays on Detective Fiction and Contemporary Literary Theory*. Ed. Ronald G. Walker and June M. Frazer. Macomb: Western Illinois University Press, 1990. 98–108.

Young, Laurel. "Dorothy L. Sayers and the New Woman Detective Novel." *Clues: A Journal of Detection* 23.4 (2005): 39–53.

Youngberg, Ruth Tanis. *Dorothy L. Sayers, A Reference Guide*. Boston: G. K. Hall, 1982.

Web Sites

Dorothy L. Sayers Society: http://www.sayers.org.uk/—Includes short biography, FAQs (accessed November 1, 2010).

Dorothy_L: http://www.dorothyl.com/—Official Web site for the Dorothy_l listserv. Includes links to archives of postings (accessed November 1, 2010).

Smith, Alexander McCall, 1948–

After a slow start, she was rather surprised to find that her services were in considerable demand. She was consulted about missing husbands, about the creditworthiness of potential business partners, and about suspected fraud by employees. In almost every case, she was able to come up with at least some information for the client; when she could not, she waived her fee, which meant that virtually nobody who consulted her was dissatisfied.

—*The No. 1 Ladies' Detective Agency,* 1998

Biographical Sketch

Alexander McCall Smith was born in Zimbabwe (then Southern Rhodesia), where his father was a public prosecutor in the then British colony. He attended the University of Edinburgh, where he received a Ph.D. in law. He then taught at Queen's University in Belfast, and, while there, he entered a writing contest in both the children's and the adult categories. He won the children's category and later became a prolific children's author. He later returned to Africa, moving to Botswana, where he helped to found a law school. In 1984, he moved back to Scotland to join the faculty of the University of Edinburgh, but he still visits Botswana yearly. Smith is married and has two daughters. He was named a Commander of the British Empire in 2007.

Although a prolific writer with many juvenile, fiction, and nonfiction titles to his credit, Smith gained international fame with the publication of *The No. 1 Ladies' Detective Agency.* The dignified Mma Ramotswe, a lady of "traditional build," captivated readers, along with Smith's positive portrayal of Botswana. Mma Ramotswe is not stumbling over dead bodies in these books—the crimes are gentler and arise out of everyday life. Critical reception has generally been positive, although some feel that Smith has not portrayed the true Africa. The first few books in the series were adapted into an HBO miniseries by Anthony Minghella. Smith's other mystery series is about Isabel Dalhousie, an Edinburgh professor of moral philosophy, and the problems arising in the books are portrayed through her moral and ethical viewpoint.

Categories: Diverse Characters, Private Detective

Major Works

No. 1 Ladies' Detective Agency series: *The No. 1 Ladies' Detective Agency* (1998), *Tears of the Giraffe* (2000), *Morality for Beautiful Girls* (2001), *The Kalahari Typing School for Men* (2002), *The Full Cupboard of Life* (2003), *In the Company of Cheerful Ladies* (2004), *Blue Shoes and Happiness* (2006), *The Good Husband of Zebra Drive* (2007), *The Miracle at Speedy Motors* (2008), *Tea Time for the Traditionally Built* (2009), *The Double Comfort Safari Club* (2010)

Sunday Philosophy Club (Isabel Dalhousie) series: *The Sunday Philosophy Club* (2004), *Friends, Lovers, Chocolate* (2005), *The Right Attitude to*

Rain (2006), *The Careful Use of Compliments* (2007), *The Comforts of a Muddy Saturday* (2008), *The Lost Art of Gratitude* (2009), *The Charming Quirks of Others* (2010)

Research Sources

Encyclopedias and Handbooks: CA (215), CANR (154, 196), CLC (268), WWW

Bibliographies: FF, OM

Biographies and Interviews

"Alexander McCall Smith: 2006 National Book Festival." (webcast) *Library of Congress.* September 30, 2006. http://www.loc.gov/today/cyberlc/feature_wdesc.php?rec=3994 (accessed November 1, 2010).

"Alexander McCall Smith: 2008 National Book Festival." (webcast) *Library of Congress.* September 27, 2008. http://www.loc.gov/today/cyberlc/feature_wdesc.php?rec=4429 (accessed November 1, 2010).

"Alexander McCall Smith." *BookBrowse.com.* June 1, 2009. http://www.bookbrowse.com/biographies/index.cfm?author_number=745 (accessed November 1, 2010).

"Alexander McCall Smith." *Bookreporter.com.* April 2004. http://www.bookreporter.com/authors/au-smith-alexander-mccall.asp (accessed November 1, 2010).

"Alexander McCall Smith." *Contemporary Writers.* 2009. http://www.contemporarywriters.com/authors/?p=authc2d9c28a16ae81fe9egtv3d0860f (accessed November 1, 2010).

"Alexander McCall Smith: The Book Show, Sky Arts." (videocast) *Sky Channel.* January 29, 2008. http://www.youtube.com/watch?v=L8NKg2AIE3c (accessed November 1, 2010).

"Alexander McCall Smith: Botswana." (videocast) *Journeyman Pictures.* December 14, 2007. http://www.youtube.com/watch?v=JtHqqRkTQIs: Alexander McCall Smith revisits Botswana. (accessed November 1, 2010).

Ashbrook, Tom. "Alexander McCall Smith." (audiocast) *On Point, NPR.* December 15, 2009. http://www.onpointradio.org/2009/12/alexander-mccall-smith (accessed November 1, 2010).

Cruz, Gilbert. "Q&A: Alexander McCall Smith." *Time.* April 30, 2009. http://www.time.com/time/arts/article/0,8599,1894458,00.html (accessed November 1, 2010).

Girish, Uma. "Bush Tea with Alexander McCall Smith." *California Literary Review.* March 31, 2007. http://calitreview.com/64 (accessed November 1, 2010).

"Interview with Alexander McCall Smith." *Readers Read.* February 2003. http://www.readersread.com/features/alexandersmith.htm (accessed November 1, 2010).

Rankan, Ian, and Alexander McCall Smith. "Why Would a Priest Want to Read about Murder?" *Spectator.* October 21, 2006. http://www.specta tor.co.uk/essays/all/25829/why-would-a-priest-want-to-read-about-murder.thtml (accessed October 31, 2010).

Simon, Scott. "Alexander McCall Smith's Mysteries of Philosophy." (audiocast) *All Things Considered, NPR.* September 30, 2006. http://www.npr.org/templates/story/story.php?storyId=6169188 (accessed November 1, 2010).

Teeman, Tim. "Exclusive Interview with Alexander McCall Smith." *Times.co.uk.* March 24, 2008. http://entertainment.timesonline.co.uk/tol/arts_and_entertainment/books/article3552303.ece (accessed November 1, 2010).

Wakefield, Mary. "The Heart of Lightness." *Spectator* 295.9176 (June 19, 2004): 22.

Welch, David. "Red Bush Tea with Alexander McCall Smith." *Powells Books.* May 6, 2004. http://www.powells.com/authors/smith.html (accessed November 1, 2010).

Criticism and Reader's Guides

Geherin, David. "Alexander McCall Smith: Botswana." *Scene of the Crime: The Importance of Place in Crime and Mystery Fiction.* Jefferson, NC: McFarland, 2008. 137–47.

LaGrand, Virginia, and Craig E. Mattson. "Peter Wimsey and Precious Ramotswe: Castaway Detectives and Companionate Marriage." *Christianity and Literature* 56.4 (2007): 633–64.

Mekgwe, Pinkie, and Alexander McCall Smith. "'All That Is Fine in the Human Condition': Crafting Words, Creating Ma-Ramotswe." *Research in African Literatures* 37.2 (2006): 176–86.

"The No. 1 Ladies Detective Agency." (reading guide) *ReadingGroupGuides.* n.d. http://www.readinggroupguides.com/guides3/1_ladies%27_detective_agency1.asp (accessed November 1, 2010).

Smith, Alexander McCall. "Precious Ramotswe." *The Lineup: The World's Greatest Crime Writers Tell the Inside Story of Their Greatest Detectives.* Ed. Otto Penzler. New York: Little, Brown, 2009. 385–402.

Web Site

Official Web site: http://www.alexandermccallsmith.co.uk/; also available at http://www.randomhouse.com/features/mccallsmith/main.php (accessed November 1, 2010).

If You Like Alexander McCall Smith

Smith's No. 1 Detective Agency series features a positive look at an African country, cozy mystery telling, and an optimistic view of human nature. His writing in these novels has a deceptively simple, lyrical style that is very appealing.

Then You Might Like

M. C. Beaton

Beaton's Hamish MacBeth series is set in Scotland but shares the gentle humor and positive portrayal of a culture that are hallmarks of Smith's novels. MacBeth is constable of a small village in the Scottish Highlands and solves the crimes he is confronted with by using his knowledge of his neighbors and their foibles, as well as his understanding of the human race in general. The series begins with *Death of a Gossip,* followed by *Death of a Cad.*

Robert Hans van Gulik

Judge Dee, who solves crimes in ancient China, was an actual person, although his adventures as portrayed by Gulik are entirely fictional. Gulik began by translating an eighth-century Chinese novel about Dee but followed up by writing his own series of novels, which have been praised for their portrayal of ancient Chinese culture and for their depiction of a shrewd protagonist. Titles include *The Chinese Bell Murders* and *The Chinese Lake Murders.*

Tarquin Hall

Hall does for India what Smith has done for Botswana. She portrays the Punjab culture through the eyes of an appealing and gently humorous detective. Vish Puri, India's "Most Private Investigator," solves his first case in *The Case of the Missing Servant.*

Michael Pearce

Set in Egypt during the early years of the 20th century, Pearce's Mamur Zapt series recounts the exploits of the British head of the Secret Police in Cairo during a time when Britain ipso facto ruled Egypt. The humorous mysteries give a good idea of the politics and culture of Egypt during that period. Begin with *The Mamur Zapt and the Return of the Carpet,* followed by *The Mamur Zapt and the Night of the Dog.*

Michael Stanley

Stanley's novels about Detective David Bengu are also set in Botswana and portray familial relationships similar to those in Smith's stories. Stanley's novels are grittier and more violent than Smith's but give an excellent sense of the culture and the country. The series begins with *A Carrion Death* and continues with *The Second Death of Goodluck Tinubu.*

Stout, Rex, 1886–1975

So beginning Monday morning we were again a going concern, instead of a sitting-and-waiting one, but I was not in my element. I like a case you can make a diagram of. I don't object to complications, that's all right, but if you're out for bear it seems silly to concentrate on hunting for moose tracks.

—*And Be a Villain,* 1948

Biographical Sketch

Rex Todhunter Stout was born in Indiana, but the family soon moved to Kansas, where he grew up. He was a math prodigy; at the age of nine, he went on an exhibition tour where he would add huge columns of numbers almost impossibly quickly. He dropped out of school to read through his father's library and was state spelling champion at the age of thirteen. He dropped out of the University of Kansas after two weeks and did not have any further formal education. He served in the U.S. Navy and then drifted around the United States, turning his hand to a number of different jobs before becoming a freelance writer in New York for four years. Looking for a way to finance more serious writing, he created and managed the Educational Thrift Service, a school banking system that eventually had more than two million children enrolled. The proceeds from that venture made him financially comfortable for the rest of his life, even before the proceeds from his popular Nero Wolfe series started coming in. He retired to France, where he lived in Paris for two years and wrote five psychological suspense novels. Realizing that he would not be a great novelist, he decided to turn to detective stories. Stout was married twice and had two daughters. He died in Danbury, Connecticut.

Stout's creation of the Nero Wolfe/Archie Goodwin duo was a stroke of genius. The stories are told through the voice of Goodwin, who is the antithesis of Wolfe. However, the two respect each other and together make a formidable team. Stout applied conventions developed by Poe, Doyle, and Christie to the hard-boiled genre to create a style that was and is uniquely his own. His puzzle plots fit comfortably in the golden age, but there is an underlying grittiness and vigor that were his unique contribution to the genre. His novels continue to be read and bring pleasure today.

Categories: Private Detective

Awards

Edgar Grand Master Award for Lifetime Achievement (1959)

Major Works

Nero Wolfe series: *Fer-de-Lance* (1934), *The League of Frightened Men* (1935), *The Rubber Band* (1936), *The Red Box* (1937), *Too Many Cooks* (1938), *Some Buried Caesar* (1939), *Over My Dead Body* (1940), *Where There's a Will* (1940), *Black Orchids* (1942), *Not Quite Dead Enough* (1944), *The Silent Speaker* (1946), *Too Many Women* (1947), *And Be a Villain* (1948), *Trouble in Triplicate* (1949), *The Second Confession* (1949), *Three Doors to Death* (1950), *Murder by the Book* (1951), *Curtains for Three* (1951), *Triple Jeopardy* (1952), *Prisoner's Base* (1952), *The Golden Spiders* (1953), *The Black Mountain* (1954), *Three Men Out* (1954), *Before Midnight* (1955), *Three Witnesses* (1956), *Might as Well Be Dead* (1956), *Three for the Chair* (1957), *If Death Ever Slept* (1957), *Champagne for One* (1958), *And Four to Go* (1958), *Plot It Yourself* (1959), *Three at Wolfe's Door* (1960), *Too Many Clients* (1960), *The Final Deduction* (1961), *Gambit* (1962), *Homicide Trinity* (1962), *The Mother Hunt* (1963), *Trio for Blunt Instruments* (1964), *A Right to Die* (1964), *The Doorbell Rang* (1965), *Death of a Doxy* (1966), *The Father Hunt* (1968), *Death of a Dude* (1969), *Please Pass the Guilt* (1973), *A Family Affair* (1975)

Tecumseh Fox series: *Double for Death: A Tecumseh Fox Mystery* (1939), *Bad for Business: A Tecumseh Fox Mystery* (1940), *The Broken Vase: A Tecumseh Fox Mystery* (1941)

Short-story collections: *Justice Ends at Home and Other Stories* (1977), *Death Times Three* (1985), *Under the Andes* (1985), *Target Practice* (1998), *An Officer and a Lady, and Other Stories* (2000)

Nonseries novels: *The Hand in the Glove: A Dol Bonner Mystery* (1937), *Mountain Cat: A Mystery Novel* (1939), *Red Threads* (featuring Inspector Cramer, 1939), *Alphabet Hicks: A Mystery* (1941)

Research Sources

Encyclopedias and Handbooks: BEA, BEB, CA (61–64), CANR (71), CLC (3), EMM, OCC, STJ, WWW

Bibliographies: FF

Townsend, Guy M., ed. *Rex Stout, an Annotated Primary and Secondary Bibliography.* New York: Garland, 1980.

Biographies and Interviews

"Authors and Creators: Rex Stout." *ThrillingDetective.com.* n.d. http://www. thrillingdetective.com/trivia/rex_stout.html (accessed November 1, 2010).

McAleer, John J. *Rex Stout: A Biography.* Boston: Little, Brown, 1977. Later reissued as *Rex Stout: A Majesty's Life."* Florence, SC: James A. Rock, 2002.

"Rex Stout." *Kansas State Historical Society.* 2010. http://www.kshs.org/por traits/stout_rex.htm (accessed November 1, 2010).

Criticism and Reader's Guides

Anderson, David R. *Rex Stout.* New York: Ungar, 1984.

Anderson, David R. "Rex Stout." *Mystery and Suspense Writers: The Literature of Crime, Detection, and Espionage, II.* Ed. Robin W. Winks and Maureen Corrigan. New York: Scribner's, 1998. 885–99.

Baring-Gould, William Stuart. *Nero Wolfe of West Thirty-Fifth Street; The Life and Times of America's Largest Private Detective.* New York: Viking Press, 1969.

Beiderwell, Bruce. "State Power and Self-Destruction: Rex Stout and the Romance of Justice." *Journal of Popular Culture* 27.1 (1993): 13–22.

Cannon, Ammie Sorenson. "Controversial Politics, Conservative Genre: Rex Stout's Archie-Wolfe Duo and Detective Fiction's Conventional Form" (master's thesis), August 2006. http://contentdm.lib.byu.edu/ETD/image/etd1340.pdf (accessed November 1, 2010).

Crais, Robert. "Rex Stout: On Archie and Me." *RobertCrais.com.* 1993. http://www.robertcrais.com/articlesandessays/stout.htm (accessed November 1, 2010).

Darby, Ken. *The Brownstone House of Nero Wolfe.* Boston: Little, Brown, 1983.

Gerhardt, Mia I. "'Homicide West': Some Observations on the Nero Wolfe Stories of Rex Stout." *English Studies: A Journal of English Language and Literature* 49.(1968): 107–27.

Isaac, Frederick. "Enter the Fat Man: Rex Stout's Fer-de-Lance." *In the Beginning: First Novels in Mystery Series.* Ed. Mary Jean DeMarr. Bowling Green, OH: Popular Press, 1995. 59–68.

Jaffe, Arnold. "Murder with Dignity." *New Republic* 177.5 (1977): 41–43.

Kagan, Donald, and Walter A. Ralls. "A Wolfe in Stout Clothing." *Armchair Detective: A Quarterly Journal Devoted to the Appreciation of Mystery, Detective, and Suspense Fiction* 28.2 (1995): 176–83.

Kaye, Marvin. *The Archie Goodwin Files.* [Rockville, MD]: Wildside Press, 2005.

Kaye, Marvin. *The Nero Wolfe Files.* [Rockville, MD]: Wildside Press, 2005.

Kinkead, Linda. "Rex Stout and Nero Wolfe." *Suite101.com.* August 25, 1998. http://www.suite101.com/article.cfm/mystery/9907/1 (accessed November 1, 2010).

Langford, David. "A Stout Fellow." *Ansible.co.uk.* 1992. http://www.ansible.co.uk/writing/rexstout.html (accessed November 1, 2010).

"Nero Wolfe and Archie Goodwin." *Thrilling Detective.* n.d. http://www.thrillingdetective.com/wolfe.html (accessed November 1, 2010).

Owens, Ron. *Stout Fellow: A Guide Through Nero Wolfe's World."* Lincoln, NE: iUniverse, 1983.

"The Psychology of Rex Stout, Nero Wolfe and Archie Goodwin." *Abelard.* November 21, 2005. http://www.abelard.org/nero_wolfe.php (accessed November 1, 2010).

Robinson, Bobbie. "Rex Stout." *American Mystery and Detective Writers* (*Dictionary of Literary Biography* 306). Ed. George Parker Anderson. Detroit, MI: Thomson Gale, 2005. 346–60.

Rollyson, Carol. "Rex Stout." *100 Masters of Mystery and Detection, vol. 2.* Ed. Fiona Kelleghan. Pasadena, CA: Salem Press, 2001. 627–34.

Stout, Rex, and Michael Lee Bourne. *Corsage: A Bouquet of Rex Stout and Nero Wolfe.* Bloomington, IN: James A. Rock, 1977.

Tuska, Jon. "Rex Stout and the Detective Story." *A Variable Harvest.* Jefferson, NC: McFarland, 1990.

Van Dover, J. Kenneth. *At Wolfe's Door: The Nero Wolfe Novels of Rex Stout.* San Bernardino, CA: Borgo Press, 1991; 2nd ed., James A. Rock, 2003.

Web Sites

Clayton, John Strother, Sr. "The House on 35th Street: Nero Wolfe & Archie Goodwin at Home." (fan site) *Johnclaytonsr.com.* No date. http://john claytonsr.com/Wolfe/Intro.htm—Includes information and diagrams of the fictional home of Nero Wolfe (accessed November 1, 2010).

The Wolfe Pack (fan site): http://www.nerowolfe.org/—Official site of the Nero Wolfe Society. Includes biographical information, links to obituaries, book information, links to other sources. Thorough and well-organized site (accessed November 1, 2010).

Wolfe World (fan site): http://www.wolfeworld.8m.com/main.htm—Includes articles by Web site owner, links to other sources (accessed November 1, 2010).

Turow, Scott, 1949–

> *I have Nico on one side making out like I'm the one who murdered her. And every jackass in the world with press credentials wants to know when we're going to find the killer. And the secretaries are crying in the johns. And in the end, you know, there's this woman to think about. Christ, I knew her as a probation officer before she graduated law school. She worked for me.*

> —*Presumed Innocent,* 1987

Biographical Sketch

Son of a physician and a writer, Scott Turow was born in Chicago. The family moved to one of the city's suburbs, and he attended New Trier High School, where, after flunking freshman English, he went on to become editor of the school newspaper. His writing prospered when he attended Amherst as an English major, and, after graduating with a B.A., Turow was awarded a fellowship to the Creative Writing Center at Stanford University. He received an M.A. from Stanford in 1970 and, after graduating, lectured at Stanford for three years while he worked on a novel. That novel received numerous rejections, and Turow became discouraged about his prospects as a writer, so he went to Harvard Law School, where he earned a J.D. degree in 1978. He was an assistant U.S. district attorney for eight years and was involved in some high-profile cases in Chicago, where he served as lead government counsel in a number of trials connected with the federal government investigation into corruption in the Illinois judiciary. He then joined the law firm of Sonnenschein Nath & Rosenthal and became a partner in 1986. He continues to work for the firm to this day. Turow is married to Annette Weisberg, an artist, and the couple has three grown children.

Turow is that rare novelist who continues to work full-time as well as to write, even after becoming a best-selling author. His legal thrillers are set in a fictional county that resembles Cook County, Illinois, and his career has given him plenty of fodder for his plots. Turow's novels have been praised by critics not only for their thrilling plots but also for the quality of writing and characterization, with both good and evil being clothed in shades of gray.

Categories: Legal, Thriller

Awards

Silver Dagger Award for Best Novel Runner-Up (*Presumed Innocent,* 1987)

Major Works

Kindle County series: *Presumed Innocent* (1987), *The Burden of Proof* (1990), *Pleading Guilty* (1993), *The Laws of Our Fathers* (1996), *Personal Injuries* (1999), *Reversible Errors* (2002), *Limitations* (2006), *Innocent* (2010)
Nonseries novels: *Ordinary Heroes* (2005)
Nonfiction: *One L: An Inside Account of Life in the First Year at Harvard Law School* (1977), *Ultimate Punishment: A Lawyer's Reflections on Dealing with the Death Penalty* (2003)

Research Sources

Encyclopedias and Handbooks: 100, BEA, BEB, CA (73–76), CANR (42, 65, 111, 137), MCF, STJ, WWW

Bibliographies: FF, OM

Biographies and Interviews

Abbe, Elfrieda. "Building a Legal Thriller." *Writer* 118.5 (2005): 18–22.
Gray, P. "Burden of Success." *Time* 135.24 (1990): 68.

Kloberdanz, Kristin. "The Angel of Death Row." *Book* (Summit, NJ) (November-December 2002): 20, 22.

"Ordinary Heroes." (videocast) *Pritzker Military Library.* May 10, 2006. http://www.pritzkermilitarylibrary.org/events/2006/05-10-scott-turow.jsp (accessed November 1, 2010).

"Personal Injuries." (audiocast) *Weekend Edition Sunday, NPR.* October 2, 1999. http://www.npr.org/templates/story/story.php?storyId=1064811 (accessed November 1, 2010).

Turow, Scott. "Ordinary Heroes." (audiocast) *Bookstreamink.* n.d. http://www.bookwrapcentral.com/authors/scottturow.htm (accessed November 1, 2010).

Vitale, Tom. "Lawyers Turned Novelists." (audiocast) *Weekend Edition Sunday, NPR.* December 1, 2002. http://www.npr.org/templates/story/story.php?storyId=862996 (accessed November 1, 2010).

Criticism and Reader's Guides

Breen, Jon L. "The Legal Crime Novel." *Mystery and Suspense Writers: The Literature of Crime, Detection and Espionage, III.* Ed. Robin W. Winks and Maureen Corrigan. New York: Scribner's, 1998. 1103–15.

Diggs, Terry K. "Through a Glass Darkly." *ABA Journal* 82.10 (1996): 72–74, 76.

Heffernan, Nick. "Law Crimes: The Legal Fictions of John Grisham and Scott Turow." *Criminal Proceedings: The Contemporary American Crime Novel.* Ed. Peter Messent. London: Pluto Press, 1997. 187–213.

"Limitations: A Reading Group Guide." (pdf) *Macmillan Picador.* n.d. http://us.macmillan.com/limitations; Also available at http://www.scottturow.com/files/rgg_limitations.pdf (accessed November 1, 2010).

Macdonald, Andrew F., and Gina Macdonald. *Scott Turow: A Critical Companion.* Westport, CT: Greenwood, 2005.

"Ordinary Heroes: Reading Group Guide." *Macmillan.* n.d. http://us.macmillan.com/ordinaryheroes (accessed November 1, 2010).

"Ordinary Heroes [reading guide]." *BookBrowse.com.* n.d. http://www.bookbrowse.com/reading_guides/detail/index.cfm?book_number=1706 (accessed November 1, 2010).

"Ordinary Heroes [reading guide]." *ReadingGroupGuides.com.* n.d. http://www.readinggroupguides.com/guides3/ordinary_heroes1.asp (accessed November 1, 2010).

Szuberla, Guy. "Paretsky, Turow, and the Importance of Symbolic Ethnicity." *MidAmerica XVIII: The Yearbook of the Society for the Study of Midwestern Literature.* Ed. David D. Anderson. East Lansing, MI: Midwestern Press, 1991. 124–5.

Web Site

Official Web site: http://www.scottturow.com/ (accessed November 1, 2010).

Vine, Barbara—see Rendell, Ruth

Walters, Minette, 1949–

It was impossible to see her approach without a shudder of distaste. She was a grotesque parody of a woman, so fat that her feet and hands and head protruded absurdly from the huge slab of her body like tiny dispro-portionate afterthoughts. Dirty blonde hair clung damp and thin to her scalp, black patches of sweat spread beneath her armpits.

—*The Sculptress,* 1993

Biographical Sketch

Minette Jeb was born in Bishop's Stortford, England, the daughter of Samuel and Colleen Jebb. Her father was an Army officer and her mother an artist. She attended Godolphin School and Durham University before marrying Alexander Walters, a business executive, in 1978, and having two sons. She has worked as a secretary, barmaid, magazine writer and editor, and freelance writer. She has also been active in local politics and school governance.

Walters's stand-alone novels have been successful from the beginning, with her first novel winning the prestigious John Creasey Dagger Award for previously unpublished authors. Her plotting and strong characterizations have been described as layered and psychologically suspenseful. The themes of her books address social and psychological issues and often result in an uncomfortable yet fascinating reading experience.

Categories: Psychological, Thriller

Awards

Gold Dagger for Best Novel (*The Scold's Bridle,* 1994)
John Creasey Dagger for First Novel (*The Ice House,* 1992)
Edgar Award for Best Novel (*The Sculptress,* 1994)
Macavity Award for Best Novel (*The Sculptress,* 1994)

Major Works

Novels: *The Ice House* (1992), *The Sculptress* (1993), *The Scold's Bridle* (1994), *The Dark Room* (1995), *The Echo* (1997), *The Breaker* (1998), *The Shape of Snakes* (2001), *Acid Row* (2001), *Disordered Minds* (2003), *Fox Evil* (2003), *The Tinder Box* (novella, 2004), *Chickenfeed* (novella, 2006), *The Devil's Feather* (2006), *The Chameleon's Shadow* (2007)

Research Sources

Encyclopedias and Handbooks: BYA, CA (160), CANR (167), GWM, MCF, STJ, WWW

Bibliographies: FF

Biographies and Interviews

Came, Barry. "Literary autopsies." *Maclean's* 112.10 (March 8, 1999): 62–63.

Gee, Eve Tan. "Minette Walters: My Glittering Career." *Crime Time.* n.d. http://www.crimetime.co.uk/interviews/minettewalters.html   (accessed November 1, 2010).

James, Dean. "Interview with Minette Walters." *Deadly Women: The Woman Mystery Reader's Indispensable Companion.* Ed. Jan Grape et al. New York: Carroll & Graf, 1998. 195–98.

"Minette Walters." *Contemporary Writers.* British Council. 2007. http://www. contemporarywriters.com/authors/?p=auth5688A7141b5e919468TxG4 21D03B (accessed November 1, 2010).

Muller, Adrian. "Minette Walters." *Speaking of Murder: Interviews with the Masters of Mystery and Suspense.* Ed. Ed Gorman and Martin H. Greenberg. New York: Berkley Prime Crime, 1998. 171–80.

Peters, Barbara. "Minette Walters Interview" (videocast—6 parts) *Poisoned Pen Bookstore.* January 7, 2008. http://www.poisonedpen.com/inter views/minette-walters-interview; also available at http://www.youtube. com/watch?v=ByW7rHwl7RY (accessed November 1, 2010).

Silet, Charles L. P. "An Interview with Minette Walters." *Armchair Detective: A Quarterly Journal Devoted to the Appreciation of Mystery, Detective, and Suspense Fiction* 27.2 (1994): 182–85.

Criticism and Reader's Guides

DuBose, Martha Hailey. "Minette Walters: Dark Shadows." *Women of Mystery: The Lives and Works of Notable Women Crime Novelists.* New York: St. Martin's Minotaur, 2000. 400–5.

Fletcher, Don, and Rosemary Whip. "Exploring Sexual Violence in The Dark Room." *Social Alternatives* 17.4 (1998): 27–30.

Fletcher, M. D., and R. J. Whip. "Minette Walter's Feminist Detective Fiction." *Clues: A Journal of Detection* 18.1 (1997): 101–12.

Forselius, Tilda Maria. "The Impenetrable M and the Mysteries of Narration: Narrative in Minette Walters's *The Shape of Snakes.*" *Clues: A Journal of Detection* 24.2 (2006): 47–61.

Hadley, Mary, and Sarah D. Fogle, eds. *Minette Walters and the Meaning of Justice: Essays on the Crime Novels.* Jefferson, NC: McFarland, 2008.

Lebihan, Jill. "Tearing the Heart out of Secrets: Inside and outside a Murder Mystery." *Journal of Gender Studies* 10.3 (2001): 287–95.

Web Site

Official Web site: http://www.minettewalters.co.uk/ (accessed November 1, 2010).

Winspear, Jacqueline, 1955–

She had found two more graves whose headstones bore Christian names only, not very far from the final resting place of Vincent Weathershaw. Three young "old soldiers" who had withdrawn from their families. Maisie sat back on the bench and started to compose her questions, the questions to herself that would come as a result of her observations. She would not struggle to answer the questions but would let them do their work.

—*Maisie Dobbs,* 2003

Biographical Sketch

Jacqueline Winspear was born and raised in Kent, England. She graduated from the University of London Institute of Education and worked in publishing, communications, and higher education in England before immigrating to the United States, in 1990. She worked briefly in business and as a personal/professional coach before becoming a full-time writer. She lives in California.

Winspear's Maisie Dobbs series was an instant success, with the first volume, *Maisie Dobbs*, being named a *New York Times* book of the year. Her interest in World War I grew out of personal family history; although the books are set after the war, the plot of each grows out of events that happened during the "war to end all wars." Maisie is a memorable character, and her personal struggles, as well as the psychological insights she gains in the situations she is hired to investigate, pull the reader into the stories. Reviewers have praised the sense of time and place that the author invokes through her stories.

Categories: Historical, Psychological

Awards

Agatha Award for Best Novel (*Birds of a Feather,* 2004)
Agatha Award for Best First Novel (*Maisie Dobbs,* 2003)
Macavity Award for Best First Novel (*Maisie Dobbs,* 2004)

Major Works

Maisie Dobbs series: *Maisie Dobbs* (2003), *Birds of a Feather* (2004), *Pardonable Lies* (2005), *Messenger of Truth* (2006), *An Incomplete Revenge*

(2008), *Among the Mad* (2009), *The Mapping of Love and Death* (2010)

Research Sources

Encyclopedias and Handbooks: CA (229), CANR (192), GWM

Bibliographies: FF, OM

Biographies and Interviews

Gurley, Doc. "Doc Gurley Interviews Jacqueline Winspear." *YouTube.com.* July 18, 2009. http://www.youtube.com/watch?v=FAwRO4UwIY8 (accessed November 1, 2010).

"Jacqueline Winspear." *Bookreporter.com.* February 20, 2009. http://www.bookreporter.com/authors/au-winspear-jacqueline.asp (accessed November 1, 2010).

Onatade, Ayo. "Jacqueline Winspear Speaks to Ayo Onatade for Shots Ezine." *Shots Magazine.* n.d.. http://www.shotsmag.co.uk/shots23/intvus_23/jwinspear.html (accessed November 1, 2010).

Scribner, Amy. "The Winds of Change." *BookPage.com.* n.d. http://www.bookpage.com/0508bp/jacqueline_winspear.html (accessed November 1, 2010).

Spencer-Fleming, Julia. "A Conversation with Jacqueline Winspear." *Juliaspencerfleming.com: The Narthex.* April 6, 2008. http://www.juliaspencerfleming.com/Jacqueline-Winspear.html (accessed November 1, 2010).

Criticism and Reader's Guides

"Among the Mad." *Macmillan Picador.* n.d. http://us.macmillan.com/amongthemad (accessed November 1, 2010).

"An Incomplete Revenge." *Macmillan Picador.* n.d. http://us.macmillan.com/anincompleterevenge (accessed November 1, 2010).

"Maisie Dobbs Reading Guide." *Penguin.* n.d. http://us.penguingroup.com/static/rguides/us/maisie_dobbs.html (accessed November 1, 2010).

"Messenger of Truth." *Macmillan Picador.* n.d. http://us.macmillan.com/messengeroftruth (accessed November 1, 2010).

"Pardonable Lies." *Macmillan Picador.* n.d. http://us.macmillan.com/pardonablelies#rggold (accessed November 1, 2010).

Sharratt, Mary. "Building a Mystery." *Historical Novels Review* 36 (2006): 5–6.

Web Site

Official Web site: http://www.jacquelinewinspear.com/ (accessed November 1, 2010).

Lists of Authors by Categories

Crime fiction includes a number of subcategories, each with its own devotees. Sometimes these cross over. An amateur detective series may also be considered a cozy series. A police procedural may also feature diverse characters. These lists identify at least some of the authors who write in each category. Some authors are primarily identified with one type, but some authors may write in more than one category. Most authors were limited to two categories each. There were some exceptions who have been listed more than twice because of the variety of their important series. Regardless, users of this book can get an idea of the type of crime fiction that each author writes and may discover new authors in that category.

Amateur Detective

Andrews, Donna
Barr, Nevada
Christie, Agatha
Connelly, Michael
Davidson, Diane Mott
Elkins, Aaron
Evanovich, Janet
Francis, Dick
Harris, Charlaine
Hart, Carolyn
Hiaasen, Carl
Jance, J. A.
Peters, Elizabeth

Picard, Nancy
Sayers, Dorothy L.

Caper

Hiaasen, Carl
Leonard, Elmore

Cozy

Andrews, Donna
Christie, Agatha
Davidson, Diane Mott
Hart, Carolyn
Pickard, Nancy

Diverse Characters

Hillerman, Tony
King, Laurie R.
Mosley, Walter
Smith, Alexander McCall

English Setting

Francis, Dick
George, Elizabeth
Marsh, Ngaio
Sayers, Dorothy L.

Forensic

Cornwell, Patricia
Elkins, Aaron
Reichs, Kathy

Hard-Boiled

Burke, James Lee
Chandler, Raymond
Child, Lee
Crais, Robert
Grafton, Sue
Lehane, Dennis
Leonard, Elmore
Muller, Marcia
Paretsky, Sara
Parker, Robert B.

Historical

King, Laurie R.
Lovesey, Peter
Perry, Anne
Peters, Elizabeth
Winspear, Jacqueline

Humorous

Evanovich, Janet

Legal

Baldacci, David
Connelly, Michael

Grisham, John
Maron, Margaret
McBain, Ed
Turow, Scott

Medical

Gerritsen, Tess

Paranormal

Harris, Charlaine

Police Procedural
(includes quasi-police roles)

Barr, Nevada
Burke, James Lee
Cornwell, Patricia
Crombie, Deborah
George, Elizabeth
Hillerman, Tony
James, P. D.
Jance, J. A.
King, Laurie R.
Lippman, Laura
Lovesey, Peter
Maron, Margaret
Marsh, Ngaio
McBain, Ed
Patterson, James
Perry, Anne
Reichs, Kathy
Rendell, Ruth

Private Detective

Chandler, Raymond
Christie, Agatha
Connelly, Michael
Crais, Robert
Grafton, Sue
James, P. D.
Lehane, Dennis
Lippman, Laura
Mosley, Walter
Muller, Marcia

Paretsky, Sara
Parker, Robert B.
Smith, Alexander McCall
Stout, Rex

Psychological

Rendell, Ruth
Walters, Minette
Winspear, Jacqueline

Romantic Suspense

Clark, Mary Higgins
Peters, Elizabeth (as Barbara
        Michaels)

Thriller

Baldacci, David
Child, Lee
Clark, Mary Higgins
Gerritsen, Tess
Grisham, John
Patterson, James
Turow, Scott
Walters, Minette

General Bibliography

Encyclopedias and Handbooks

Ashley, Mike. *The Mammoth Encyclopedia of Modern Crime Fiction.* New York: Carroll & Graf, 2002.

Barnett, Colleen. *Mystery Women: An Encyclopedia of Leading Women Characters in Mystery Fiction.* 3rd ed. 3 vols. Scottsdale, AZ: Poisoned Pen Press, 2006. Vol. 1 includes characters who appeared between 1860 and 1979. Vol. 2 covers 1980–1989, and Vol. 3 deals with 1990–1999. Has descriptive entries about each character plus essays covering historical aspects of each decade.

Beetz, Kirk H., ed. *Beacham's Encyclopedia of Popular Fiction: Analyses Series.* Osprey, FL: Beacham, 1996. Includes analyses of individual titles by selected authors.

Beetz, Kirk H., ed. *Beacham's Encyclopedia of Popular Fiction: Biography Series.* Osprey, FL: Beacham, 1996. Includes biographical information and resources on selected authors.

Bleiler, Richard J. *Reference and Research Guide to Mystery and Detective Fiction.* 2nd ed. Westport, CT: Libraries Unlimited, 2004.

DeAndrea, William L. *Encyclopedia Mysteriosa: A Comprehensive Guide to the Art of Detection in Print, Film, Radio, and Television.* New York: Prentice Hall, 1994.

Drew, Bernard A. *100 Most Popular Genre Fiction Authors: Biographical Sketches and Bibliographies.* Westport, CT: Libraries Unlimited, 2005.

Herbert, Rosemary, ed. *The Oxford Companion to Crime and Mystery Writing.* New York, Oxford University Press, 1999.

Herbert, Rosemary. *Whodunit? A Who's Who in Crime & Mystery Writing.* New York: Oxford University Press, 2003.

Klein, Kathleen Gregory, ed. *Great Women Mystery Writers.* Westport, CT: Greenwood, 1994. Bio-critical essays of several pages on included authors.

Landrum, Larry. *American Mystery and Detective Novels: A Reference Guide.* Westport, CT: Greenwood, 1999.

Lindsay, Elizabeth Blakesley. *Great Women Mystery Writers.* 2nd ed. Westport, CT: Greenwood, 2007. Updates Klein, *Great Women Mystery Writers,* for those authors still working and adds new ones.

Macdonald, Gina, ed. *British Mystery and Thriller Writers since 1960.* (*Dictionary of Literary Biography*, vol. 276). Detroit, MI: Gale, 2003.

Murphy, Bruce F. *The Encyclopedia of Murder and Mystery.* New York: Palgrave, 1999.

Pederson, Jay P. *St. James Guide to Crime and Mystery Writers.* 4th ed. Chicago: St. James Press, 1994.

Sobin, Roger M. *The Essential Mystery Lists: For Readers, Collectors, and Librarians.* Scottsdale, AZ: Poisoned Pen Press, 2007.

Swanson, Jean, and Dean James. *By a Woman's Hand: A Guide to Mystery Fiction by Women.* 2nd ed. New York: Berkley Prime Crime, 1996.

Swanson, Jean, and Dean James. *Killer Books: A Reader's Guide to Exploring the Popular World of Mystery and Suspense.* New York: Berkley Prime Crime, 1998.

Bibliographic Sources

Burgess, Michael, and Jill H. Vassilakos. *Murder in Retrospect: A Selective Guide to Historical Mystery Fiction.* Westport, CT: Libraries Unlimited, 2005.

Fantastic Fiction—Author bibliographies with cover views and brief biographical information. http://www.fantasticfiction.co.uk/. (accessed November 1, 2010)

Herald, Diana Tixier, and Wayne A. Wiegand. *Genreflecting.* 6th ed. Westport, CT: Libraries Unlimited, 2006.

Heising, Willetta L. *Detecting Men: A Reader's Guide and Checklist for Mystery Series Written by Men.* Dearborn, MI: Purple Moon Press, 1998.

Heising, Willetta L. *Detecting Women: A Reader's Guide and Checklist for Mystery Series Written by Women.* 3rd ed. Dearborn, MI: Purple Moon Press, 1999.

Huang, Jim. *100 Favorite Mysteries of the Century: Selected by the Independent Mystery Booksellers Association.* Carmel, IN.: Crum Creek Press, 2000. Essays about the titles included are written by the booksellers.

Keating, H. R. F. *Crime & Mystery: The 100 Best Books.* New York: Carroll & Graf, 1987. This list was selected by Keating and includes an essay about each title.

Niebuhr, Gary Warren. *Make Mine a Mystery: A Reader's Guide to Mystery and Detective Fiction.* Westport, CT: Libraries Unlimited, 2003.

Omnimystery—Bibliographies arranged by author with reference to award-winning titles. http://authors.omnimystery.com/. (accessed November 1, 2010)

Penzler, Otto, and Mickey Friedman. *The Crown Crime Companion: The Top 100 Mystery Novels of All Time; Selected by the Mystery Writers of America.* New York: Crown, 1995. Annotated entries include background information, very brief plot summaries, and information about media adaptations. Also included are the top 10 books per category with an essay for each category.

Stilwell, Steven A. *What Mystery Do I Read Next? A Reader's Guide to Recent Mystery Fiction.* Detroit, MI: Gale, 1996.

Trott, Barry. *Read On... Crime Fiction: Reading Lists for Every Taste.* Westport, CT: Libraries Unlimited, 2008.

Biography and Interviews

Carr, John C. *The Craft of Crime: Conversations with Crime Writers.* Boston: Houghton Mifflin, 1983.

Contemporary Authors. Detroit, MI: Gale Research, 1981–. Also available online; check availability at your library.

Contemporary Authors, Autobiography Series. Detroit, MI: Gale Research, 1984–1999. Each volume contains about twenty autobiographical essays written especially for the series.

Contemporary Authors, New Revision Series. Detroit, MI: Gale Research, 1981–.

Gorman, Ed, and Martin H. Greenberg, eds. *Speaking of Murder: Interviews with the Masters of Mystery and Suspense.* New York: Berkley Prime Crime, 1998.

Gorman, Ed, and Martin H. Greenberg, eds. *Speaking of Murder, vol. 2: Interviews with the Masters of Mystery and Suspense.* New York: Berkley Prime Crime, 1999.

Herbert, Rosemary. *The Fatal Art of Entertainment: Interviews with Mystery Writers.* New York: G. K. Hall, 1994.

Kaminsky, Stuart, and Laurie Roberts. *Behind the Mystery: Top Mystery Writers Interviewed.* Cohasset, MA: Hot House, 2005.

The Poisoned Pen—Includes extensive video interviews by Barbara Peters, owner of the Poisoned Pen bookstore. http://www.poisonedpen.com/interviews. (accessed November 1, 2010)

Wired for Books—Audio author interviews by Don Swaim. Sponsored by Ohio University. http://wiredforbooks.org/swaim/. (accessed November 1, 2010)

YouTube—Short interviews with many current authors can be found on YouTube in addition to the more substantive ones found in the author entries mentioned here. For best results, search by using quotation marks around the name in natural order (e.g. "John Smith"). http://youtube. com (accessed November 1, 2010)

Criticism and Interpretation

Anderson, George Parker, ed. *American Mystery and Detective Writers (Dictionary of Literary Biography 306)*. Detroit, MI: Thomson Gale, 2005. Extensive bio-critical essays on selected writers.

Anderson, George Parker, and Julie Anderson, eds. *American Hard-Boiled Crime Writers (Dictionary of Literary Biography 226)*. Detroit, MI: Gale, 2000.

Bargainnier, Earl F. ed. *10 Women of Mystery*. Bowling Green, OH: Popular Press, 1981.

Benstock, Bernard, ed. *Art in Crime Writing: Essays on Detective Fiction*. New York: St. Martin's Press, 1983.

Benstock, Bernard, and Thomas F. Staley, eds. *British Mystery Writers, 1920–1939 (Dictionary of Literary Biography 77)*. Detroit, MI: Gale Research, 1984.

Benstock, Bernard, and Thomas F. Staley, eds. *British Mystery and Thriller Writers since 1940, First Series (Dictionary of Literary Biography 87)*. Detroit, MI: Gale Research, 1989.

Contemporary Literary Criticism. Detroit: Gale Research, 1973–. Also available online; check availability at your library.

Delamater, Jerome H., and Ruth Prigozy, eds. *The Detective in American Fiction, Film, and Television*. Westport, CT: Greenwood, 1998.

DeMarr, Mary Jean, ed. *In the Beginning: First Novels in Mystery Series*. Bowling Green, OH: Popular Press, 1995.

Dove, George N. *The Reader and the Detective Story*. Bowling Green, OH: Popular Press, 1997.

DuBose, Martha Hailey. *Women of Mystery: The Lives and Works of Notable Women Crime Novelists*. New York: St. Martin's Minotaur, 2000.

Geherin, David. *Scene of the Crime: The Importance of Place in Crime and Mystery Fiction*. Jefferson, NC: McFarland, 2008.

Gillis, Stacy, and Philippa Gates, eds. *The Devil Himself: Villainy in Detective Fiction and Film*. Westport, CT: Greenwood, 2002.

Glassman, Steve, and Maurice O'Sullivan, eds. *Crime Fiction and Film in the Sunshine State: Florida Noir*. Bowling Green, OH: Popular Press, 1997.

Irons, Glenwood H., ed. *Feminism in Women's Detective Fiction*. Toronto: University of Toronto Press, 1995.

Jakubowski, Maxim, ed. *100 Great Detectives, or The Detective Directory*. New York: Caroll & Graf, 1991. A collection of essays written by crime novelists about fictional detectives.

Kelleghan, Fiona, ed. *100 Masters of Mystery and Detection, vols. 1 and 2.* Pasadena, CA: Salem Press, 2001. Extensive multipage bio-critical essays on selected authors.

Klein, Kathleen Gregory, ed. *Diversity and Detective Fiction.* Bowling Green, OH: Popular Press, 1999.

Klein, Kathleen Gregory, ed. *Women Times Three: Writers, Detectives, Readers.* Bowling Green, OH: Popular Press, 1995.

Nichols, Victoria, and Susan Thompson. *Silk Stalkings: More Women Write of Murder.* Lanham, MD: Scarecrow Press, 1998. Lists major characters appearing in crime fiction by women with descriptive entries for each.

Penzler, Otto, ed. *The Lineup: The World's Greatest Crime Writers Tell the Inside Story of Their Greatest Detectives.* New York: Little, Brown, 2009. Extensive essays by authors about their main characters.

Priestman, Martin. *The Cambridge Companion to Crime Fiction.* Cambridge, U.K.: University Press, 2003. Features a timeline and extensive essays on categories of crime fiction.

Reynolds, Moira Davidson. *Women Authors of Detective Series: Twenty-one American and British Writers, 1900–2000.* Jefferson, NC: McFarland, 2001.

Rzepka, Charles J. *Detective Fiction.* Cambridge, U.K.: Polity Press, 2005.

Twentieth-Century Literary Criticism. Detroit, Mich.: Gale, 1978–. Also available online; check availability at your library.

Walker, Ronald G., and June M. Frazer, eds. *The Cunning Craft: Original Essays on Detective Fiction and Contemporary Literary Theory.* Macomb: Western Illinois University, 1990.

Winks, Robin W. *Detective Fiction: A Collection of Critical Essays.* Woodstock, VT: Countryman Press, 1988.

Winks, Robin W., and Maureen Corrigan, eds. *Mystery and Suspense Writers: The Literature of Crime, Detection and Espionage.* New York: Scribner's Sons, 1998. 2 vols.

Indexes and Databases

Biography Reference Bank Select. H. W. Wilson. Incorporate materials from Wilson's biographical publications as well as indexes of articles and books, some full-text. *Online resource available by subscription only; check your local library for availability.*

Literary Reference Center. Ebsco. Includes articles from Magill's literary survey titles as well as indexing articles and books. Some available full-text. *Online resource available by subscription only; check your local library for availability.*

Literature Resource Center. Thomson Gale. Incorporates materials from the *Dictionary of Literary Biography,* as well as other Gale resources. *Online* resource available by subscription only; check your local library for availability.

MLA International Bibliography. Modern Language Association and Ebsco. Index to periodicals and books, some available full-text. *Online resource available by subscription only; check your local library for availability.*

Magazines and Scholarly Journals

Alfred Hitchcock Mystery Magazine—Short-story magazine with fiction ranging from hard-boiled to classic puzzlers. Appears ten times per year. http://www.themysteryplace.com/ahmm/. (accessed November 1, 2010)

Clues: A Journal of Detection—Produced by McFarland, this is the only scholarly journal being published in the United States on the subject of crime and mystery fiction and film. http://www.mcfarlandpub.com/clues. html. (accessed November 1, 2010)

Deadly Pleasures—a fan-oriented mystery magazine with articles, reviews, and so on. http://www.deadlypleasures.com/. (accessed November 1, 2010)

Ellery Queen Mystery Magazine—Includes stories by professional authors in a monthly format (10 issues per year). Also includes reviews and a crossword puzzle. http://www.themysteryplace.com/eqmm/. (accessed November 1, 2010)

January Magazine—An online magazine that includes news, reviews, and interviews in all genres of fiction and nonfiction. http://januarymagazine. com/. (accessed November 1, 2010)

Mystery Readers Journal—a fan-oriented magazine with themed articles, short articles by crime authors, reviews, and columns. Published by Mystery Readers International. http://www.mysteryreaders.org/journal.html. (accessed November 1, 2010)

Mystery Scene—A long-running magazine with interviews, articles, reviews, and coverage of books, media, and children's books. http://www.mys teryscenemag.com/. (accessed November 1, 2010)

The Strand Magazine—Published four times a year, this glossy magazine has stories in various genres by professional writers. Also included are true-crime articles and reviews. http://www.strandmag.com/. (accessed November 1, 2010)

Crime Fiction Organizations and Conventions

Bouchercon World Mystery Convention—Held annually, the convention is named in honor Anthony Boucher, a prominent crime fiction editor, reviewer, and author. http://www.bouchercon.info/. (accessed November 1, 2010)

Crime Writers Association—A British organization whose aim is to "promote the crime genre and support professional writers." The Dagger awards are given by this group. http://www.thecwa.co.uk/. (accessed November 1, 2010)

International Thriller Writers—An organization of professional authors from around the world. The organization sponsors Thrillerfest, an annual conference. http://www.thrillerwriters.org/. (accessed November 1, 2010)

Left Coast Crime—An annual convention held in the western United States, defined as the Mountain Time Zone and points west. The Lefty award is given each year by attendees to the most humorous crime novel. http://www.leftcoastcrime.org/. (accessed November 1, 2010)

Malice Domestic—This conference has been held annually since 1989 in the metropolitan Washington, D.C., area. The focus is on the traditional mystery in the spirit of Agatha Christie. The Agatha Awards are given by attendees each year. http://www.malicedomestic.org/. (accessed November 1, 2010)

Mystery Readers International—A fan organization open to all. Macavity awards are voted on by membership. http://www.mysteryreaders.org/. (accessed November 1, 2010)

Mystery Writers of America—A U.S. organization for professional writers, other professionals related to the field, and fans. MWA gives the Edgar Awards and the Grand Master recognition. http://www.mysterywriters.org/. (accessed November 1, 2010)

Private Eye Writers of America—This organization was founded to recognize the private-eye genre and its writers. Membership is open to writers, fans, and other professionals. The Shamus awards are given by this association at Bouchercon each year. http://www.pwanewsandviews.blogspot.com/. (accessed November 1, 2010)

Sisters in Crime—Founded by Sara Paretsky in 1987 with the support of other women authors to fight discrimination against women crime-fiction authors, especially in the areas of reviews and awards. A detailed history of the organization and its efforts to support women authors can be found on the Web site. http://www.sistersincrime.org/index.cfm. (accessed November 1, 2010)

The Wolfe Pack—An organization founded to provide a forum for those who appreciate the works of Rex Stout. The Nero Awards are given by this group. http://www.nerowolfe.org/. (accessed November 1, 2010)

Web Sites

G. J. Demko's Landscapes of Crime—Settings of crime novels are highlighted in this site with lists of stories set in various locales. Also includes essays and articles by the site's author. http://www.dartmouth.edu/~gjdemko/. (accessed November 1, 2010)

A Guide to Classic Mystery and Detection—A fan site with voluminous information about authors and topics about classic crime fiction. http://mikegrost.com/classics.htm. (accessed November 1, 2010)

Hidden Staircase Mystery Books—This site has a wealth of resources, including bibliographies, new releases, a current bestseller list, and contests and games. http://hsmb.omnimystery.com/. (accessed November 1, 2010)

Mystery Ink—Includes author interviews and awards. This site spotlights the Gumshoe Award. http://www.mysteryinkonline.com/. (accessed November 1, 2010)

Stop, You're Killing Me—This Web site includes bibliographies, awards lists, new releases, and resources. A well-designed site that is easy to navigate. http://www.stopyourekillingme.com/. (accessed November 1, 2010)

Major Awards

There are numerous awards given each year for crime fiction and various subgenres that fit into the crime-fiction milieu. The awards listed here are the most prominent or best known and include both fan-voted awards and those given by professional writers' associations. Award information was compiled from the Web sites of the respective organizations that administer the awards.

Agatha Awards

Started in 1988, the Agatha Awards focus on traditional mysteries and are named in honor of Agatha Christie. Registered attendees of the annual Malice Domestic conference vote on the fan-generated nominees. Works considered typically fall into the "cozy" category and do not contain gratuitous violence or explicit sex. These works usually feature an amateur detective, although police or private detectives may be present. Hard-boiled detectives will not be found here. Dates given in the text for awards are as listed on the award Web site. http://www.malicedomestic.org/agathaawards.html. (accessed November 1, 2010)

Anthony Awards

Started in 1986, the Anthony Awards are voted on by attendees of Bouchercon, the World Mystery Convention, and are named in honor of Anthony Boucher, a well-known author, critic, and fan. http://www.bouchercon.info/history.html. (accessed November 1, 2010)

Barry Awards

Given by the editorial staff of *Deadly Pleasures* magazine since 1997, the Barry Awards are named in honor of Barry Gardner, a long-time devoted mystery fan. From 2007 to 2009, the awards were cosponsored by *Mystery News.* The awards are presented at Bouchercon. http://www.deadlypleasures.com/barry.html. (accessed November 1, 2010)

Crime Writers Association (U.K.)

The Crime Writers Association gives a number of awards. Judges for these awards are primarily book critics. The awards given and, in some cases, the names of the awards have changed over the years. Often the name of the sponsor is attached to the name of the award, and these sponsors have changed over time. Awards are listed here by the most prominent name. Sponsors' names are left out for the sake of clarity. http://www.thecwa.co.uk/daggers/index.html#international. (accessed November 1, 2010)

Edgar Mystery Awards

The Edgar Awards are considered the premier American crime fiction awards. Given since 1946, they are voted on by the Mystery Writers of America. They are named in honor of Edgar Allan Poe and are awarded in numerous categories, only some of which are listed for the authors in this book. http://mysterywriters.org/?q=AwardsPrograms. (accessed November 1, 2010)

Lefty Awards

The Left Coast Crime annual convention gives an award for best humorous mystery. This award has been given since 1996. http://www.leftcoastcrime.org/history.html. (accessed November 1, 2010)

Macavity Awards

These awards are given by Mystery Readers International, whose members nominate and vote for the recipients. The awards, started in 1987, are named for the mysterious cat in T. S. Eliot's *Old Possum's Book of Practical Cats.* http://www.mysteryreaders.org/macavity.html. (accessed November 1, 2010)

Nero Awards

This award is given by the Wolfe Pack, a fan group devoted to the works of Rex Stout, for the book that best represents the spirit of the Nero Wolfe novels. The award has been given since 1979. http://www.nerowolfe.org/htm/ neroaward/awardees_chron.htm. (accessed November 1, 2010)

Shamus Awards

Beginning in 1982, these awards have been given by the Private Eye Writers of America (PWA). Membership is not limited to authors. The organization does not currently have a Web site for the awards, but lists can be found at http://www.thrillingdetective.com/trivia/triv72.html (accessed November 1, 2010), as well as at many other locations.

Index

About the Author

ELIZABETH HAYNES, Ph.D., is associate professor of library and infor-
mation science at the University of Southern Mississippi in Hattiesburg.
Dr. Haynes received her degree in library and information science from the
University of Texas, Austin. She is the author of *User's Guide to Sears List of
Subject Headings* and coauthor of *Unlocking the Mysteries of Cataloging: A
Workbook of Examples*. Prior to coming to USM, in 1998, Dr. Haynes was an
employee of the El Paso Independent School District in El Paso, TX. In addition to being a lifelong reader of crime fiction, Dr. Haynes teaches a readers'
advisory course for genre fiction.